Close Enough for Jazz

Close Enough for Jazz

Mike Zwerin

Quartet Books
London Melbourne New York

First published by Quartet Books Limited 1983
A member of the Namara Group
27/29 Goodge Street, London W1P 1FD

Copyright © 1983 by Mike Zwerin

British Library Cataloguing in Publication Data

Zwerin, Michael
    Close enough for jazz
    1. Zwerin, Michael   2. Jazz musicians –
    United States – United States – Biography
    I. Title
    785.42'092'4   ML410.Z/

    ISBN 0-7043-2400-8

Typeset by A.K.M. Associates (U.K.) Ltd, Southall, London
Printed and bound in Great Britain
by Mackays of Chatham Ltd, Kent

For: Benjamin Marcel

Thanks to: Richard G. Stern, Paul Haines, Jason Weiss, Stan Getz, Gene Lees, Jim Haynes, Jean-Louis Aubert, John Hammond, Martine Zwerin and most of all to Anne Zwerin for her support above and beyond the call of duty and love.

Portions of this book have appeared in the *International Herald Tribune*, the *Village Voice*, *Mademoiselle* magazine, the *Paris Metro*, *Jazz Forum*, *Passion* magazine, *Jazz Hot* and the *Holland Herald.*

Contents

TAGS

'We cannot get away from the critic's tempers, his impatience, his soreness, his friendships, his spite, his enthusiasms, nay his very politics and religion, if they are touched by what he criticizes . . . It should be his point of honour not to conceal them.'

GEORGE BERNARD SHAW

'Mike, you've got good time for a white cat.'   MILES DAVIS

'Think of your ears as eyes.'   GERTRUDE STEIN

'A jazz musician is a combination orator, dancer, diplomat, poet, dialectician, mathematician, athlete, entertainer, educator, student, comedian, artist, seducer, and general all-round good fellow.'

STEVE LACY

'The holes in your Swiss cheese are somebody else's Swiss cheese.'

MELVIN FISHMAN

'Once we had the Mona Lisa, now we also have the Mona Lisa with a moustache.'   JOHN CAGE

Meet: 'Fatha' Hines, Claude Thornhill, Miles Davis, Maynard Ferguson, John Lewis, Gunther Schuller, Budd Johnson, Eric Dolphy, Michel Petrucciani, Sonny Stitt, Joe Newman, Alan Silva, Charles Mingus, Bob Wilber, Albert Mangelsdorff, Jimmy Knepper, Ravi Shankar, Ted Curzon, Zoot Sims, Kenny Clarke, Bud Powell, Steve Lacy, Barre Phillips, George Wein, Archie Shepp, Hans Dulfer, Allen Eager, Baba Ram Dass, Gerry Mulligan, Polish jazz, Sugar Blue, Roswell Rudd, Larry Rivers, Paul Desmond, Arnie Lawrence, Alexis Korner, John Surman, Telephone, Django Reinhardt, Count Basie, Chet Baker, John Cage, Manfred Eicher, Jimmy Gibson, Elvin Jones, Jaco Pastorius, Adolphe Sax and Sun Ra.

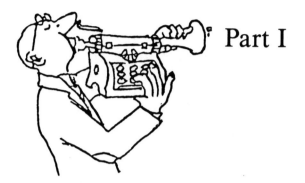

Part I

Part I

Have a Nice Day at the Office Dear

The staff had scratch pads handy. Fred Mann called time: 'Please take notes, gang.' Everybody's Only President drew a staff and notes . . .

Fred was very excited: 'We are very excited, gang. Dome has entered the steel joist business.' Steel joists are open beams of welded angles and bars which support lightweight floors and roofs and look like this . . .

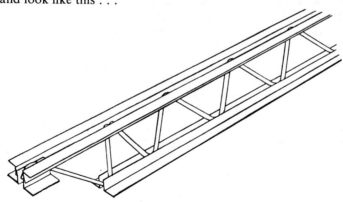

'Let me describe our sales approach as we see it.' Fred flashed his profits-are-good-for-you smile: 'We say to the contractor, let's call him Contractor X . . .'

Fred liked to get in the office earlier than usual on Monday mornings so he could get 'a good jump on the week'. I tried getting in even earlier than Fred to prove how dependable I was, but Fred was more dependable than me.

'Any questions so far? Yes Bud.'

Bud Scheister had been briefed to ask: 'Does our joist design conform to Institute specifications?' (It did not; we were cutting some corners.)

Fred looked at everything from all angles: 'We've looked at this from all angles, Bud, checked our arithmetic time and time again and time and time again . . .'

There is a jazz record released under my name with the biographical note: 'In his spare time, Mike Zwerin is president of Dome Steel Corporation.' Spare time . . . how can time be spare? If it can be spare it can also be killed. Brother can you spare a time? A spare time was had by all. Spare time is not good time. Good time is very important to someone involved with the art of music. 'You got good time for a white cat,' Miles Davis told me.

Turning the time around is playing one and three where two and four should be. When you have good time, even for a white cat, you never turn it around. Not once. Not for a measure. What happened? How had my time turned around? Worst of all it was my own fault. I was serving time behind steel bars of my own fabrication. I was guilty, swinging at the end of my tether, hung up you could say, for having committed the capital crime of killing time.

Swing is the sum of good time. People with spare time do not swing. Fred Mann putters in his spare time. If time can be spare, it cannot be good. The possibility of puttering time aside does not exist for someone with good time. You must follow the forward dance. To question it is to go into spare time. Calling time does not swing. *Time* magazine does not swing. Killing time does not swing. One and three do not swing. Fred Mann lives on one and three. One and three plod. Two and four swing – the second and fourth beats of the bar, the weak beats push. Generally people called 'hip' swing, or try to, though both 'hip' and 'swing' have been deformed by 'hippy' and 'swinger'. Swing in its good time sense is an instinct. You either have it or you don't. Money does not swing, though what it buys certainly can. Bach swings, Mahler doesn't. Russians do not swing. Generalizations do not swing – I'm sure it's possible to find one swinging Russian. If you are wondering what I'm talking about, you probably don't swing. Black people tend to swing, it is less instinctive for whites. Uncle Toms try to forget how to swing on purpose. People who call themselves 'swingers' swing in spare time. We are talking about good time – the dance of time, a cosmic stance. Gypsies swing. New York Jews can swing if they're also funky.

Funk swings. Funk can be defined as a sort of healthy dirt. Babies are funky. (Babies swing.) Keith Richard swings. (Keith Richard is funky.) Animals are funky. Funk is an attitude towards dirt, towards life-substance. Cunnilingus is funky, but the word isn't. Garlic is funky. Americans get less funky all the time, though they can still swing. A smile swings. Farts are funky. People can be funky without swinging, Lyndon Johnson for example, though you cannot swing without at least a smidgeon of funk. Funk, like swing, can be evil. You often hear swinging soundtracks with violent movies. Hitler was funky, Iago swung. Funky Charles Manson swung. The devil swings hard. (Perhaps God is not funky enough.) Corporations don't swing . . . the heart of my problem.

Fred did his homework: 'We've done our homework, gang, and we hope so will you.'

I stifled an impulse to hide my staff and notes from my father, staring sternly down from the founder's plaque on the wall behind me. My life was one big stifled impulse.

The board buzzed . . . important call for Prez. 'Excuse me, gang. I'll take it on my line, Hilda.'

Lew Anderson, credit manager of Bethlehem Steel: 'Oh hi there Lew, how the hell are ya? Right, sure is a good day for hitting a few.' Lew was a golf nut. Dome bought the bulk of its steel bars from Bethlehem, which controlled the market on the East Coast. Pleasing Bethlehem was not the least important part of my life. I cut my hair to their specifications, discussed the game of golf (which does not swing) with their executives, avoided calling them 'man' and made sure not to say anything nice about anybody as far left as John F. Kennedy in their presence.

'Frankly, Michael,' said Lew, 'we were wondering when we could expect a cheque from you folks.'

'Look, Lew . . .' I opened my second pack of cigarettes of the day. Along with pastel button-down shirts, a silver cocaine box, cowboy boots and an FM receiver in my office, my presidential style featured Gauloises Disque Bleu cigarettes: 'We're suffering from the same credit crunch as everybody. Never seen brea . . . money so tight.'

'Yes, but you boys are averaging seventy days and it's not that tight. Say, is there any truth to the rumour that Dome is taking over the Daisy joist operation?'

How the fuck did he know that already? 'Yes, Lew, as a matter of fact Fred and I were hoping to go over it with you next week at the convention in the Greenbriar.'

'By the way, give old Fred my regards.' Fred Mann was Jewish with a Christian name, which Lew found sneaky. Fred told dirty jokes to Lew's wife. Lew's wife thought Fred was cute.

'Michael, you realize . . . I'll be blunt. The first question to pop into our heads when we heard about Daisy was your cash-flow position. Are you fellows fluid enough to take on that extra volume?'

(. . . *dontcha worreh mastah boss, we knows oweh place, we gwanna be good boys, shucks, hehehe, bwanna, everythin' gwanna be juss fiiine* . . .)

'No need to worry, Lew. When we can sit down and lay out all the facts, I'm sure you'll agree.'

'How did you fellows do in the second quarter?'

(. . . *blew our dicks off in the siezecond quiezarter Lew biezaby, solid bruz, swung like a motherfucker, de pots was on* . . .)

'Our auditor's preliminary figures indicate a decided improvement over the first quarter . . .'

(. . . *which was really fucked-up, you should know how bad, Lew, you'd shit* . . .)

'Which wasn't too bad at all considering the cold weather. Construction pretty much froze up around here. How was yours?'

'Our hotbeds were busy, but cash-flow is just awful. Frankly, we're tightening up.'

'Lew, we're in good shape, nothing to worry about. Do me a favour now, forget about business this afternoon and hit 'em good for me, OK?'

My spare-time buddy Solly the accountant was going to have to – excuse the expression – jazz up the figures somehow. Solly: 'The market has been rather good to me lately, Michael, as soon as Dome can reverse these losses, it might be well to consider going public.'

Reverse *this*, Solly.

The *American Flyer* was due to dock Thursday with 2,000 metric tons of French reinforcing bars we didn't need. In addition to shoving it up Bethlehem's ass, I loved to buy foreign – excuse me, Fred said always use 'imported', sounds classier – imported steel because it was romantic and involved trips to Europe. I usually bought too much. I made a note. 'Fred/short-term bread,' and dialled Jennifer Smollett. Jennifer's hotbed was always busy. She was always ready to take on extra volume. No need to lay anything out. No answer. I snorted a fast two and two, wiped the dust off my nose and dashed back to the staff meeting the way a dashing young president should.

'You're just in time, Michael,' Fred Mann greeted me. 'We're on purchasing, that's your bailiwick.'

'Thisoperationisgearedtohighstrengthimportedangles . . .'

I had known 'the gang' ever since my father let me play with his calculating machines on Saturdays. Uncle Morty was traffic manager. Aunt Goldie was in charge of 'the girls'. I went to camp with Charlie Baldick. I exchanged salesman jokes with the salesmen. Dome Steel Corporation had just leased a fleet of air-conditioned Dodges for their greater comfort and efficiency. Fred said it would 'pay off in spades'. Fred Mann had given me a musical slide-rule for my fourteenth birthday so I could transpose tonalities more efficiently. Fred liked to tuck a *Wall Street Journal* under his arm to 'duck into the little boys' room'. He sipped a Presbyterian before dining out with his 'child bride'. Director of the PTA, ADA, AMA and the Concrete Steel Bar Institute despite a Jewish nose, Fred knew deep down at gut level that go-out-and-nab-that-order Fred Mann and not this spare-time son of the boss deserved to be president of Dome Steel Corporation.

I gave Bud Scheister the floor: 'Yes, Bud.'

'The gang might be interested to know about how we are planning to run other items on Daisy's welders in the slow months so that . . .'

'Excuse me Bud, but I'd like to assure everyone that we won't be making any chains over at Daisy.' The gang laughed except for Fred who looked nervously at Goldie who was quite deaf but laughed anyway. Nothing like a bawdy joke to amuse the troops, and to cut off Bud who had been instructed not to discuss future plans at this meeting: 'Let's call it a day, gang.'

Back in my corner office overlooking romantic Sixth Avenue, I closed my *shoji* screens and lit the indirect lighting. Hilda buzzed: 'There's a Mr Hamburger to see you.'

'I'm expecting him. Send Mr Hamburger in, please. And Hilda, I'll be working late tonight, please leave me the first line.'

Hilda was black and married to a trumpet-player. I had hired her because she was black and married to a trumpet-player, integrating the joint and gaining an ally at the same time. Hilda was in a position to guess who or what Hamburger was, and that I wouldn't be 'working' late.

Hamburger charged $70 an ounce, high back in 1963. He delivered. I was his only president: 'Would you like a sample, Mr President?'

'No thank you Mr Hamburger, your quality-control programme is well-known. However I'm sure you won't mind if I verify your tally sheet.'

'Not at all Mr President.'

Saying goodnight to Uncle Morty on the way to the mail-room, I came back with the scale. The count read light. Hamburger scratched his head and checked the tare.

'Maybe I will have a sample after all,' I said.

'Why Mr President . . .' Hamburger looked hurt.

'No no, it's OK, anybody can make a mistake.' I didn't really mind the light count; Hamburger was in a hole and if I was in spare time, I also had spare cash. 'I just thought a smoke might help solve my backhaul problem.'

Hamburger lit a pipe: 'What's a backhaul?'

'Returning from a delivery with an empty truck. It's throwing out good money.'

'Personally, I always charge the round-trip cab-fare.'

I did not laugh. This 'Businessman' game was no longer funny.

Hamburger no longer smiled when he called me 'Mr President'. It wasn't funny; you are what you do. I was a Jewish businessman. I was the only president my friends knew. They hustled me with business ideas. Hamburger was currently pushing a venture called 'Cosmobild', which held the patent to a design for corrugated-paper houses that could be sold for a thousand dollars each. Hamburger wanted to build them in Israel. He said paper houses would solve the Palestinian problem in five years by eliminating Arab slums: 'People who live in paper houses don't throw bombs,' he said. He asked me if I'd studied their prospectus.

'Not yet,' I answered. 'Not from all angles.' Actually I had discussed it with Fred Mann, who said: 'In my humble opinion we shouldn't touch it with a ten-foot pole.' Fred held the ten-foot pole gold medal.

'One final word, Prez,' said Hamburger before leaving. 'Seems to me your organization chart is out of focus. Presidents shouldn't worry about below-the-line shit like backhauls. Don't you have a traffic manager?'

Uncle Morty couldn't manage the traffic from here to the little boys' room. I settled back into the red leather swivel chair formerly occupied by my father ('I'm sure Dad would be proud to know you are sitting in his place') and rolled a joint. Hamburger was right. Something was wrong. Everything. All wrong. I was aware of blowing something, I wasn't sure what. Money. Time. Privilege. Youth. Talent. I wasn't doing something I should be doing, I should be doing something I wasn't. Four letters to dictate, all of which absolutely had to go out tomorrow. Two projections to complete before the weekend. I stretched out on my Bloomingdale sofa and began to study the giant photos of steel reinforcing bars on my wall. I was planning an advertising campaign around the aesthetics of steel for concrete. As with my daring plan to redesign our letterheads, Fred said it was 'throwing out good money'.

Good money. Make good money in your spare time. Check your arithmetic. Look at everything from all angles. Do your homework. I switched on the FM receiver – John Coltrane playing 'Giant Steps' – and considered Bud Scheister's request for a raise. Would that be throwing out good money? Goldie was recommending computerized billing. 'Giant Steps' is the synthesis of the turnaround. Fred Mann thought Dome should consider going into the erection end. Coltrane was burying changes more than running them. The first line rang. Probably some contractor complaining; we were having flatbed problems. I closed my eyes.

'Hi, Prez.' A happy young freckled face at the door. Jennifer Smollett, of the Odessa, Texas, Smolletts, had ended a series of crushes on football-players after screwing Charlie Barnett's trombone-player. Jennifer was no intellectual, though she was smart enough to know that her body was more interesting than her mind. She made it her currency. She and I arrived at occasional transactions.

The word 'screw' in this context may offend some female readers. Let me insist on it, however. It is precise. I would not use it about my wife. She and I did not screw, we made love. We liked each other, gave to each other, touched with emotion. Whatever you call it, though, she and I weren't doing it any more and so this evening I would screw Jennifer.

I was Jennifer's only president. I was everybody's only president. Everybody's Only President was having trouble presiding. He was presided upon to moan. There was an offer of cheap South African steel. Was it immoral to buy South African steel? Lee Morgan got off on 'The Rumproller'. If Dome went into the erection end, it would require more flatbeds. Jennifer laid out some facts. Computerized billing might improve fluidity. She pushed his head down and Everybody's Only President did not come up smelling like a rose. She pulled him over on top of her on his fifty-inch Itkin desk. A good jump on the weak. He had his back hauled. Cache flowed. Papers flew. And in the course of spare time his projections crumpled.

2
What Do You Want to Be when You Grow up?

High-school hipsters slouched through my living-room, eyes red, leaning forward with horns in gig-bags cradled in their arms. They wore goatees and Dizzy Gillespie berets. Those who were not already junkies scratched themselves and spoke with the rasp to make believe they were. Charlie Parker was a junky and that was good enough for us.

'Groovy, man, what a gas!' they'd say as my father looked over his evening paper in disbelief. They'd climb the stairway to my little attic studio where there was a wire recorder, an upright piano and pictures of jazz giants on the walls. Earl Brew burned some piano keys but my mother did not say anything because Earl was black and she was liberal. She thought the burns were from cigarettes.

When we weren't playing music we were listening to or talking about it. 'What do you want to be when you grow up?' was not something that had to be asked.

We had cards printed with 'music for all occasions' on them. We took professional names. Bob Milner became Bob Mills, Frank Hamburger chose Duke Frank, I was Mike Wayne. Al Goldstein picked Al Young in honour of his hero Lester Young, but everybody called him Lester Goldstein.

My attic room overlooked the Forest Hills Tennis Club. The tennis-players complained because our jamming jammed their concentration. We were the first Jewish family in Forest Hills Gardens, an exclusive semi-private enclave. My father suspected the tennis-players were anti-Semitic. The tennis-players accused him of operating a rehearsal studio in violation of zoning laws. Lester Goldstein loved to honk out the window during crucial rallies and Lester really knew how to honk.

I cut high school to catch noon shows at the Paramount, the Capital, the Strand – Broadway theatres in which my models rose hungover from pits for the first of five daily shows playing 'Blue Flame', 'Skyliner', 'Take The A Train' and 'Let's Dance', my 'Star-Spangled Banners'.

I was dazzled by the sparkle of spots off brass. I daydreamed of future hungover noons rising from pits. I knew name-band personnel like other kids know big-league line-ups.

My parents took me to a Catskill Mountain hotel for a summer holiday. After breakfast one morning, walking into the early mountain air, we passed the hotel band bass-player coming in with a dazzling woman on his arm. We had talked and he knew I wanted to be a musician. 'Boy, you're up early,' I said.

He hesitated: 'Yes . . . early.'

Later I realized he had not in fact been to sleep. How I envied grown-ups who could stay up all night playing music and be with such beautiful women. Now when I think back at what life must have really been like for that hack working the Jewish Alps for the summer, I wonder how children survive their fantasies. I was in love with music; she was my obsession; I could not see straight for the love of her.

But if music is, as Duke Ellington put it, my mistress, we have had a stormy relationship. I cheated on her, lied to, neglected and beat her. On the other hand, she was too demanding. When she nagged I left her and when I neglected her she left me. I was to spend my time under too many hats, between too many stools. It would be a stormy affair.

In the summer of 1949, I was in New York on vacation from the University of Miami where I was majoring in sailing. No. Actually, sixteen of us were on scholarship to play for dinner in the student cafeteria which was cantilevered over an artificial lake. When we played the way we wanted we sounded like Stan Kenton. The band was called 'Sonny Burnham and his Sunmen'. It was sort of like sailing at that.

In those days I played my horn like a kid skiing down a slalom, with more courage than sense. Falling on my face never occurred to me. One night I climbed up to Minton's, where bebop was born, in Harlem. A lot of white cats considered Minton's too steep a slope, but I never imagined that somebody might not like me because I was white or Jewish. I was absolutely fearless. I walked in, took out my horn and started to play 'Walkin' ' with Art Blakey, then known as Abdullah Buhaina, a fearful cat, I was later to learn.

When I noticed Miles Davis standing in a dark corner, I tried harder because Miles was with Bird's band. He came over as I packed up. I slank into a cool slouch. I used to practise cool slouches. We were both wearing shades; no eyes to be seen. 'You got eyes to make a rehearsal tomorrow?' Miles asked me.

'I guess so.' I acted as though I didn't give one shit for his stupid rehearsal.

'Four.' Miles made it clear he couldn't care less if I showed up or not.

Driving home over the Triborough Bridge to the house by the tennis courts, I felt like a batboy who had been offered a try-out with the team.

The next day at four I found myself with a band that would come to be called 'The Birth of the Cool'. Gerry Mulligan, Max Roach, John Lewis, Lee Konitz, Junior Collins, Bill Barber and Al McKibbon played arrangements by Mulligan and Gil Evans, who was musical director.

Miles was . . . cool. Pleasant, relaxed, diffident, it was his first time as leader and he relied on Gil. He must have picked up his famous salty act sometime later because he was sweet as his sound that summer.

It did not seem historic or legendary. A good jazz gig, but there were plenty of them then in New York. We certainly did not have the impression that those two weeks in a Broadway joint called the Royal Roost would give birth to an entire style. It was fun being on a championship team, and when Gene Krupa's entire trumpet section took a front table to hear us I was proud, but my strongest memory of those two weeks is the one we played opposite Count Basie, who then had Wardell Gray on tenor saxophone. Like a later summer spent listening to John Coltrane with Thelonious Monk at the Five Spot, Wardell with Basie is a sound that has never left my head and I will go to my grave with it.

I call that sound that stays in my head 'the Cry'. I seem to remember somebody else once talking about the Cry so if I'm stealing I apologize. Anyway, stealing is the essence of literary love. You cannot patent licks, just shove them out there and hope they are stolen. The Cry is everywhere. The Rumanian pan-pipe-player Gheorge Zamfire has it – Zoot Sims, Ray Charles, Bruce Springsteen. Bob Marley had it. The blues are the classical incarnation of the Cry. You could also call it 'the Wail', a direct audial objectification of the soul. You know it when you hear it. Billie Holiday had it, to die. I wonder whether to include Mozart's operas, which might be a bit too structured to fit my definition of the Cry. The Cry must be a bit off, informal, direct, not stifled by structure or commercial considerations. Glenn Gould had it, Trane, Bix, Bird, Hendrix, Prez, Monk. Indian ragas have it, Flamenco singers, Milton Nascimento (all Brazilian singers seem to have it), Jewish cantors, black gospel singers. I could go on but you get the idea. Miles Davis certainly had it.

How would my life have changed had I stayed in New York to pursue the Cry after the summer of 1949 instead of going back to Miami and college like a good boy? A few months later, Miles made that 'historic' *Birth of the Cool* record with Kai Winding on trombone, and I became a footnote to jazz history. Do I have the Cry? Perhaps it is here on a few pages. Will I ever get into the body of the work?

Back to shoeless life in Coconut Grove, to the sweet mildew there, to being a big fish in a calm pond. We had our groupies, girls in gypsy skirts who said 'groovy' too. They could not clap on two and four and I avoided them until one told me about another kind of swing made by people like T.S. Eliot and Bach. She was tall, blonde, Catholic, with twin girls by a former husband, and when we ran away to Georgia to be married, my father cut me off.

My childhood ended checking into a motel near Jacksonville. From now on I would be checking myself in, nobody to do it for me. Having fought for freedom, I was no longer sure I wanted it. I understand why people bury themselves in corporations or career military service; it is comforting to take orders. For years I took comfort there myself. My eyes opened with fright the following morning. More often than not I have opened my eyes with fright ever since. Think of what I have done wrong, what I haven't done at all, what has to be done today. If only somebody would tell me what to do and not do. Or better yet, do it for me. I always thought this my own private fear, and I had not intended dealing with it here until I read an interview with Gabriel Garcia Marquez, the writer of *One Hundred Years of Solitude*, in *Playboy* only yesterday. He said: '*Everyone* is afraid of solitude,' and that he too wakes with fear in the morning.

Eleanor and I woke up before sunrise and delivered the *Miami Herald* door-to-door. It took an hour to fold the papers in the Veedol Station on the corner of Coral Way and 17th Avenue, longer when it rained and they had to be stuffed into plastic bags. Then we inched our Chevy along lawn-lined streets tossing papers.

There was the smell of bougainvillaea as the tropical sun rose and dogs barked chasing us. We lived in a $60-a-month crooked wooden house with a big sea grape tree in the front yard. All of a sudden I had a wife with three sisters, a brother and friendly parents and I was no longer a lonely only child. Main childhood memories are of afternoons and early evenings with maids while my parents went to work and theatres. People said I was throwing away my life marrying early, but I needed company. We had a dog named Bird.

I worked in Minsky's Burlesque backing strippers for a season. We played 'Dawn on the Desert' behind Dolly Dawn, who thought it was very funny to say 'fuck you' to the band instead of 'good evening'. So did we. One season was enough. I was smart enough to get through college with Cs without learning anything.

The good boy drifted with neither thought nor protest into Dome Steel Corporation ('Steel for Concrete'), in return for which his father forgave him his Catholic wife. We had a daughter of our own as I started working my way up the executive ladder. After my father died of overwork we moved into the big house by the tennis courts in Forest Hills.

I had a closet full of neckties, custom shirts and a suit for every day of the week. By the age of twenty-three my ambition was to grow old. Responsible people called it 'responsible . . . mature, serious'. Youth was a liability, music a tangent and vacations were spent to work more efficiently when they were over.

You might ask whatever happened to my burning love of music. I asked myself. When I read about Gerry Mulligan's success with his pianoless quartet in *Time* magazine, I moaned. That could have been me.

I jammed here and there with amateurs but I'd rather not play at all than sound amateurish so I stopped jamming. My father had not pressured me to go into his business. He was pleased enough once it happened, but he already had an heir in Fred Mann, who was more like the son he should have had. My mother just wanted me to be happy and she has always supported me no matter what. There had been no pressure there either. Eleanor did not care about financial wealth. She said (more and more often) that she should have married a 'creative person' and why didn't I go back to music. But playing music was fun; I could not consider that a 'serious' career. It was comforting to rely on a pay-cheque in an organization where my name precluded any danger of dismissal. Had I committed myself to jazz at that point I think that today I would be one of the ten best trombonists in the world. I had everything but the conviction. It was an unforgivable crime and I'm still paying for it. Never once, to this day, have I played jazz six nights a week for as long as two weeks running. I've read music with big bands, toured with rock bands, played with jazz bands in which I had a chorus or two a night, but I've never blown, stretched out, stayed in the slot, put my own pots on for as long as two straight weeks. I abused my muse and retribution was pitiless. 'You're an underrated trombone-player,' a customer in an Amsterdam club recently told me. 'It's better than not being rated at all,' I answered. I'm not so sure.

Leaving the Russian Tea Room after a three-martini lunch with Lew Anderson, I crossed Miles and Gil Evans arriving. By now I had a familiar stomach-lump in such situations. I had to break bread with the likes of Lew to be able to afford the Russian Tea Room; Miles and Gil did it with jazz. I was increasingly aware of the fact that I had made somebody else's mistake. It's terrible having nobody to blame. Miles and Gil had followed their forward dance, I had 'egg on my face', which is how Fred would have put it. I was a poacher.

It was a bright autumn afternoon and Miles looked as though he had just stepped out of the pages of *Esquire* magazine. He wore a flared suede single-vent jacket and leather driving gloves with belts on them. The doorman was parking his Ferrari. I was afraid he would not acknowledge recognizing me; we had not met since the cool had been born, but he poked my stomach and said in that sandpaper voice of his: 'You're getting fat, Mike.'

'Have a nice day at the office, dear,' my better half said as I left for work.

'Bye bye, wifey,' I answered, pecking her cheek. 'Have fun ironing my shirts.'

We were both increasingly aware that we were stuck in roles we did not have the courage to opt out of. When I called her 'the little woman', she would pull out the blade and twist it back: 'It's a bird; it's a plane; it's BUSINESSMAN.'

We stayed home nights reading. Reading is what Eleanor does. It is her occupation, her commitment, her passion. She is still reading every day until this day. You are what you read. 'Wouldn't you hate to die while you were reading a bad novel?' she once asked me. I was in the middle of *Marjorie Morningstar* at the time. I never finished it. Flirting with the intellectual wing of the Catholic church, Eleanor read Christopher Dawson, Simone Weil, Jacques Maritain and the entire *Summa Theologica*. We subscribed to *Commonweal* and the *Partisan Review*. We caught foreign – imported – films on weekends. I ferried baby-sitters home, children to dance-classes. We held hands listening to Bach, Rameau sustained us for a while. We discovered Scarlatti, who sustained us for months. We discovered Beethoven's late string quartets. Then she took the kids to Miami for a short vacation and never returned.

I could hear Fred Mann's clichés: 'Back to square one . . . it's a whole new ball game.' Finding yourself in Paris is a cliché in itself but none the less good for it for that reason, and I went there. I took mistress music out to lunch, bought her flowers, kissed her every day, moved into a musicians' hotel called the Crystal. Stephane Grappelli practised Bach sonatas in the next room on his violin. Allen Eager could be found in the Old Navy Café. William Burroughs and Brion Gysin were cutting up words in the Beat Hotel. I practised scales, arpeggios, patterns and old Lester Young solos.

Word spread that Miles Davis was coming for a concert at the Olympia Theatre and three weeks in the Club St Germain, across

Rue St Benoit from the Crystal.

But no Miles by the afternoon of the concert. Speculation focused on what kind of number he was running. Still no sign of him by the half hour. When the curtain went up, only sidemen on stage. I've always somehow been waiting for Miles Davis. As you may have guessed by now, he's no great friend of mine, yet I've always known him and he will always be close to me. Nasty son of a bitch or not, he's touched and formed me more than many of my great friends. Like family, he may disappear and ignore me but I can count on his return. I imagine Miles slinking down dark streets, the collar of his Burberry raincoat turned up. There he goes roaring into the Malibu sunset in his Ferrari. Now he lounges days away in some pneumatic retreat, puffing an opium pipe, surrounded by perfumed and shiny things.

Recently I was with Chet Baker in the Club Dreher on Place Châtelet in Paris one afternoon, alone there, interviewing him. He stopped talking when the tape played Miles's record *The Man with the Horn*. (Note the definite articles; no false modesty there.) Chet stared at the bottles for a while and said: 'That sure is romantic music.'

And it's true. Miles Davis has in fact never played bebop, cool, fusion or funk. He has always been a flat-out up-front romantic. Miles recorded a tune called 'Willie Nelson' in the seventies and Nelson, the country music star, praises Miles. They have been rumoured to be planning a project together. What does the bad black dude have in common with the redneck picker? In addition to grainy textured voices, restrained tension, staying-power and the uncanny ability each has to transmogrify standards (compare Miles's 'If I Were a Bell' to Nelson's 'Stardust'), each of them is an incurable romantic.

That is why Miles and Coltrane made such a timeless team – the nineteenth and twentieth centuries in tandem. And like a true nineteenth-century romantic, Miles is always disappearing with a wave of his cape and a Byronic consumptive cough into the mists, on some brave, secret, lonely mission. Always to reappear just when you need him.

Meanwhile, back in the Olympia Theatre, Barney Wilen was playing the blues on his tenor saxophone; Kenny Clarke, Pierre Michelot and Rene Urtreger behind him. Milesless in Paris. But you could feel the breeze from the cape. When the blues came to the dominant on Barney's last chorus, he moved back and Miles emerged from the right wing. It took him just exactly those four bars to reach the mike and hard – not easing in, not warming up, not even very cool – he began to machine-gun the Cry.

Actually his total absence would not have been a total surprise. Miles, who James Baldwin called 'a miraculously tough and tender man', was having hard drug problems. He talked about it to a journalist named Cheryl McCall who interviewed him for *Jazz Hot* magazine: 'Max Roach put $200 in my pocket and said I looked good. This disgusted me so much I went right home to my father in St Louis. I said to myself that son of a bitch gave me $200 and said I looked good. I was strung out and he knew it. And this was my best friend, right? I died with embarrassment. I looked at myself in the mirror and I said: "Godamn it, Miles, come on." '

'Was kicking junk terrible?' she asked him.

'Yeah, it was awful . . . but I had a plan. I was going to jump out the window and break my leg and then with a little luck they'd give me a painkiller for my leg and everything would be OK. But then every day it got a little better . . . I'd had enough of seeing myself that way. I was a pimp too. I had lots of girls. I did this and that . . . I had more money than I have now. That's right, I had about seven girls. I can't even remember their names now.'

In Paris in the winter of 1957 his drug problems were obviously over. He danced there like an in-shape champ, jabbing and undercutting notes that stung and burned. Now and then he would stand still, wiping his lip, staring, lay out for five or six measures – a long musical space – as though waiting for his opponent to tire. The Man with the Horn.

Miles has been called 'the Prince of Silence'. 'Don't play what's there, play what's not there,' he'd tell his musicians – and 'Don't play what you know, play what you don't know.' He once said: 'I have to change, it's like a curse.' He is known for caustic putdowns, turning his back on the audience, showing up late or not at all, refusing to play encores, driving fast cars, being a clothes horse, womanizing, getting in trouble with the law; his financial negotiating prowess is legendary. He can be tyrannical.

The first night at the Club St Germain, Barney Wilen came over to me at the bar, shook his head and said: 'You won't believe what

Miles said to me after my last solo.' Barney was a hot young tenorman oozing confidence and he actually thought this was funny: 'He said "Barney, why don't you stop playing those awful notes?"'

This sort of Miles line always leaves me like one of those motel massage-beds right after the money runs out. You don't know quite how to feel. On the one hand it's sensual being launched out into that still space, on the other hand it was such a disappointment when the vibrations stopped. His lines leave you hanging like that. Towards the end of John Coltrane's period with Miles, Trane was searching desperately to find his own personality. His solos were getting longer and longer, sometimes lasting for forty-five minutes in the middle of a forty-five-minute set. Miles said to him: 'Man, why don't you try playing twenty-seven choruses instead of twenty-eight?' Trane answered: 'I get involved in these things and I don't know how to stop.' Miles said: 'Try taking the saxophone out of your mouth.'

It was once said of a playboy: 'He would rather not make love to a beautiful woman and have everybody think he had than make love to her and have nobody know it.' There must be a little bit of that in every man. Even though wooing Eugenia and Ursula had produced no physical contact with either, I revelled in my big splash descending into the basement Club St Germain, one on each arm. Everyone would think I was making it with both of them at once; an entrance worthy of Allen Eager.

'Allen Reluctant' we used to call him, the granite-faced tenorman who played more like Lester Young than Lester Young. The first time someone told me about Stan Getz, he was described as 'playing even better than Allen Eager'. There were many other white Presidents – Stanley Kosow, Brew Moore, Johnny Andrews – and I had played with all of them in Brooklyn strip clubs. They had taught me tricks like running augmented arpeggios on dominant seventh chords; listening to them had been my school, but none of them had taught me more than Allen Eager. Allen was my Joe Dimaggio; I modelled my swing after his. He listened to Prokofiev, drove racing cars (once won Sebring), frequented Swiss ski resorts, lived with high fashion models (boy were they high), patronized the best English custom tailors. He could also be a nasty bastard when strung out, which was not infrequent. Miles kept trying to find out the name of Allen's tailor but Allen wasn't talking. This was no nodding-out, nose-scratching junky fixing in dirty toilets. He was always sharp, bright, on top of it. He could hold his own with poets, writers and classical musicians. He was a model to me of what hip should be. How have I survived my heroes? How I envied Allen Eager. Much later, not too many years ago, I ran into him living in a broken-down house in the black slums of Coconut Grove. He had lost his teeth, was a born-again Christian, on welfare and the food-stamp programme.

In Paris in 1957 Allen Eager was rooming with Beat poet Gregory Corso in the 'Beat Hotel' and I was pleased to imagine myself in his image walking into the Club St Germain with Eugenia on one arm, Ursula on the other. Miles was between sets in a dark corner. I always seem to see Miles in dark corners. He put his arm around my shoulder, asked about my health and generally made it clear that he was concerned with my welfare. His smile went a long way with the ladies. A club-owner once said to him: 'The trouble with you is that everybody *likes* you, you little son of a bitch.'

He joined us after the first set. I had to take Eugenia back to her university dormitory, where there was a curfew. When I returned I found Miles and Ursula in deep eye-contact. With his best evil ray, he looked at me and asked her: 'What do you see in a dumb cat like this? He's too fat anyway.'

I could never take his salty act seriously. He was so up-front about it for one thing. They were more jabs than anything. It was not really a knock-down round, he was just sparring. He went back for another set.

'Well I guess I have a decision to make,' Ursula said. Was it possible? She was deciding between me and Miles. You can understand the nature of groupiedom from the beginning of time when I tell you I almost recommended Miles, pleased to be able to furnish him a beautiful woman. As we walked up the stairs together, Miles squinted at us from the bandstand. He looked so tragic, so Byronic, like a little lost poet as he opened up the melody of 'When I Fall in Love' like a flower.

Back in New York, I hung around the Local 802 union floor with my newly in-shape embouchure. The union floor was packed with guys who knew 300 tunes but could not make music. I was part of the minority who could make music but had an awful lot of trouble making money at it. We huddled together, picking up the scraps. Local 802 rented the Roseland Ballroom during the day for their union floor. I played the Roseland at night for several weeks. I forget the name of the band; it was a forgettable band. People nostalgic for the big band era forget how many forgettable big bands there were. I went out with 'weekend bands' like Urbie Green, Billy May and the Commanders. Forgettable bands. Yet here I was finally a working musician, waking up hungover at noon. I could not believe my luck.

When I finally made my first big name band, the name had faded and the band was shrunken.

3
Claude Thornhill: The Square on the Lawn

Claude Thornhill loved confusion. It seemed to be his only remaining pleasure. His mistress had abandoned him too. All his creativity went into the deliberate cultivation of confusion.

He never called out the number or the name of the next arrangement. Each started with a piano introduction and we had to recognize it. He tried tricking us with oriental, Flamenco or atonal disguises. He could be pretty clever about it. We would wait for Squirms, the lead trumpet-player who had been with Claude so long he could hear through him, to shout 'Lover Man' or 'Witchcraft' and then we scrambled to pull out the chart.

When we were ready, Claude modulated with grace and musicality into another introduction and watched our confusion. Eventually Squirms screamed another title and we scrambled again. It could go on three or four times. In the meantime, Squirms might grab a fast blast from the portable leather bar he always carried – 'my band aid' he called it – and groan: 'This band should disband.'

Claude adored the confusion setting up. Combination french horn-player and bandboy, Nooch would be unpacking while musicians ran scales and stage hands fussed. Once Claude grabbed a microphone, announced: 'Testing, testing onetwothree,' and then, looking totally revolted by the results, began shouting firm and completely unintelligible instructions to nobody in particular. He looked up, pointing with horror: 'What the blirdy spidle restitrew?'

'You're putting me on,' said the drummer.

'Are you kidding? Who'd want to wear a drummer?' Claude laughed to beat the band.

'Put on' is originally jazz slang. It is at the root of the irony of jazz humour. We would laugh at what was not supposed to be funny. Being put on was passing a test. We'd tell 'sick' cancer-, multiple sclerosis- and elephantitis-jokes just because they were not supposed to be funny. This expressed our anarchistic life-view. Lenny Bruce and Lord Buckley took 'hip' humour out of the closet so perhaps we should drop it here.

Though one more example serves. The writer Terry Southern (*Candy, The Magic Christian*) could carry sick humour to new lows. He called me for a period of months seriously suggesting we form what he called 'the Alltime Allstar Fuckup Band'. It would include Allen Eager, Squirms, Tony Fruscella, Phil Seaman, Jimmy Ford, Chet Baker and all those outrageous fucked-up heroes. Laughing at them is like laughing at spastics, acceptable 'hip' humour it's true. Perhaps I wasn't hip enough. Sometimes Terry would call in the middle of the night: 'What about Junior Collins? Gotta have Junior Collins.' He thought it pretty funny to assemble these nodding-out, throwing-up, nose-scratching wasted souls on one bandstand. Terry was writing for *Esquire* magazine at the time and he was sure they'd go for an article about the Alltime Allstar Fuckups.

Considering the context of sick humour jazz musicians exist in, it was odd that I could not laugh at Claude Thornhill's sick jokes. One time he went down in the diving bell they used to have in Atlantic City, off the Steel Pier. There was nothing much to it – you just went down under the pier and right back up again. There was a microphone in there and the people on the pier could hear the 'oohs' and 'ahs' of that incredible experience. We heard Claude's voice among the others, getting louder and louder, until it became a scream drowning out everything: 'Look, look, water, water. There's a leak. Oh my God! Help! Please somebody help me. We're all going to drown like rats in a trap. HEEEELLLPPP . . .'

That might have been an amusing little number had it not been for the fact that he sounded like he thought he was really drowning. He could see the water coming to drown him. He really did need help.

Claude died a few years later, but he was already dead musically by the fall of 1958 when I toured with his band for six weeks in Texas, Oklahoma, Louisiana and states like that.

Claude had been a pioneer, the first commercial dance band to play bebop arrangements and Charlie Parker tunes as early as the late forties. They were good, too, by Gerry Mulligan and Gil Evans. They were still in the book in my days but rarely pulled out. Claude was highly amused when we played 'Walter Winchell Rhumba' instead. He saw it as a huge joke on the public. But when he was drunk, nostalgic, or we pestered him enough, he sometimes launched into an introduction even Squirms couldn't remember, until he'd finally yell: 'Anthropology' or 'Yardbird Suite' and we'd find those yellow, fading, stained parts; but this was not often.

He was then a small, shrunken man with a W.C. Fields nose and there was quite a bit of Fields in him in general. His hair was combed straight back and the hairline was receding. His waistline was expanding. His eyes were often glazed, which I attributed to excessive alcohol but Squirms told me that Claude once suffered a nervous breakdown and had had electro-shock therapy, although he drank enough too.

The band's basic style was built around a soft, smooth sound obtained by a french horn playing the melody with harmonized saxophones. Glenn Miller with brains. Claude had been on top for a while with that sound, playing the best theatres, clubs and hotels. His theme song 'Snowfall' was on juke boxes and Fran Warren and Gene Williams were popular when they sang with him. But by my time his fortunes had taken a decided and, as it turned out, permanent turn for the worse.

Arrangements written for full sections were being played by only one trombone, two trumpets, four saxophones, a now guitarless rhythm section plus the essential french horn. We worked country clubs, American Legion halls and high-school gymnasiums in provincial towns where Claude Thornhill was still a name. Referring to more successful 'ghost bands' – Sam Donahue and the Tommy Dorsey Orchestra, Ray McKinley and the Glenn Miller Orchestra – Claude once said to me after a particularly grungy affair: 'I guess you have to be dead to make it these days.'

All twelve of us travelled in two cars and a supply truck, which was driven by Nooch. Claude's road manager, Kurt, who also played saxophone, was a fat nervous type who kept trying unsuccessfully to look cool. We started to tour one wet November night at the Nevada Hotel, a dive which many musicians called home, on Broadway and 68th Street. Kurt sipped coffee, sneaking looks at his watch and out the luncheonette's foggy window. 'Jeezus H. Keerist, where the hell is Claude?' he muttered. Squirms pulled me aside and said he had just grabbed a double in a little bar across the street and, look, Claude was there. We could see him peeking out the window, a pixyish smile on his face watching Kurt freak.

I learned about the day sheet. In those days, if you checked into a hotel at 7 a.m. you could check out as late as four the following afternoon and pay for only one night. With a little planning and a missed night's sleep here and there, it was possible to check in only three times a week. And ghosting. Ghosting is when two guys check into a double room and some time later four more wander through the lobby looking as though they are checked in somewhere else. By staggering their entrance into the elevator, they could usually get to the room without detection. Then they slept on a couch or the floor and the cost of the room got split six ways instead of two.

After a three-day drive interrupted only once by some boss ghosting we arrived in Port Arthur Texas just in time for the day sheet. Squirms and I were wary of ghosts, so we decided to room together alone, cost notwithstanding. We went to sleep, leaving a 5 p.m. wake-up call. I unpacked my horn beforehand. The hardest part about practising is taking the monster out of the case; it is often an unsurmountable psychological block. By 5.30 I was warming up.

Admiring the shine of my trombone's polished brass, I remembered a line by the poet (Eleanor taught it to me) Gerard Manley Hopkins that described something pure 'like shining from shook foil'. We are living in the age of shiny things, we define ourselves by the shiny things we accumulate. The brainwash is reinforced daily. Even those who consider themselves 'liberated' are raped by the shiny things dazzling them continually from all sides. But a trombone is one noble shiny thing. I can think of none nobler. A simple assemblage of tubing with no mechanical equipment of any kind; kiss it and it makes music.

A cruddy instrument makes cruddy music. My trombone is

always polished. I am not one to admire Charlie Parker's habit of playing on a cruddy saxophone held together with rubber bands and chewing gum. Bird would have played even better on a shiny saxophone. The shine reflects a certain cleanliness of the soul. It is a sparkle of honour. I love these machines you kiss in order to make music like my father loved the efficient click of calculating machines. Gun-lovers polish their rifles with the same sort of affection I lavish on my slush pump.

'Slush pump'. I don't know where the name came from; it is jazz argot for trombone. Not current argot; it implies a certain archaic irony. It probably has something to do with 'sludge', maybe unblocking a toilet. A trombone is not terribly sexy, it is in fact humorous like an accordion. You pump it, bump into things with it. It's also called a 'bone' and the dixieland-style 'tailgate trombone' comes from the fact that during those old-time New Orleans funeral parades, the only place the trombone-player had enough room to pump was over the tailgate of the waggon. It is on the other hand considered the instrument closest to the human voice; a nineteenth-century composer called it 'the voice of God'.

I fastened the slide to the bell at varying angles until it fit my hand, lubricated the stockings, put vaseline on the tuning crook so it would move easily but only when desired, passed a brush through the tubing, polished the balance-weight and made sure the spit-valve was properly corked. I shined the bell inside and out with a chamoix cloth, caressed it and might have even kissed it had not Squirms finished throwing up in the toilet and emerged groaning: 'I'm sick and tired of waking up tired and sick.'

Now here was a hero. My roomie, Squirms's definition of a square was someone who doesn't like to throw up. A funky road-rat with bleary eyes and a green complexion testifying to a dedicated pursuit of happiness, Squirms was laying low from the day. Daytime was not his friend. Under cover of darkness, he consumed small packages of powders and liquids in vials. He almost never ate and yet he was overweight. If the gin people had added vitamins to their product he would not have eaten at all. He ate out of a sense of duty. His idea of a meal was one Drake's Cake.

Squirms poured himself a libation from his band-aid, a quadruple. Four fingers, no fucking around. The smell of alcohol joined that of codeine syrup and the dyspeptic cloud which surrounded Squirms at all times. Even a ten-foot pole was not enough to escape its touch. The fact that the lead trumpet-player sits in the middle of the brass section made playing a brass instrument hazardous with Squirms, who would joke: 'My mouth feels like dinosaurs are walking around in it.' (Trombone-players have been known to bribe bandboys not to set their chairs directly in front of Squirms. Trombones sit in front of trumpets.) Squirms smelled like catfood. He even looked like catfood, the yuckie kind that comes out of a can. My roomie. And I'm allergic to cats – you figure it out.

Squirms won farting contests, which involve big-league farts with road-rats. And road managers have used the threat of riding in the same car with him to keep unruly players in line. 'Not that, Kurt, anything but *that*.'

Affectionately called 'Filthy McSwine', Squirms believed that playing a saxophone held together by rubber bands and chewing gum was *essential* to Charlie Parker's genius. He thought that the new brand of educated, punctual, well-mannered and responsible jazz musicians would be the death of the music. He considered himself to be preserving tradition, upholding true values. Everybody was too *clean*, that's why jazz was in trouble. His theory was that soap is bad for the skin, that it contains chemical impurities that interfere with natural body juices. 'Look at cats,' he'd say, 'they wash with their own spit.'

His fierce and dependable lead trumpet playing was a miracle. The lead trumpet-player of a big band must be a concertmaster and quarterback in one. He must be clear-headed with fast reflexes and great strength. The chair requires a unique and demanding combination of physical conditioning, tact, leadership and intelligence. Lead trumpet-players often lift weights. A heart attack is the occupational disease. There was controversy over Squirms in the band business, much like over fast-living quarterbacks such as Joe Namath in the sports world. Is it possible that dissipation can help not hinder performance? In certain cases involving genius, this may be true; one element of genius is excess, after all. Geniuses by definition are abnormal. How can they be expected to conform to norms? Physically, however, geniuses are mortal and, in addition to his not being a genius, the wonder was how Squirms's heart could take it. Kurt suggested he leave his heart to science.

'Are you kidding?' Squirms laughed. 'I have to jerk off to get it started in the morning.'

I have neglected to mention Squirms's legendary 'cough syrup switcheroo'. It went like this. Place a can of Tab on a table next to a bottle of maximum codeine cough syrup. Bury your head in the sports page. Read for a while and then absent-mindedly reach for the Tab. This avoids the awful anticipation of the syrup's sweet and sickening consistency. Pick up the syrup by 'mistake' and 'discover' the 'error' after it's all down. Act surprised. Swear. Burp. Wash it down with the Tab.

It went like this three times a day when Squirms could not score anything harder (sometimes even if he could). After only one day sheet, empty syrup bottles would be rolling around under the bed and in dresser drawers. Chambermaids gave him knowing winks: 'Cough any better?'

This did not embarrass him, on the contrary. He was proud of his excess. He gloated and joked about it: 'My stomach may be a mess, but I haven't had a cough in three years.'

Getting ready to go to work I realized that Fred Mann was probably just getting in bed. Fred went to bed at eight sometimes. Good old Fred. Team-player down the line, Fred believed in the collective good. Although he would be horrified at the mention of the word in connection with himself, Fred was something of a socialist. He believed that business has an obligation to contribute to the community, and to the well-being of employees. He believed in profit-sharing plans, in rewarding people for work well done. He tended to be soft-hearted with requests for a raise. He was in fact an easy touch. Although he believed in the old values as taught in the synagogue, he was not repressive when his daughter announced her lesbianism. He had his doubts about her prospects but he did not deny her his support. Fred contributed something to humanity. He created jobs and set an honest example, raised the tone of the business world. He honoured his word and contracts. Business contacts were embarrassed about lying and cheating with him around. They did not stop doing either, but he made them conscious of what they were doing. I thought about my roomie Squirms. What did he accomplish? Contribute? What did he

29

believe in other than self-gratification? And most of all I wondered why I was so attracted to him.

Some context is necessary. Squirms is an exception, not the rule. He was both larger and smaller than real life. Most jazz musicians are somewhere in between. They are for the most part more or less normal blokes who take no more drugs than advertising agency executives. They might drink a bit because the road is tough, but so do truck-drivers. They have neither the courage nor the desperation it takes to live like Squirms, one long chemical Russian roulette game. Obviously I am not speaking about the great names, but by far the majority of jazz musicians are normal guys who found a way to live outside organized society – to avoid work in banks, record company offices or music stores. This takes a certain amount of sanity. Writing about Squirms is like telling a multiple sclerosis joke. Squirms was one big sick joke, and thus of some interest. But it's past interest, this type basically plays rock today. Rock stole our excess like our licks. So here we are preserving some exotic folklore about an endangered species. I felt pleased being finally part of that folklore, even only to observe it.

Claude Thornhill was not interested in how his band sounded in the autumn of 1958. He never gave any instructions about vibratos, phrasing or dynamics, if he ever even thought about such details. When someone was out of tune – not unusual – Claude would pound an 'A' on the piano. Over and over, two and sometimes four octaves. The customers usually looked perplexed, as if they did not understand modern music. At no time would he say or do something to improve the intonation, just pounded those notes and laughed. Once it got so bad he stopped pounding and rose from the piano bench waving a white handkerchief in unconditional surrender.

We were protected by a thick coat of provincial ignorance. Once in a while, a group of local musicians came to hear the famous Claude Thornhill orchestra, and then he went out of his way to play the dumbest arrangements in the book, which was pretty dumb. We did have our moments, and some nights for four or five minutes we could come close to a reasonable facsimile of the Claude Thornhill of yore. We were like an expansion team, over-the-hill veterans, rookies, and a few like myself who had other things on their minds. Bill's drumming varied with the quality of the girls on the dance floor. If they excited him the time would speed up, if pickings were lean it would be like walking through thick mud. The bassist was a nineteen-year-old hippy (and I use the word in the failed hipster sense) from the Bronx who was also on his first name band. He flew over all sorts of marvellous notes, few of which had any relation to the relevant chord.

I was loafing by the bandstand on a break between sets at the Fort Worth Country Club when Claude, looking elegant in his tuxedo and giggling into the palm of his hand, walked up to me and pointed to a pale, blue-haired little old lady at a nearby table. She had a carnation in her white gown and eyeglasses with fake jewels on the rim. He said she had just requested 'Chloe'. Claude said he politely answered that we had no arrangement for this composition and thus could not play it for her. She looked disappointed for a minute, but then cheered up, snapped her fingers and said: 'Fuck it. Play "Anthropology".' He looked into my eyes unblinking: 'Do you believe *that*?'

'Sure I do,' I answered. 'I believe it.'

The next set we played 'Anthropology'.

We bought an arsenal of cherry bombs in one of those southern counties where they were legal and tossed them out the window with lit fuses on lonely roads. Outside Holdenville, Oklahoma, we spotted Claude's car behind us and tried timing the fuses to explode under it. In Holdenville he jumped out, did a little dance and said: 'Hey fellows, you can't beat fun now can you?'

The acceptable limit of ambition for someone who wants to be called 'hip' is to do what you want as well as possible and if you get rich and famous from it so much the better. Eschew the accumulation of capital or power for their own sake. Conniving for either is considered 'square', though if they arrive on their own so much the better.

The Rolling Stones obtained the fruit of ambition by doing what they wanted to do anyway. They thumbed their noses at square society and were rewarded for it. This was a victory for our side. We formed our resistance behind the Stones. What else could a poor boy do? But once we get what we want we wonder if it is in fact what we need because it is finally not too different in kind from what Richard Nixon got. Like him, we then look around and sigh: 'Now what?' What shiny things do we need next? Bob Dylan said 'Money doesn't talk, it swears;' the problem is deciding how much money is enough – and to keep it from talking dirty. How many shiny things do I really need? What's my purpose in life?

Everyone has their own way of escaping such questions. Keeping on the move is one. Congressmen go on the campaign trail every weekend. Normal people visit ten cities in twelve days on their vacations. Young men ship out to sea. Working-class families live in trailers. Dictators visit their provinces. Beatniks went on the road. Hippies crashed in Goa. Copping out of straight society is central to the 'hip' ethic and playing with a road band is as good a way as any.

All you have to do is show up on time and sober and not all that much of either at that. Alienation is no longer a problem; no need to worry, you are alien everywhere. You travel thousands of miles from Bangor to Baton Rouge (or Berlin to Barcelona) and end up in a hotel exactly like the one you just left. You speak to and play for people exactly like the people you just left. You cannot be reached, mail does not catch up. You skim more than read, pass out rather than fall asleep. You work when everybody else is off, breakfast in the evening dinner at dawn. Disorder is the order, physical alienation is so powerful, so omnipresent, that no treatment seems too extreme. Nobody can even question the need for treatment. Playing chess will not do the trick. You've got to find a familiar internal place to hang on to, it's a matter of survival. And there is one place, a warm corner called stoned.

I shiver remembering one hop we made with Squirms at the wheel. 'Wake me up when we get there,' he'd said starting out. His band-aid was empty by the time we reached the outskirts of Dallas, and he was complaining about the absence of coke to tone up his smack.

'Look at that fucking square,' he snarled, pointing to a man in an undershirt watering one in a line of small lawns. He looked square all right, watering his lawn at seven in the morning. He did not look like he had been up all night. Battling heartburn, I put on shades. The square stooped to smell a flower. His better half was probably cooking ham and eggs, maybe waffles. I could smell them blend with the odour of perking coffee in a sparkling kitchen, flooded with morning sun. It did not seem as square as it would have a few weeks earlier, and I did not feel as hip as I would have liked. Wouldn't it be hip, I thought, if 'hip' turned out to be square?

We pulled up at a light on the corner of 'Shoe City' and 'Hamburgerville'. American commercial enterprises often take names which hopefully put them on a larger map. Shoe Village, Bargaintown, Foam Rubber City, Disneyland, Miss Universe. This sort of geographical exaggeration is all over our culture. An adjective can cover square miles – Dullsville, Fat City.

Squirms extended it to cosmic proportions with a game he called 'Wordgrad'. After a gig he'd kick it off by saying something like 'Tired Hollow, man', or, seeing a beautiful woman, 'Stacked Junction'. As we started driving towards the last date, even Squirms squirmed with the ultimate Wordgrad: 'New York City *City*, baby'. It wasn't so absurd at all if you consider the real-life 'Roseland Dance City', two Wordgrads in one. Spooky Landing.

The last hop was from Dallas to Midland, Texas. We checked out of the White Plaza Hotel late in the afternoon planning to drive at night after the gig to open the day sheet in Midland. Claude passed out in the back seat at two when we finally left. He stayed that way the entire drive. We had to shake him awake in Midland. Eventually he flopped out of the car, entered the hotel and staggered towards the elevators. In the middle of the lobby he stopped, seemed to remember something, and approached the desk. 'Let me have my key,' he stuttered. The clerk looked puzzled and asked his name. Standing nearby, Kurt explained that this was Mr Thornhill who was expected. The clerk asked what kind of room Mr Thornhill would like. 'Look just let me have my key,' Claude repeated, getting red in the face. 'I like my room, I don't want to change it.' Claude had not checked out of the White Plaza and did not realize he was now in Midland, 300 miles west.

I was reminded of how old and tired Claude looked that morning in Midland when I recently purchased a record called *The Billie Holiday Story* and saw his picture in the enclosed booklet. He had accompanied her on a number of recordings and the photo shows a clean-cut cherubic face with a winner's smile. The contrast between those two images tells the Claude Thornhill Story.

But he kept his dignity as his audience dwindled. His hair was always combed, his suits pressed, his face shaven, his bow-tie straight. I marvel at how much control that must have involved, considering the skid he was on. He knew he had been something special. It had taken imagination, taste, talent and courage to play Charlie Parker's 'Anthropology' at fancy hotels and supper clubs when people had paid to hear a band that had won two *Billboard* magazine polls in the 'sweet band' category. The distinctive, softly dissonant swing he had pioneered anticipated 'cool' jazz by several years. In fact Claude Thornhill not Miles Davis had given birth to the cool.

His closest friends were the most alienated guys on the band. He loved Squirms, for example. Claude was attracted to people who were defeated, cynical, dissipated – who were, like himself, victims of changing public taste and their own inability to adapt to it. Road-rats, they appeal to me too. Losers appeal to me. Perhaps it can be explained by paraphrasing R.D. Laing – if an alienating society calls those who cannot adapt to it 'losers', does this not make them winners in a larger sense? In any case road-rats were to become so alienated that they were not even aware of the fact that some square folkie named Bob Dylan was singing about them: 'How does it feel to be without a home, like a rolling stone.'

4
Maynard Ferguson: Not Frank Sinatra

Frank Sinatra used to deliver a line between songs. Maybe he still does. I heard it one night in Atlantic City years ago. He was sitting on a bar stool, a whisky glass and a cigarette in the same hand. Bathed in smoky spots, he sneered: 'A friend in need is a *drag*.'

He obviously could not accept the premise that he himself would ever be in need. He has total faith in the force, persistence and justness of his lucky star. That's a sick joke. It implies that the sick, poor or lonely have nobody to blame but themselves.

One night in Birdland ('the jazz corner of the world') Buddy Rich finished a set by announcing: 'And now ladies and gentlemen, we turn you back to our genial master of ceremonies, Pee Wee Marquette.' Pee Wee was a black midget; God forbid he should ever be in need. Buddy raised the microphone to its maximum Wilt-the-Stilt height and walked off. Everybody laughed when Pee Wee arrived.

You may consider Frank Sinatra and Buddy Rich oblique leads into a chapter on Maynard Ferguson. Like Buddy, with some taste and humbleness, Maynard would have been a genius. And both of them have basically never forgiven the Creator for not creating them as Frank Sinatra.

In 1959, Maynard Ferguson had the hottest big band a white musician could hope to play with. There was still Woody Herman, true, but Maynard was zappier, integrated and younger. Forte was about as quiet as it got and allegro was a slow tempo, but there was Joe Farrell on tenor, Jaki Byard, piano, Frankie Dunlop, drums, Don Ellis, trumpet, Charles Greenlee, trombone and the altoman/singer Jimmy Ford, who used to be called 'White Bird' back in Houston.

There were no racial quotas; Maynard had a certain innocence (or was it guile?) that was quite attractive. I don't think he ever really noticed colour. You were you. Once we arrived for a concert at the University of Virginia and a student said: 'I hear you got coloured musicians.' Maynard answered: 'Yep. We have a green trumpet-player and a purple singer.'

There were times when Jimmy Ford made me think that the Alltime Allstar Fuckups had become a reality. Jimmy had about as much class fucking-up as possible, he could make it seem positively polite. Blond locks fell boyishly over his forehead as he'd drawl: 'Pleased to meet you, ma'am', when introduced to a woman, kissing her hand. There was a rumour that his family had oil money but I think it was only a rumour. Last I heard, he was back in Texas selling used cars. Like Chet Baker; two redneck disaster areas, they could both sing, had looks, talent, intelligence and good time but they both self-destructed.

There's a type here . . . Jimmy Ford, Chet Baker, Brew Moore, Johnny Andrews . . . redneck jazz musicians often have, shall we say, negative tendencies. Having grown up white in a segregated society, playing music invented by blacks can cause complexes. And Jimmy Ford, the purple singer, did not exactly have his muse to the grindstone.

Maynard's sick humour could be terminal. He put some Desenex foot powder in a small vial and pretended to spill it by accident next to Jimmy's seat on the bus. The floor was anything but clean, which did not stop Jimmy from pouncing and snorting a few pinches. Maynard roared, as did Willie Maiden ('Willie Makeit' we called him), Maynard's arranger, general court jester and chief beer-taster. Jimmy looked like he needed a hug.

He had a nickname for everybody. I was Mike the Knife. Rick Kiefer was Admiral Rickover. I loved to listen to Jimmy talk. Like some of Jimi Hendrix's song lyrics, it did not matter what he said, the way he swung saying it mattered. He had that natural sense of poetry a lot of southern whites are not aware they have. Once he announced: 'Ahm gonna buy me a pair of ground-pads,' and went to find a pair of shoes.

On a bandstand that needed considerable cheering up, Jimmy began gesturing frantically to Frank Hintner, the baritone saxophone-player who was on the aisle. He mouthed the words;

'Reed reed, I need a reed' in the middle of a tune. Frank could not figure out why Jimmy needed a baritone reed and he couldn't stop playing without the whole bottom falling out, but he got up anyway and went to fetch one in the dressing-room. The first rest, Jimmy reached under his chair, pulled out a container of ice cream and used the baritone reed as a spoon.

Finally Maynard could no longer put up with such capers and Jimmy was fired. I can't say I blamed him, but the soul seemed to go out of the band when Jimmy left.

Then there was nothing left but the void. It was always present, but it now became unavoidable. There was a great big void where thought and sensitivity should be. Joseph Conrad once described an orchestra: 'They weren't making music, they were murdering silence.'

I jump at unexpected noises. Fast cuts into violent scenes make me shiver. Two drivers arguing over a parking space scares me . . . kids tailgating an elderly couple on Main Street. I cannot dismiss these events as mere parenthetical aberrations. Such events are trailers for a violent feature, the inevitable gory coming attraction. It might even be a double feature. Maynard's band would make the perfect soundtrack. It was an air-raid more than music. Maynard slashed and strutted like a lion-tamer. His music accused you of being a sissy for not liking it. Maynard's trumpet is one kissing machine unlike the others. Duck when you hear it. Do not turn your back on it. Playing with that band was like being an American adviser.

But how I loved being in the middle of those twelve-part chords, even as frenetic as Maynard's. I soaked in trumpets above, saxophones below, I felt safe in that warm bath. Twelve human beings kissing their machines in the interest of the collective good. This was the beautiful part, the ease with which even the most stubborn or selfish characters could compromise. Sharp? Pull out. No point pretending you're right. No sense fighting over it. Doesn't matter who's wrong if the total doesn't add up right. Everybody listens. Bullheadedness gives way to universal reason. Everybody becomes interested in what the other person has to say, everybody becomes a pacifist.

Being in the middle is wonderful. It is no spectacular position, only perceptive listeners appreciate it, but a rich trombone section makes the whole band rich. I am here, I am doing something beautiful, it is up to you to find me. I will not oversell you. I do not play the guitar or the saxophone like everybody else. Most trombonists are nonconformists. Here I am, find me.

During my sophomore year at the High School of Music and Art I passed the audition for the senior symphony orchestra. I was proud to announce it when I came home that evening.

'How many trombones are there?' my father asked me.

'Three,' I said.

'And which are you?'

'Second.'

He reopened his paper to the business page without comment. I loved the anonymity of being in the middle. How could I ever explain this to him? How could such an over-motivated person understand? See how miscast Everybody's Only President was? I felt strength in anonymity. I had no desire to be biggest, first, strongest, richest, most famous. I thought I would love living in the country for that reason. My heroes were strong people who did not flaunt their strength. J.D. Salinger retired from public view. He would not puff his chest for Dick Cavett. Sonny Rollins disappeared for a few years. Charles de Gaulle disappeared when he saw it was time. Marlon Brando faded out of focus when that became possible. I am a moving target. Finding myself in a crowd waiting to do something, I automatically lose interest in doing it. I like dark horses, underdogs, lost causes, fallen heroes. Not that I want to follow. I am an unreliable follower. I would not stay out of jail one year in the Soviet Union. I can be counted on not to follow. I'm sort of French that way. I want to lead from a corner – from the middle of the chord. If only my father had been alive so I could have told him how happy I was to be in the middle of the chord.

Maynard on the other hand was a leader, a front man in every sense of the word. He wanted to be on top and bottom at the same time. (In the middle too for that matter.) He could hit a double high C and then without missing a beat drop down to a low G with a fat symphony sound. He had learned circular breathing. He could read fly shit. He could switch between trumpet and valve trombone without a hitch. He was a virtuoso, the complete instrumentalist; even his improvising was not bad for a bandleader. Why then has he left me with so little to remember?

Although Timothy Leary once called Maynard's wife Flo 'the most intelligent woman I've ever met', I don't remember many incisive insights on the part of either Ferguson in a year and a half. Is this their fault, or my faulty memory? It's true, she used to read a lot, or at least she carried books – Sartre's *No Exit* for one – but I recall few conversations worth recalling. There was an attractive complicity between them, however; they were a tight family with four or five kids from previous matings and of their own. When one of them became ill and the best doctor they could find lived in England, they moved there and Maynard had an English band for a few years until the child was healed.

The band of my time has since been called 'legendary'. People often ask me to talk or write about it. Why is there so little to say? It was like a bright shiny package which, when opened, does not fulfil the external promise. It can shake your faith in legends.

A young trumpet-player was auditioning one night, sight-reading the book on the job. Maynard's trumpet section played standing up. The music stands were very short, barely off the floor. Parts were in poor condition: torn, faded, smudged by leaky spit-valves. The trumpet book was very difficult: lots of flag-wavers mostly in the stratosphere, a tough book to sight-read under any conditions. But this young fellow was in awful shape. He had a nose-blowing cold, his eyes were tearing and he breathed like a groaning seal. Chet Feretti, the lead trumpet-player, was something of a hypochondriac. To play lead on Maynard's band you had to be a powerhouse and Chet was built like a bull. Short and stocky, he lifted weights, made sure to get his sleep and he practised breathing exercises. Chet looked at this auditioner and saw nothing but a big juicy germ. The guy asked the usual sight-reading questions: 'Do we start at letter A? Is this repeat good? Where's the coda sign?' Each question was punctuated by coughs, sneezes and wheezing. Chet was concerned with only one thing, contamination. He answered the questions ambiguously or not at all, moving further away, which pushed Rick Kiefer, who was on his other side, close to the riser's edge. Finally they began to look like they were in two different trumpet sections. He did not get the job.

Like Claude Thornhill's, Maynard's band travelled in cars. Also like with Claude, everybody fought to get into Don Ellis's car.

(Don was on both bands.) He did not drink or smoke and was always wide awake and perky; driving with him was certain to improve life-expectancy projections. Chet was not a bad driver himself, and also a health nut. But he could be, well, unpredictable. Lost, Chet pulled to the curb so the guy in the death seat could ask a pedestrian for directions. As the pedestrian pointed and spoke, Chet took his foot off the brake. The car began to creep. At first the friendly pedestrian creeped with us, then he had to walk to keep up. Finally he found himself running. Speeding away finally, Chet looked at the pedestrian standing hands on hips in the rear view mirror, and cackled: 'Stupid asshole.'

Rick Kiefer went on the road with Buddy Morrow when he was fifteen. When I met him with Maynard, he was twenty and had been on the road for five years. He would order 'a cup of dust, please, ma'am' in a restaurant because 'that's what I'm going to get anyway'. But Rick was as hooked on playing with big name bands as I was. Despite its faults, Maynard's band could swing hard. There were no Rolling Stones at that time and we were what was happening. We knew it, Maynard certainly knew it. It was the best you could do in the sleepy fifties. 'You guys play with Maynard?! Wow!' He could pay us less because his charisma felt so good to be around. If he pulled too many practical jokes, he could take it as well as dish it out.

It could get out of hand. New Year's Eve, the Red Hill Inn, Camden New Jersey. We forged a plot on a gospel-type tune called 'Got the Spirit', on which we repeated the same riff over and over behind Maynard's solo until he gave us the cue to take it out. This was New Year's Eve, though, and we decided to celebrate. We moved the figure up a half-tone every time. Maynard found himself playing in such keys as B and F-sharp. He managed pretty well until about the tenth time when he moved up but we didn't. He turned his back to the audience, gave us the arm laughing and shouted: 'You're all fired.'

We played Cincinnati. We left New York Friday night, drove through a driving snowstorm and arrived late for the soundcheck. We drove back through the same storm on Sunday. I happened to drive one of the cars that weekend. Monday I went to Maynard's house to pick up my cheque. There were two of them – one for driving, $105, the second $35 for playing. I looked at the two cheques.

40

My Maynard Ferguson period ended with two weeks in Birdland, opposite Miles Davis. Coltrane was with Miles then and the Cry was all over the joint. Miles and I were sitting together at the musicians' table on the side, in a dark corner once again, listening to Wynton Kelly, Jimmy Cobb and Paul Chambers, his rhythm section at the time, play 'Oleo'. Miles had not greeted me once in a week, and we were not really together at the table. He looked furious. 'What the hell is Paul doing with the time?' The time sounded pretty good to me, but I said nothing. Before he bounded towards the stand to do something about the time, he patted my knee and said: 'You're still too fat, Mike.'

5

A Bisocial in the Steelpile

Pasquale Cardenale passed his usual sawbuck to the head waiter. We were at his usual choice table. The room hummed with business lunch. 'Led me tell ya sumpm, Michael,' said Pasquale. 'Dere's good money ta be made haulin' gabbidge.'

I licked my chops: 'Is your mouth as dry as mine?'

Although he was now developing eight-figure properties along Madison Avenue, Pasquale will always be a deze dem and dozer. No need to spell that out forever however, so from now on he will appear to speak good English: 'I'm serious. Listen to me for a minute. You could make millions. You're not in the steel business, you're in the money business. All business is the money business. The sooner you understand that, the sooner . . .'

Pasquale had an idea from somewhere that he should be my father figure. He hesitated, attempting to swallow: 'My mouth *is* dry. Let's get something to drink. Call the waiter, Mike.'

'*You* call the waiter, motherfucker. It's your club.'

He grabbed my collar: 'Nobody calls me fothermucker and gets away with it.' Tears came to our eyes, laughing. I began to feel conspicuous. Pasquale grabbed my collar again: 'Nobody calls me a fuckerfocker and . . .' He knocked over the flowers laughing.

After the waiter cleaned up, I fingered Pasquale's white-on-white tie with disapproval: 'You've got to clean up your act.' I dusted dandruff off his shiny suit and removed the fat cigar from his mouth: 'You could be cooler, you know. You've got Mafia written all over you.'

Pasquale glanced over his shoulder, then whispered: 'That's my cover. Don't blow my cover. I look so much like Mafia nobody believes I really am. Where's this week's protection by the way?'

An indignant aside: 'By gum, I think he's serious!' I got up as though to leave: 'As a two-fisted above-the-belt American businessman, I refuse your three-million-dollar order. You can't buy *my* integrity. You dirty rats will destroy this beautiful country of ours.'

Pasquale grabbed my collar once more: 'Listen buster, you'll take that order or . . .'

'Or what?' I moved my arm as if going for an arm.

He indicated three harmless-looking Ivy League types a few tables away: 'The boys know what to do.'

My face turned into a mask of fear: 'No, not the boys! Please not that. Anything but that.' I took a contract out of my pocket: 'I'll take your three-million-dollar order after all. Only promise you'll call off the boys.' I handed him the contract: 'Sign here.'

'Not so fast, Jewboy.' The contract was thirty thousand not three million but Pasquale Cardenale had not become king of garbage by forgetting the line between a joke and reality. The brotherhood of marijuana goes only so far.

I do not like being called Jewboy, except maybe by another Jewboy, and even then I don't like it much. Pasquale accepted 'Wop' from me though, so I laughed: 'Nobody calls me a Blueboy and gets away with it.'

He dusted off my sleeve with his napkin: 'Sorry, sir, no racial slur intended. Some of my best friends are Blueboys. Would you like to join my club, sir? How about marrying my daughter?'

We occupied ourselves with our snails. Snails give me the creeps. I only ordered them because they are so presidential.

'Where was I?' Pasquale had lost his train.

'Garbage.'

'Right. Just say the word and I'll fix up a meeting with the big boss. There's heavy bread to be made in garbage, Prez.'

Pasquale once fronted an all-girl band. He sang like Julius La Rosa, worked around Queens Village until TV and rock put him into his father's foundation company. Cardenale and Sons can dig a hole faster than just about anyone. Pasquale told Fred that he only bought from Dome because he 'dug' the way I played the blues. Get it? (Fred didn't.)

From their foundation base, Cardenale was granted the garbage-removal concession in several north Jersey towns. The money rolled in, the company spread out and began building shopping centres for its own account. Charging it to 'entertainment', I once gave Pasquale two ounces of Acapulco Gold, stoned on which he had put together a condominium package he named 'Acapulco Towers' in gratitude.

Fred Mann will freak if he happens to read this. He has his principles. He did not even approve when salesmen got girls for customers, though everybody does that so he looked the other way.

'I tell you, Michael, if your father was alive today he'd be hauling garbage.'

It sort of started with garbage at that. My father found one of those holes through which pluggers can slip a class up. The scheme, at the end of the Second World War when steel was gold, illustrates the fact that your rejects are somebody else's primes. Construction codes were 'imaginative' in Central America. Sam Zwerin convinced the rolling mills to sell him rusty coils of wire rods waiting on the scrap pile to be remelted into ingots. He straightened and cut them and exported them to Central America as reinforcing rods. 'Rust helps bond with concrete,' he told me, and it's true. The rods were out of round or too rusty to make nails or bailing wire but they were more than adequate to be buried in columns or slabs. Perfectly moral and legal everywhere. His ingenuity was universally admired. A leftist, my father was often heard to say how embarrassed he was to be making so much profit.

In the fifties, however, as Fred Mann said: 'The bloom went off the rose.' Dome's export trade faded when rebuilt Japanese mills booked large chunks of business on daring credit terms. During his last years, my father saw it coming and started retooling for the domestic market.

'Buy from one of your own, it won't cost you any more,' he told Jewish contractors.

'Buy from Dome. We are geared for faster, more personal service than the big boys,' he told small contractors.

'I can save you steel if you let Dome engineer your job,' he told all contractors, studying their plans and specifications far into the night. He was a tireless scrambler, a fast-moving linebacker, a play-calling genius. But he could not cope with posthumous formations. And Dome was suffering the consequences of one of his rare mistakes. Following his heart instead of his head, my father established a subsidiary in Israel which was eating up a lot of good money. After he died of a stroke, my mother made a worse, almost fatal mistake. She appointed me president.

Yes, that's right, I had deserted my mistress again. That drive to Cincinnati with Maynard had done it. When my mother wanted to step down from the presidential post she had assumed right after my father's death and offered it to me, I thought I'd rather be president than a chauffeur. The square on the lawn also had something to do with it. Hip seemed less hip all the time. I thought I'd be able to work five hard years, get Dome to the point where it could pay me a substantial honorarium for doing substantially nothing, give myself a subsidy as it were. There seemed to be all sorts of good reasons but in fact what happened is that I was in spare time.

Otis Dinwiddie loomed over our table. Otis is Atlanta society filtered through Princeton, where he played tight end. Otis was not as different from Squirms as might appear. Their ability to handle being blasted, though on different chemicals, put them both ahead of the competition. I had watched Otis negotiate a million-dollar bridge order after drinking five vodka martinis. Steel executives take pride in being hard drinkers, they are quite macho about it. One qualification for moving up the executive ladder is the ability to absorb more liquor than the next guy. The deal falls to the survivor. Last one conscious wins. They brag about it. So long as they stayed absolutely smashed, their normal condition in any case, Otis Dinwiddie and Squirms would have understood each other very well.

Otis had been with two Bethlehem vice-presidents on the other side of the restaurant. 'You guys are in a good mood today,' he said, looming even larger. 'The way y'all were breaking up back there, I wondered what the hell you were smoking.'

'Just a little of that ole wacky weed,' said Pasquale, touching my knee conspiratorially. 'Sit down, Otis. What's your poison?'

'Vodka martini, thanks.' He turned to me: 'How's your Israel operation?' He pronounced it 'Izyreel'.

'Top notch.' Taxes were up, the Israeli pound was down, the construction market was off. Top notch.

'You fellows worried about the political situation over there?'

Otis adjusted the carnation in his lapel. Bethlehem likes its executives tall. I was the only customer Otis had who was taller than himself, but he managed to loom over me anyhow. Was I a customer? Our relationship was schizophrenic. Dome bought from Bethlehem's rolling mills and competed with their fabricating division. They wanted our business but not at the expense of their own. We never gave our best price to a contractor Bethlehem sold. Sometimes Bethlehem 'allowed' us to take a job because they'd sell the raw material anyway in that case. In one way we were just another Bethlehem sales office. If we went too low, Lew Anderson could always tighten the credit screws. One of Fred Mann's greatest talents was knowing how to Tom Bethlehem Steel.

Otis Dinwiddie was organizer and enforcer of what were euphemistically known as 'industry meetings'. The reinforcing bar fabricators got together every so often in the interests of an 'orderly' market. You don't come into our customer's office, we won't go into yours. Don't cut your prices, we won't cut ours. Questionable ethics of course, but it did not matter because everybody was going in everywhere, prices were being slashed and the market was anything but 'orderly'.

I reassured Otis: 'It's safer on the streets of Tel Aviv than in an industry meeting.'

Otis winked and roared: 'That's not saying much.'

'What's an industry meeting?' Pasquale asked. Whoops! If he knew about that he'd absolutely blow his stack. Those meetings were costing Pasquale maybe $5 a ton.

Otis changed the subject: 'Bye the bye I went to hear your boy Miles Davis last night.'

Pasquale, proud as a papa: 'Mike played with Miles. He's a swinging fothermucker . . .'

ORDER! CUT! Order in the fantasy factory. There was no Pasquale Cardenale – though Otis Dinwiddie is unfortunately real enough. I made Pasquale up. If I had had somebody like Pasquale, I might have been able to make good money. My time could have been less spare. All I needed was to see someone remotely like myself during a business day. There are good people and bad people in the steel bar business like any business but I never found one who shared my exile. They were all on home turf. Why had I exiled myself?

I tried not to brag about it but I had had an affair with one of Marlon Brando's girlfriends. She was a woman of some strength and character and she lived with Brando off and on for years. Sometimes I'd drop this 'credit' just a bit too eagerly, like I'd make sure to tell people I'd played with Miles Davis. I held on to these old credits. I had no new ones. They added up to the exotic image I liked to encourage . . . the jazzy president making love to star women, holding my eclectic own on the top. Unfortunately, the president part was essential. This had something to do with why I did not just open my cell door and walk out. President was one credit I was afraid I could not operate without. Of course it was a phony credit, snuck up on the marquee at night when nobody was looking, pasted over the name of the real star. The credit had little to do with the actual movie running because in reality I was playing a Jewish businessman behind steel bars for the crime of killing time.

Cut to a fat thirty-four-year-old executive rattling around his expensive townhouse in Greenwich Village. After flashing back, we have now returned to the day of the staff meeting in chapter one. Everybody's Only President had married a second time while performing the supporting role of slush-pumper with Maynard Ferguson. Another failure, they had just separated. More fear and indecision. He had once more put himself safely behind Dome's steel bars. This man was changing roles, hats and stools so fast, the film seemed to be tearing the projector apart.

Close-up. He looks in the mirror. A mature fat man. Camera pulls back . . .

Sam and Mike Zwerin and Fred Mann inspecting the Jersey yard. From time to time they disappear behind high piles of inventory.

SAM: We are running low on number three bars, Michael, please make a note to call Bethlehem.

Mike salutes Sam. He searches in vain for a pencil.

SAM: If I've told you once I've told you a thousand times, an executive should never be without a writing implement. Never.

Zoom in on Sam fingering a holster hanging from his belt.

SAM: I suggest you purchase one of these immediately.

Close-up. The holster's bulging variety of writing hardware of many sizes and colours dissolves slowly into a six-shooter. Camera pulls back to show Sam Zwerin in full dress general's uniform. The general draws. Freeze, prez.

I was starring in many such short subjects at the time. If some were musical, they were no comedies and were often screened through tears. I took a wet sponge, which is what I felt like, wiped the dust off my trombone, rinsed the slide, swabbed the mouthpiece with a Q-tip.

I began squeezing in an hour's practice here and there. Sometimes I stayed home from the office to practise. ('I'll be working at home today, Fred.') Driving to a district sales meeting, I played long tones on my mouthpiece behind the wheel. I positioned an imaginary slide talking to customers, memorized Bird lines during sales meetings. I approved an order for twelve hundred dollars over cost.

'What happened?' Fred Mann was appalled.

'Don't worry Fred, we'll make it up in volume.'

I started to work every Monday night at the Five Spot on the Bowery with the 'Upper Bohemia Six' which featured wrong changes, time turned around, forgotten key signatures and misplaced bridges. Our star, painter Larry Rivers, played the saxophone like a Caribbean revolution. That is to say his mistakes were laughable, but they were passionate. Another painter Howard Kanovitz played another trombone. The band with the painters and the president began to draw attention.

There was rapport between painters and jazz musicians in New York in the early sixties. Jackson Pollock was said to have approached painting like a jazz musician – dancing and improvising over his canvas. The Five Spot had been a painter's bar until the customers talked owner Joe Termini into hiring a solo pianist Saturday nights. Thelonious Monk. Hard to believe now, for a fifty-cent glass of beer you could go in, sit down and listen to Monk. It grew to weekends and a quartet, finally to six nights a week. (The Upper Bohemia Six had the off-night.) When Ornette Coleman first came to New York he played the Five Spot and it was the painters who spread the news to Leonard Bernstein and the intellectual community in general. Larry Rivers, who painted a portrait of Elvin Jones, had a foot in both camps and was thus at the centre of the fusion.

Late one night, about eight of us were lying around Larry's loft waiting for a bass-player to start jamming. I was directly in front of one of his enormous works, overflowing with October colours and shadowy shapes. It was done with fine technique, imagination and humour. (I don't know anything about art but I know what I like.) A face had one eye finished in exquisite detail; the other was nothing but a smudge. This was as though to say – I showed you I could paint an eye, what's the point of doing two of them?

I asked Larry: 'Why do you play jazz? Don't you get enough satisfaction doing *that*?'

'It's physical. I don't identify with jazz the same way I once did, but once I get over the nervousness of what am I going to play and who am I playing with and what are they going to think – all of that social paraphernalia – when I begin really playing and it seems to be going right, it's fantastically satisfying. I suppose jazz is the closest art to sex. When I was younger, my playing related to feelings – loneliness or beauty for example – but now it doesn't seem to be that way. Now it's mostly pure physical release.'

In the years before he became one of New York's best-known, expensive and respected painters, Larry had played saxophone with Herbie Fields, Jerry Wald, Johnny 'Paradiddle Joe' Morris and Shep Fields. It must be added that this was during the war when a lot of lightweights were in the big bands and the big leagues thanks to armed-service drafts. Larry mistreated his musical mistress too and began to draw. But he could not leave her for good. Though violently undisciplined, his solos were always imaginative. Polytonal flurries would be followed by squeaks, honks or a sweet little melody. When he played the melody of a standard, it would be extremely personal and ironic. Were they quarter tones or was he out of tune? Probably the latter but the fact remained you could interpret it either way. Larry's ambiguity was innate, he could be nothing less than original. On hearing Archie Shepp for the first time, a friend of Larry's exclaimed: 'Hey Larry, he plays just like you!'

'Playing jazz is like you're *married* or something,' Larry said. 'One reason I think I got so involved with painting is because it's more self-sufficient. You hang *yourself* up, nobody else can hang you up. You have nobody else to blame. Jazz is social. You have to deal with people who have to play in tune and show up on time and listen to you and so on. I think my relationship to jazz has a lot to do with my relationship to black people. I'll bet that the whole story of *your* relationship with jazz is so intertwined with your relationship with blacks and your response to their place in American society that it's almost impossible to talk about one without the other. I don't worry about whether or not it's *their* music I'm playing. I mean . . . who owns painting for Chrissake? I don't think most black musicians really think that way, and if they do it's self-pity on a very dopey level.'

Even though it may not be their music, on a per-capita basis blacks certainly seem to play jazz better. Stop screaming in the bookstalls. The hand-wringing is deafening. People of all hues get quite touchy on this subject. In any event, the between-stool front-line of the Upper Bohemia Six was smart enough to know it needed all the help it could get. We hired the best black rhythm section available. Usually this was Freddy Redd, piano, Richard Davis, bass, and Joe Chambers, drums.

Archie Shepp caught us live as a guest reviewer for *Down Beat* magazine. He wrote: 'Mike Zwerin is the president of a steel company I understand. Well, he seems to be an intelligent man. I assume he's a sensitive man. If he ever starts to share a few of the shares, his music might get better. He's going to play stronger. That's right, you've got to be a little poor to play jazz.'

Share the shares. How many shares of frustration equal an asset? I would have gladly traded whole blocks of Dome Steel shares for just one of Archie Shepp's. If only I had known where such business might be transacted. If only I had known how easy it is to transact if you want it badly enough.

Larry Rivers invited me to a loft session in the west 20s. It was packed with bisocials. Bisociality is principally an American phenomenon. A steel company president who plays jazz trombone is bisocial. Bisocials swing both ways, they are downwardly mobile. A bisocial hangs out in Harlem with a necktie in his pocket just in case he should run into a midtown party later. Poverty can be romantic under certain conditions, temporary for example. There are two kinds of bisocials. The kind that goes 'slumming', dabbles in the romance of underground culture, invites a painter for dinner once in a while. Bisocials are rich, have a certain standing of one kind or another or have access to power or money. Woody Allen plays clarinet in a jazz club once a week, an example of the second kind. Some people are not satisfied being locked into any one endeavour, spending time with lawyers or travel agents like themselves. I know a banker who deals drugs because he likes gangsters more than for the money (he likes drugs too). One very rich and ambitious literary agent who will sell any garbage whatsoever if it can make him richer insisted on the best struggling writers available when he edited an underground paper for a year (not giving any of them a shot at his rich garbage). Sometimes bisociality remains only a fantasy. Nobel lauriate Gabriel Garcia Marquez says that if his literary career should suddenly take a nosedive he would like to play cocktail piano in a bar 'to make people happy'. The King of Siam, who played jazz saxophone, once told a touring American jazz musician who had jammed with him that if he ever lost his kingdom he'd like to drive a New York taxi during the day and blow his saxophone at night. It does not work in the other direction; poor people who try and spend time with the rich are just pushy. For example it's easier to make a hippy out of a Lord than a Lord out of a hippy. On the other hand it's easier to make a businessman out of a musician than the other way around. Bisociality has its twists and vagaries but one thing sure, a chic party in a funky loft is bisocial.

The party drew half of every Dr Feelgood office in town, including one in person – a certain Dr Bent, currently employed keeping casts of *Hair* feeling good worldwide. Feelgoods are doctors you go to, or went – this particular medical speciality was phased out with the criminalization of amphetamine – when you were feeling not bad but wanted to feel better. They tuned the nervous system to cope with the constantly escalating stress and multiplication of choice contemporary society inflicts on bisocials. It was their theory that negative chemical changes take place in people hustling towards a top spinning ever faster. They sought to rebalance these chemicals. They never pretended the treatment was for everybody. It was an exceptional treatment for exceptional people. Dr Bent was an erratic old Russian with a dishevelled head of steel-grey hair who had trouble seeing through a microscope, though he could spot a hundred-dollar bill at fifty paces. Some considered him simply a legal speed connection. His magic elixir consisted of calcium, nyacin, bone-meal and B-12, on top of the essential base. Amphetamine: what made you feel *good* as opposed or in addition to whatever else may or may not have made you healthy. Good or healthy, either way, it was one star-spangled flash.

One 7 a.m. in Dr Bent's office, a delivery boy came in with pastrami sandwiches and coffee. That's right, pastrami sandwiches at 7 a.m.; Dr Bent kept himself feeling good all night long. The boy put down the brown paper bag and rolled up his sleeve. He had a big grin on his face. He'd delivered here before. Dr Bent selected a syringe from the large pile and hit him ('You have magnificent veins, my boy') with his delivery-boy special. The boy swooned for a few seconds and left like a shot.

'Fastest delivery service on the East Side,' Dr Bent explained.

Bent's office has been compared to a Harlem rooftop. The poor, however, were rare there. The comparison is valid only to illustrate a state of mind. Speed, like cocaine, is not for the poor. Hippy speed-freaks in the Haight soon saw they were going in the wrong direction to cure what ailed them and turned to heroin and religion. Except for delivery boys, truck-drivers, front-line troops and other such peculiar job specifications, speed does not suit the lower rungs of the ladder. Running faster down there only means faster circles to nowhere. It is rather for those in sight of the top, or already at the top who must keep running to stay there. It is the drug of bisocial Manhattan.

Dr Bent disappeared into a side room, a line of bisocials at the door. The party was twitching rather than jumping. I came out with my nervous system burning. Five sleek young black musicians were setting up and my heart sank when they started to play. I'd never be able to keep up with them. Their elastic time stretched to the breaking point, the harmony was deeply ambiguous. Larry Rivers did not even open his case, he hid it under a bed. Larry was not about to stake his stability on somebody else's territory. He knew he was a good painter, I knew I was a bad businessman, we were not analagous. Larry would wait for his own terms, he was really good at that. He once asked a society matron for $6,000 to paint her portrait and when she balked he sounded surprised: 'I'll bet that's not twice as much as you expected.' She paid it.

A steel executive playing jazz has an advantage because the people who have work to give tend to be bisocial themselves. Any work he finds probably takes work away from a black musician who may then have to deal, steal or carry heavy objects to make a living. But I would have no peace unless I tried. Notice how I change from first to third person. My personal reference was anything but clear. Bisocials have trouble knowing who they are at any given moment. Give me a moment, I'll prove who I am to you if I can only prove it to myself. I must prove myself to myself all the time – every day, hourly. When I lose at tennis this proves I am a loser. (I do not play tennis any more.) One argument with my son proves I am a bad father. Flubbing one note makes me a lousy musician. It only takes one rejected article to prove what an incompetent journalist I am. If I didn't get into the office earlier than Fred Mann one morning, this proved how unreliable I was. I keep telling myself that I like being between stools, that between stools is a good place to be. But there's no place to park your ass there; I am always half-up half-down, always wondering why it is so hard to find a simple thing like a stool to sit on. So now at the party I was going to cut through what Larry Rivers called 'all of that social paraphernalia' and prove to my mistress that I really loved and was worthy of her even though I deserted her so heartlessly and so often. But if I am on the one hand continually testing myself, on the other I am a severe grader. Mind blank with fear, mouth drying from feeling too good, I moved in on a blues I thought I could handle. Brass-players need saliva to lubricate their embouchure. The trombone-player with the dry mouth and a heavy load of bisocial paraphernalia gave himself low marks. He had not done his homework.

6
A Quiet Getaway

Dome Steel had an enlightened sick-leave policy; if you weren't
sick you got the days anyway. Thanks to Dr Bent I had not been
sick for years. I may have been a speed-freak but I never caught
colds. Policy was democratic, it applied to everyone up and down
the line.

'I'm taking my sick-leave this week, Fred.'

'What about our trip to Pittsburgh?'

That's right, we were supposed to discuss the coming year with
United States Steel: 'Bail me out on this one, Fred, will you? It's a
personal problem. I'd rather not talk about it now. It's the kids,
you see. I want to leave for Florida this afternoon.'

'I understand.' With Fred, only family business comes before
business business: 'Any way I can help?'

'Yes, don't tell my mother. It's sort of, er, delicate.'

Fred Mann and my mother were friends. Fred sent her flowers
for Mother's Day (I forgot), made out her tax return (I could not),
visited her more often than I did.

'Where shall I say you went?' Fred's pencil was poised as usual.

'I'll think of something.'

Fred opened up his United States Steel file. Fred keeps his files
handy: 'What about your usage projections? I'll need them.'

'Let me check them out one last time.' Actually there were no
projections. I skidded back to my office and copied last year's
figures, adding and subtracting arbitrary percentages. It was all
make-believe anyway. I was playing office. Plus five per cent here,
minus seven there.

I buzzed Hilda at the board, asked her to get relief right away
and sneak my trombone downstairs to Ricardo's bar. My trombone

was hidden in Hilda's closet, sneaking it out was part of her job.

The object here was an Orchestra USA record-date. It had come up at the last moment, missing it was out of the question. John Lewis, Eric Dolphy, Phil Woods, Richard Davis and Thad Jones, among all the others, were in Orchestra USA and playing with it was keeping me sane at that time. I grabbed my attaché case and phony projections and flew back into Fred's office: 'I'll swear by these figures.'

Or at them. I'd never get out of that place alive; that terrible, stifling, profitless place where life seemed to be spending me rather than the other way around. This record-date was home leave from basic training, parole, a pardon. Just then Uncle Morty arrived with a stack of traffic folders and a pocket calculator.

Uncle Morty shared a communal cubicle with Charlie Baldick. Charlie's job was to make sure the material arrived on the job site when required. Early was no good, you cannot tie up busy New York streets with idling flatbeds. Late was worse, there would be backcharges. Scheduling was a tough job calling for tact, intelligence, luck and a working-class vocabulary. A typical scheduling conversation with the field went something like this.

'Where the hell is our goddamn third-floor column steel?'

'It's on the way. You guys won't even have time to jerk off before it gets there.'

'We said nine. When we say nine it don't mean nine fucking ten.'

'Hold it, I'll check with the Jersey yard.' Charlie checks with Bill Simpson on the other line, starts screaming: 'SHITSHITSHIT' and talks to the job again: 'Now don't blow your stack, Joe, this is *force majeur*. An act of God on the Pulaski Skyway, haha . . .' There is no laughter on the other end. 'Traffic's backed up for miles. The yard says you should definitely have the load in half an hour.'

'HALF A FUCKIN' COCKSUCKIN' HOUR??!!'

Charlie holds the receiver away from his ear.

'IF WE DON'T HAVE THEM CUNT-LICKIN' COLUMN BARS WE CAN'T POUR NO CONCRETE. I GOT HALF A MIND TO TELL YOU BASTARDS TO STICK THEM CRUDDY BARS UP YOUR CRUDDY ASS.'

Uncle Morty never learned to appreciate American street poetry. He listened to Mozart, read Proust and Kafka. Charlie

Baldick's scheduling conversations seemed to harm him physically. Poor Uncle Morty, how he suffered sharing a communal cubicle with Charlie Baldick. As a boy, I loved to watch Uncle Morty run up and down his long columns of figures. He explained figures to me in such a caressing voice. Uncle Morty was my favourite uncle. I was happy to have been able to arrange a cubicle for him. It was one of my first acts as president.

'It's good I caught you two together,' Uncle Morty said to Fred and me. 'I would like to go over the backhaul situation.'

'Wonderful,' I said. 'We are very concerned about that situation.' I started to leave.

'What shall I tell your mother?' Fred looked between me, the projections and Uncle Morty, trying to assign priorities.

Aunt Goldie, office manager, appeared with a flushed face: 'I don't know how I can be expected to run an efficient office when the girls just feel free to leave whenever they . . .'

I had hired Hilda for the switchboard over Aunt Goldie's head. She had wanted to promote one of the bar-list girls. Typing bar-lists was so boring, the switchboard was considered interesting. Goldie looked faint. She had a lung condition. She had all sorts of conditions. Fred was concerned. She was falling apart condition by condition. She and Uncle Morty listened as I told Fred: 'Tell my mother I'm attending an American Management Association seminar. I'll be gone the rest of the week.'

'I didn't know there was an AMA seminar this week,' Aunt Goldie said. 'Nobody tells me anything. How can I plan the workload for the girls if I don't know which executives are in or out? How long will you be away?'

'I said the rest of the week.'

'Please let me have your itinerary.'

'I'll give it to Hilda.'

'No, not Hilda. To me please. I'd like to talk to you about Hilda.'

'Next week.'

'I don't think she should be allowed to leave her post whenever the spirit moves her. The other girls are talking. They says she's your favourite. Really!'

'I'd better come back,' Uncle Morty winked at me. Goldie's tantrums were to be avoided. As Morty started edging out of

Fred's office, Gloria arrived with a chin-high stack of bar-lists. They fell over each other. Just then Fred's line rang. He pressed the button of his speaker phone and got up to help Gloria. It was Faye, alternate switchboard girl, with a question for Goldie: 'Bud Scheister wants to call Denver. Is that all right?' Gum-chewing could be heard over the speaker phone loud and clear. Uncle Morty giggled. Faye squeaked with a Bronx accent: 'You said I should screen all long-distance calls.'

'I thought we agreed not to put Faye on the board any more,' I said to Goldie. 'I've nothing against her personally but that accent is not exactly the image I have in mind for Dome. And for Chrissakes tell her to stop chewing gum on the board.'

The speaker phone being open, Faye heard everything. She started to cry. Outside lines began to ring. Faye sobbed: 'I will not be treated this way. I will not. Hello. Dome Steel Incorporated.'

'She doesn't even know the name of the fucking company,' I screamed at Goldie. 'Dome Steel *Corporation*, not fucking Incorporated. What sort of dumb bitches are you hiring anyway?'

'What did he say? What did he say?' Goldie started to faint. Uncle Morty came to her aid with a small tango step. Fred switched off the speaker phone and spoke softly to Faye through the mouthpiece: 'It's all right, Faye. Now try and calm down. You can put through Bud Scheister's call to Denver.'

'A little calm, please, gang,' Fred said. Fred automatically included me as part of the gang. I was certainly not its natural leader. Fred Mann was the natural leader. He rose to occasions. If it had been up to me to appoint a president of Dome Steel, I would have appointed Fred Mann. Fred would have made a perfect president. Wait a minute. It *was* up to me!

'I know we're all under a lot of tension these days.' Fred draped an arm flirtatiously over Goldie's shoulder. 'But yelling at each other won't help. Let's save our energy for the competition.'

'I wish you'd tell Michael to watch his mouth,' Goldie sobbed. 'If he's so concerned about image he might start with his own.' She had a point there.

'Bye bye folks.' I deserted the trenches. Maybe I'd be shot for it later but that was later. Hilda was waiting in Ricardo's bar with my trombone: 'What's up, Prez?'

'You're going to have a little problem with Goldie when you get back upstairs, but don't worry, I'll take care of it.' I kissed her on the forehead: 'Just making a quiet getaway.'

7

Up the Third Stream without a Paddle

I would probably worry about being late for my own execution. Always early, I even rush the beat. A therapist once explained this to me. Nobody will wait for me, they will all leave and reject me like my father rejected me. Everybody will reject me sooner or later. Or another way to look at it – if I'm late I reject them, and how can I do to them what he did to me? Understanding it did not help, I'm still always early. I still have few close friends. Fewer friends means fewer rejections.

I was always early for Orchestra USA rehearsals. This was a large ensemble (as opposed to a big band, very opposed) containing thirty of the busiest and brightest recording and jazz musicians in New York, and we are about to take a plunge into that tributary of classical and jazz music known as the Third Stream.

But first, as they say, this message from our sponsor.

Between wives number one and two, just after Claude Thornhill, I lived down the hall from King Curtis in a West 70s brownstone. Curtis was king of the R&B tenor saxophone, a lot of honkers modelled their style after him. He growled his low-down dirty licks with the Coasters ('Yakety Yak') and on such R&B locomotives as 'The Hucklebuck'. He hollered a lot with the beautiful tan lady he was living with, and they almost brought down the floor making love. Once when making I passed him on the stairs, Curtis told me he enjoyed my practising, except it made him feel guilty because he never practised at all.

While living there I rehearsed for three straight days with Woody Herman, who was putting together a new Herd. Other auditioners came and went but I remained, I was sure I'd nailed

59

down the lead chair until Woody flew in Bobby Burgess instead and paid me off . . . after which I polished off a bottle of cough syrup. Bobby Burgess was one of the best players in the business, tough competition. I should not feel bad losing out to him. Why had I shot for the lead chair in the first place? Nobody put me into it, I just sat there. This was before I had worked out my existential aesthetic for the middle of the chord.

Curtis's woman knocked on my door that evening. Black and blue, she said Curtis had beat on her and split. She needed ice. We talked about our bad day. She said cough syrup destroys the stomach lining. We laughed a lot and we might have gone to bed together had I not been too wary of rejection to suggest it.

Then I met the woman who would become my second wife. We moved into a building on Tenth Avenue and 58th Street during my Maynard period. John Lewis lived upstairs. Nowhere like it. In any other city the guy down the hall works at the zoo or something, and if your upstairs neighbour is putting together a band it will play Saturday-night dances. In New York City City, *voilà*, King Curtis is down the hall and not only is John Lewis putting a band together upstairs, he's your wife's friend.

I'd been hoping to spare you this relationship, but it's too revealing about the central character of this book, about New York and why he was beginning to think about leaving there. My second wife had been with a well-known jazz musician for years before me, a kind and intelligent man I considered it an honour to follow. Following him had something to do with my falling for her. New York flourishes on such associations. I was also desperate to remarry before Eleanor – I'll show *her*. All this only in the harsh light of hindsight, of course. At the time I reacted to intelligence and beauty and felt true love. We hung out with the cats, she knew them all. We discussed the state of the world. We were buddies. John Lewis told her an apartment was free in his building. We were good agents for each other. Living beneath John Lewis is a negotiable credit in New York. Everybody knew I was living under John Lewis with Soandso's ex-girl.

My second wife turned out to be the first woman I ever rejected. Again with the clarity of hindsight, I may have rejected her before our marriage was unsavable just to get a good jump on rejection for a change.

This is difficult to write about, she's alive and I do not want to hurt her. Maynard Ferguson is alive, so is Fred Mann (though that is not his real name). I do not want to hurt them either. I do not want to hurt John Lewis, whom I respect a great deal, but once you begin tasting the past you cannot leave certain dishes untouched on the table. Otherwise you end up with one more unsavoury memoir, the sort that can be summed up: 'I love everybody, everybody loves me and look what a wonderful life I've led.' Duke Ellington wrote one like that, so did Yehudi Menuhin. How can people who would never consider lying with music lie so blatantly with words? They crumble words like some sort of soft, unconvertible currency.

On Tenth Avenue one evening I went upstairs to ask John Lewis if he couldn't stop playing his harpsichord at 3 a.m. because it was directly over my pillow. He apologized, explaining he was preparing a piece to a tight deadline and it would all be over tomorrow. We were in his doorway. To be polite, I asked him if my trombone practising was too loud. He shook his head in that kind, diffident manner of his. Oh yes, I seem to have forgotten to mention that Miles Davis lived on the same floor as John. Just then a grumpy voice behind me rasped: 'Yeah, it's too loud,' and Miles dumped a bag of garbage down the incinerator.

It was then that John asked me to join his Third Stream ensemble, Orchestra USA. Having just left Maynard, I had been magically transformed into Everybody's Only President. Wife number two and I were in the process of buying a townhouse in the Village. Why do I avoid mentioning her name? Am I afraid she'll sue me? But I like her, I consider her a friend. Will she sue me so she too can finally reject me? Maybe she won't like it when I say I left her. I'm not even sure who left whom any more. Her name is Charlotte and I hope I have made her laugh by now.

I've often wondered why John Lewis asked me to join Orchestra USA. We'd played together with the Birth of the Cool and he knew I could read and improvise, but there were plenty of homosocial trombone-players around who were in better shape than me. He must have known that anybody Charlotte married could not be a complete idiot. I wonder if he hired me despite my being a steel company president or because of it. Third Stream music could without doubt be described as bisocial. But he saw something in me, heard something, to him I was more than just another Jewish businessman. His acceptance meant a lot to me, and the fact that this story just might be considered 'snitching' gives me pause. Pause.

Why tell it at all? Fucking fink! Here I was invited inside a challenging and exciting situation with elite company and now I roll up the carpet so you can all see the dirt under there. It is some strange compulsion. There are some stories I just have to tell. If I need a rationalization – and I certainly do – it is that I reveal my own dirt at least as much as other people's, though the other people might answer: 'We do not remember you asking our permission.'

I once wrote a story about Jann Wenner, founder and publisher of *Rolling Stone* magazine. It did not reveal Wenner's best side. I knew when I was writing it (for the *Village Voice*) that it would probably get me into trouble, but there was no way I could not tell it. Once the insight hit me, it would have been total cowardice to be 'prudent'. I never write for *Rolling Stone* now.

Hugh Heffner visited London while I was writing for the *Village Voice* from there in the seventies. If I had wanted to try as hard as possible to be banned from the pages of *Playboy*, I could not have done it better. Call it a bad joke – on me. Heffner was only the vehicle, not the object. It was a funny little twist I thought he might appreciate. In any case, once the idea hit me it could not be ignored. I had by chance interviewed a poor black worker in Brixton on the same day that Heffner gave a press conference in the London Playboy Club. Hef talked about the wonderful life he had – the girls, the private jet, the swimming-pools and so on. I think he was trying to tell people that with some initiative and a little luck these things were potentially available to one and all, but on the other side of the same cassette the poor black talked about his life and it was not so wonderful. I decided to make believe that the two interviews got mixed up somehow and interwove quotations from each. Without polemic, it made a bisocial statement. I never wrote for *Playboy* again.

Now we are at last ready to plunge into a current of music for which great hope was held in the early sixties. Third Stream combined jazz and classical music through a new breed of musician who could in theory be equally at home in each, though as it turned out the stream took far too much paddling to negotiate.

As I said I was always early for Orchestra USA rehearsals, which were held at ten o'clock Sunday mornings. You might be thinking it's hard to be early for a rehearsal at ten Sunday morning and it was, but I managed. Rehearsals did not generally get going until half an hour late but this was fine because, I told myself, ignoring the deeper implications of why I have this *compulsion* to be early, it gave me time to grease my slide and warm up.

One Sunday morning, my Lambretta scooter stalled crossing 23rd Street. (We had moved down to our Village townhouse by then.) I kicked the starter for ten minutes before realizing I was out of gas. I parked the machine, hailed a cab, got to the West 73rd Street studio twenty minutes late, and walked into my nightmare.

For once they'd started on time. Assistant conductor Harold Farberman stopped the music and gave me the ray from the podium. All those high-powered professionals seemed to be leering at me through a fish-eye lense. 'Where the hell have you been?' Farberman asked me.

'I ran out of gas.' Lame.

'Sure.' He shrugged his already rounded shoulders: 'Well, what are you waiting for?'

Rejection distorted my vision. I looked at the other musicians, who, it should have been clear to me, didn't give a shit what time I arrived. But sweat oozed from the peer disapproval I imagined.

Other types with other-type disorders would have reacted in other ways. There's this story about the bass-player who arrived half an hour late for a jingle date. Not just a rehearsal mind you, the kind of recording-session on which everybody is making double or triple scale and the meter is ticking really fast. That conductor stopped also. Smiling, the bass-player unzipped his cover and said, calm and in control: 'Sorry, folks, but my wife caught me jerking off and made me fuck her.' Everybody laughed. It's a true story.

Me, instead of coming I sweat. I picked my way through the

rows of musicians and the floor littered with cases and instruments and went out of my way to hit some clinkers on Farberman's composition 'Double Concerto'.

This may seem like an unhealthy attitude, counter-productive, unprofessional. I was late. I was wrong. Period. However you can understand now how traumatic it was, and there had been provocations.

Orchestra USA was a co-operative. Its purpose was to play contemporary music of all kinds as well as classical music and, unstated but at the core of it, to prove that jazz is in fact the classical music of our time. The prospectus went: 'In its fusion of heretofore separate elements of music-making [Orchestra USA] provides an exercise of mutual respect and compatibility between classical azz forms; the particular property of today's thoroughly trained instrumentalists.'

Statements of purpose containing that sort of information were printed in concert programmes in Philharmonic Hall, Carnegie Hall, Hunter College and the Brooklyn Academy of Music. Many statements of purpose were issued during the orchestra's three-year life. In plain English the idea was to play both classical music and jazz as well as they had ever been played, and to explore new music as well. The patent impossibility of that should have been apparent from the beginning, and I think it was to most of us. But we were not interested by statements of purpose, we only wanted to play. Both John Lewis and Gunther Schuller – his partner here – are creative musicians and intelligent human beings. So what if they were statement-prone? I went into rehearsals with great enthusiasm.

A power play immediately became evident. Any organization develops power plays. Take me and Fred Mann in Dome for example. If I was absolutely forced to state my political affiliation, I would say 'anarchism'. (Not anarchy, look it up.) Anarchism is 'a society based on voluntary co-operation and free association of individuals and groups' (*Webster's*). Somebody once said that there was only one thing wrong with anarchism: 'Neighbours.' It obviously cannot work, but I obviously cannot relate to chiefs – even when the chief is me. There were disputes over what music to play, who the soloists would be and in general who would benefit most from the fact that we were so starved for interesting music to play that we were willing to rehearse for free on Sunday mornings.

Attendance record was phenomenal. Eric Dolphy and Richard Davis would usually arrive early like myself, even if they had worked until 4 a.m., which was often, the previous night. Phil Woods drove from New Hope, Pennsylvania (or slept in town overnight) to make it. Herb Pomeroy came from Boston for a while.

Each of us had two shares of stock in the orchestra, which was why the union allowed us to rehearse gratis. The corporation was managed by a board of directors which should have been elected by the stockholders. In fact, John – who had breathed life into it by depositing some thousands of dollars in a bank account – appointed a 'temporary' board. The promised election somehow never materialized. 'It's just like a fucking junta,' an astute political observer in the trumpet section observed. Conversation in general in the brass section began to take a cynical turn. Parallels with Fidel were drawn. This was very embarrassing for Everybody's Only President because he was one of John's appointees.

A violinist I'll call Nathan who also played the big board tried to organize a stockholders' revolt. Nathan said he'd joined the orchestra for the money not the music. He thought it had a chance to become an established full-time repertory organization. But *we* were all in it for fun and we chose to ignore his talk of exploitation. If it was true after all that the composer was getting his music rehearsed for free, it was also true that the composer in question was John Lewis and it was something of an honour to have the opportunity to play it.

There was as much talk as music; board meetings, stockholders' meetings, committee meetings. We were always voting on something or other. Important decisions were, however, generally imposed from above as accomplished facts. What music to play, for example, where it would be performed and who the soloists would be. We were once informed that an invitation to play the Antibes Jazz Festival on the French Riviera had been turned down because 'we aren't ready'. I for one felt perfectly ready.

John loved to make idealistic speeches during board meetings or at the end of rehearsals. 'Loved' is not quite accurate. He seemed so terribly shy making a speech, it must have been agony (perhaps therapy) for him. I still think they were sincere, but despite the facial tics, palm-rubbing and the retiring posture that accompanied his words, John knows what he wants and how to get it. He was uncompromising and even dictatorial whipping the Modern Jazz Quartet into their superb shape, but they would never have come anywhere near that shape without him. He told Connie Kay what sticks to use, what part of the cymbal to hit with them, and when. The bass-lines were often written (not just chord symbols). He rode herd continually and rumour had it this was resented. Jazz musicians tend to be undisciplined – 'voluntary' might be a better word, in the anarchist sense – and the transformation of interesting anarchy into organized anarchism is only achieved by a leader to whom the music is important enough to justify taking the risk of becoming unpopular in the process.

When John spoke you sensed that perhaps he was using his sensitivity as an arm to disarm you. How could such sensitivity be concerned with power? You let your guard down. His will of iron and great ambition can be discerned through the name he chose – Orchestra USA. What cheek! I could never pronounce it without flinching. He talked about changing the course of American musical history, about adding new dimensions to the past. For the first time anywhere, he said, Orchestra USA had assembled a body of top jazz musicians who were also schooled in the classics. Looking back, I'm surprised it wasn't Orchestra World.

My first trombone teacher played with Toscanini's NBC Symphony and one of the first things he taught me was how to shoot spitballs through the slide without getting caught by the conductor during 104-bar rests. With Orchestra USA, I could make use of that information. Monotony is inherent playing classical trombone parts. Richard Wagner, whose music I despise, wrote interesting trombone parts. Mozart, whom I adore, did not. Obviously classical trombone was not for me. But it goes deeper. Classical musicians rehearse and work hard trying to play music like it has been played before. Jazz should be different every time. Orchestra USA was dedicated to uniting those two diametrically opposed streams.

John Lewis loves the sound of a string section. Many jazz

musicians make this mistake. They think strings provide class. Even Elvis Presley eventually sang with a string section behind him. This comes from basic insecurity, that jazz and rock are both lowbrow music. But strings just seem unable to swing in this twentieth-century context. They swing playing Bach and Stravinsky but that's not the same sort of swing. John cajoled our strings, clapped his hands for hours to no avail. Perhaps it has to do with the way fiddle-players bow – straight-backed, neck taut, arms stiff. More likely it involves the personality of the person who picks that instrument in the first place.

Maynard Ferguson tells the story of the time Stan Kenton added a string section. Forty musicians travelled in two buses. It was decided at the outset that one bus would be for sleeping, the other for partying. Except for one renegade cellist, the entire string section rode the sleeping bus.

Orchestra USA rehearsals could be like a sleeping bus. For the first four weeks we rehearsed just one piece, John's 'Three Little Feelings'. He explained that this was the only way to develop our own ensemble personality, otherwise we would merely be one more competent orchestra. He was looking for *his* sound. To achieve this we apparently had to become acquainted with boredom. If he was aware that we were bored, he probably considered us a bunch of complainers. Musicians are notorious complainers, particularly jazz musicians who are not getting to play enough. Four weeks on one piece of music did not improve personnel relations.

It was like the joke musicians tell about the bebopper who died and went to hell. He was led through fire and brimstone into a studio with a big band rehearsing in it. All the cats were there – Bird, Monk, Tadd – all of them. There was one vacant chair for him. He thought – far out, if this is hell fuck heaven. He unpacked his horn, sat down and played the chart. They ran it down several times without stopping. During a solo, he asked the guy next to him: 'Where's the coda? I can't find the coda.'

'There is no coda.'

Orchestra USA had three conductors – John Lewis, Gunther Schuller and Harold Farberman. The talented young composer/

arranger Gary McFarland was around for a while as assistant something but disappeared without explanation. One nasty rumour went that Gary left John's publishing company when he got a better offer elsewhere and sanctions were imposed.

John called a meeting and made a speech in which he said that his short conducting experience with us had convinced him he had too much to learn and so Farberman and Schuller would conduct until his own technique would develop through the lessons he was starting immediately with the latter. This was attractive modesty; we were encouraged.

But the junta was becoming unstuck. They second-guessed each other in public. If one was absent from the rehearsal, the other would countermand previous instructions. This was more inefficiency than a palace revolution but it comes to the same thing.

Scholar, composer, teacher, writer, historian, Gunther Schuller is the compleat musician. No doubt about it, he's got class. But he insisted on conducting through improvised solos. Herein lies the tragic flaw of Third Stream music. You cannot conduct swing, it must be channelled with care. Swing is too elastic to conduct. Conducting swing is like clapping on one and three, it drags instead of pushes. We buried our heads in the music stands to avoid being seen laughing, or losing our place. Gunther Schuller trying to conduct an Eric Dolphy improvisation put the Third Stream irrevocably up the creek. He should have ducked, or jumped up and down like Lionel Hampton.

Gunther's 'Journey into Jazz' was one of our hits. This was a sort of hip 'Peter and the Wolf', with Skitch Henderson reading Nat Hentoff's narration. There was nothing wrong with this modest attempt to teach children how jazz works except that we were not rehearsing without pay every Sunday morning for the pleasure of being Skitch Henderson's backup band.

Gunther soon announced he had no more time for Orchestra USA. A whiff of failure was in the air, leaks were springing in the gunwales. What can only be described as the 'regime' of Harold Farberman began.

Farberman was an ambitious and talented tympanist, composer and budding conductor. He wanted to be one of the boys, telling jokes from the podium. Conductors who tell jokes from the podium are not generally so funny. Put in the position of being more or less obliged to laugh, musicians abhor them.

When John left to tour Europe with the Modern Jazz Quartet, we found ourselves playing more and more Farberman compositions. His wife, a singer, was brought in as soloist. Discipline disintegrated. Harold told us we had 'bad rehearsal manners'. 'Gentlemen, please!' he shouted.

Orchestra USA lasted as long as it did because we played Darius Milhaud's 'Creation of the World', Charles Ives's 'The Unanswered Question', Igor Stravinsky's 'Ragtime' and 'Ebony Concerto' and Paul Hindemith's 'Kammermusik Number Three for Cello and Ten Instruments' in addition to Benny Golson and John Lewis. Goodies, treats, not everyday stuff.

But we also played the 'Star-Spangled Banner'. As with our name, this was a calculated political move to score a much-discussed State Department tour abroad. It was like an ambush. You should have seen the looks on the faces of some supposedly cool jazz musicians as parts titled 'National Anthem' were handed out towards the end of our first recording-session. My reaction was that some copyist was having a little joke. Or that maybe John had delved into the Yugoslav National Anthem. But it was the 'Star-Spangled Banner' all right, the version you hear at ball-games. It did not get us the tour.

Nick Travis played the first five notes of the 'Star-Spangled Banner' on his trumpet, then switched to 'I'll Be down to Get You in a Taxi, Honey' – they are the same first five notes for each. It could have been worse. We almost recorded Harold Farberman's jazz version of Beethoven's Fifth Symphony, which was however mercifully left on the rehearsal-room floor. We played the 'Star-Spangled Banner' straight but jazzed up Beethoven Five. Think about the implications of that and you go a long way to understanding why the Third Stream dried up. Our version of the 'Star-Spangled Banner' can be heard on the Colpix album: *Debut, Orchestra USA*.

Charter members began to turn in their stock. The stockholders who replaced them at first considered themselves fortunate, though some of us old-timers were by then calling it 'Orchestra USSR'.

Eric Dolphy. Young musicians now say to me, awestruck: 'Did you really play with Eric Dolphy?' They consider me some sort of living legend. It seems like another life. Eric was a charter member of Orchestra USA, though I cannot remember him saying a word at stockholder meetings. If I am reluctant to use the word 'genius' to describe him, he is however without doubt a legend and was probably on the brink of genius when he recorded my versions of the Berlin Theatre Songs of Kurt Weill in 1964.

How to record your first album. You need passion, hustle, confidence and a gimmick; a number, a reason to be put at the head of the line. I went to the library and copied out parts of Kurt Weill operas like *Mahagony* and *The Threepenny Opera*. That music was ripe for the picking, I could not get it out of my head in any case. I paid to make a demo of 'Alabama Song' with Barry Harris, Frankie Dunlop and Peter Ind. We recorded it in Peter's little lower East Side studio, and if you can imagine him playing bass and working the mixing console at the same time you can imagine that it could not be sold.

Then Jim Morrison and the Doors recorded 'Alabama Song' on their first album. My number was overtaking me.

Finally I approached John Lewis with the proposition that if he and other Orchestra USA members would be willing to record for minimum union scale, I would finance the date. If the tape was sold, the record would be issued under the name 'Sextet of Orchestra USA'. I wrote the arrangements (in spare time) and paid Hall Overton to check them out. I told Eric Dolphy that 'Alabama Song' was about how two Germans (Bertolt Brecht wrote the lyrics) who had never been there, viewed the corruption in Florida. I suggested he play about the corruption of Berlin. Eric Dolphy was to die in Berlin six months after recording the Berlin Theatre Songs of Kurt Weill.

Three tunes were cut in three and a half hours. New York City. Not one rehearsal, sight-reading, first or second takes. George Avakian sold the tape to RCA and I got my cash back; plus union scale for arranging, playing and contracting. It was one of my few smart investments. RCA paid for the other side in the normal fashion but by that time the two other members of the front line – Nick Travis and Eric Dolphy – were dead and Jerome Richardson and Thad Jones replaced them. Jimmy Raney replaced John.

RCA insisted for commercial reasons I add 'Mack the Knife', a nice enough song I had wanted to avoid because it had become a cliché after Bobby Darin, Louis Armstrong and Ella Fitzgerald had hits with it. It was a small enough compromise. The record came and went very fast, like my books, with excellent reviews. It is currently out of the catalogue everywhere but Japan. It is my masterpiece. Eric Dolphy the legend never played more exciting, accessible solos. Kurt Weill's irony was made for him. I am told it is the only record on which he can be heard reading music. It is also the only record on which Tom Dowd engineered one side and Phil Ramone the other. These two have become producers and stars on their own. French RCA reissued the album in the seventies, called simply *Mack the Knife by Orchestra USA*. Photos of John Lewis and Eric Dolphy split the front cover, Kurt Weill, Berlin and Michael Zwerin were only to be found inside the double jacket. I never received a royalty statement. Now you know how to make and lose your first record.

To be just, the record's aesthetic success is largely due to John's piano. He is a meticulous player, wipes the keys with an oily rag before playing. He rarely plays unnecessary notes, never omits essential ones. I have trouble ending phrases properly, tend to dissipate good ideas by overextending them. John made that impossible. His accompanying often consists of deceptively simple single-line counterpoint. Because of these interweaving melodies, my solos had better shape than usual. I could not overstate a phrase or start another prematurely without tripping over John. He forced me to play at my best on that record. He controls his musical environment by choice comping, a perfect example of how less can be more.

But on a personal level his control can be very obtrusive indeed, and I was shocked by how hard he could clamp down on Eric.

The large bump on his forehead exaggerated Eric's eager tilt forward. His instruments were like an extension of his body; he was never without one. I once saw him walking down 48th Street playing his flute.

He was a reedman, not in the sense that he played reed instruments. He was *made* of reed instruments. He did not speak, he blew. He played what might be called the Dolphyphone; whatever instrument was in his hands sounded as though he had invented it. In the New York *Herald Tribune* of 30 October 1963, Eric Salzman reviewed an Orchestra USA concert: 'Mr Dolphy, for those who don't know, is a brilliant wildman, an undisciplined musical genius who produces frantic, incredible cries from the bottom to the tip-top of a whole range of woodwind instruments . . . Mr Dolphy can no doubt produce his fantastic sound on anything you can blow a noise out of; he could, I'm sure, play with the same extreme expressive intensity on a pop bottle . . . you never know if he'll make it, but when he does — WOW!'

I met Dolphy when we were both part of a package tour called 'Jazz for Moderns'. I was with Maynard Ferguson, he was with Chico Hamilton. We travelled by bus or chartered DC3 for three weeks. Eric practised his piccolo travelling, while his buddy Ron Carter, bassist with Chico, had long and bony knees. By our coincident preference for the back of vehicles, we often found ourselves a row apart – Ron's knees in my back. Eric's piccolo was in my ears for three weeks. It still is. I can still hear its tension and polytonality. Like Lee Konitz, Eric Dolphy was one of those few musicians who could be polytonal a capella. I'm not talking about multiphonics, playing one note and singing another at the same time. Tonality is a natural force, like gravity, and Dolphy had more than one centre.

Genius is intangible, by definition it does not fit in. Eric did not fit into the prejudgements of the Orchestra USA power structure. He tried, it's sad how hard and futilely he tried to please the bosses. But his own orbit was already inevitably fixed. The orchestra's instrumentalists were more necessary tools than vital cogs, and Eric was a hand-made product in any case.

Nothing sadistic about it, Eric was feared. How could you be sure what he'd come up with next? Let's hear one for reliability. Eric *was* a 'wildman' who could never adapt to the calm currents of the Third Stream. John asked Phil Woods to play one solo after another. This is not to denigrate Phil, a thrilling player, but Phil was not, like Eric, in the process of changing our ears.

On one of Eric's rare solos, Gunther asked him to 'play closer to the melody'. The mind boggles recalling it. Here was a musician who could invent melodies never before conceived. We should have played closer to *his* melody. Imagine what Eric might have done with Darius Milhaud's saxophone melody at the beginning of 'Creation of the World' had he been permitted to stretch out on it. Jerome Richardson, who did play it, was told to use his 'classical sound'. This in an ensemble formed to explore new musical forms and bring older ones closer together.

Eric loved to play the classics. He became totally immersed in his flute part on a Mozart work we prepared for several weeks, practising it during breaks and while everyone else was packing up. Although he was no Jean-Pierre Rampal, his classical flute playing lacked experience more than ability. He played Mozart appoggiaturas inside out, but then for a long time many experts thought Glenn Gould played Mozart wrong too. If Eric's intonation was questionable at times, he did get a fat sound and was in any case a charter member, and some of us back in the brass section thought it was shameful when, after Eric had rehearsed the part for weeks, a classical flautist was brought in to play the concert.

Besides hurt sensitivity, this was directly contrary to the announced purpose of the orchestra, which was to be 'an exercise of mutual respect and compatibility between classic and jazz forms'.

Orchestra USA was very important to Eric. He was involved on some deep level with it. It failed him like it failed most of us. When the classical flautist took Eric's chair, he walked up to me, looked over his shoulder, pulled up his collar and asked: 'You feel a draught?'

Before leaving for Berlin on what turned out to be his last trip, Eric asked a friend in the reed section: 'Make sure my chair's still here when I get back.'

He could not know that all the chairs were about to disappear.

8
On the Moon

'I'll be fucked if I'm going to spend my life saving for a rainy day,'
Maynard Ferguson had told me. 'What if there's a drought? Won't
I feel silly then?'

Saving for rainy days was the *cause* of my drought. Living like I
was, in spare time, gave me a stake in rainy days. I was in the
position of having to hope for rain. Like those fanatics who run
away to some holy mountain in order to escape predicted
doomsdays, you feel silly when the sun shines. Sillier still to regret
the sun. Stockpilers against disaster consider themselves aware.
Non-believers are considered fools. But believers at least have
their faith to keep them warm, it was my fate not even to have the
comfort of faith. I have no constituency. I could never plunge in,
not even in the society of jazz musicians. Crowds make me uneasy.
I find excuses to leave early, always sit on the aisle or near the door.
I had hoped that being president of Dome Steel would give me the
benefits of organized society without organizational attachment.
In fact it had turned me into an old man in a dry season by the age
of thirty-six; attached and committed to nothing, and there was
not even a young boy waiting for rain reading to me.

What do you want to be when you grow up, old man? There was
still one more stool now, I had begun writing a jazz column for the
Village Voice. Perhaps multiplicity was the answer, playing and
writing about jazz together might get me through a Domeless life.
The odds were low – jazz and journalism are two risky endeavours.
And a part of me still thrived in jail. No odds to worry about in jail.
My jail was built with my own steel bars. I had busted myself,
convicted myself. How silly, then, to be shaking the cell door
shouting: 'I'm innocent I tell you, innocent. Let me out of here.'

The cell door was not even locked. The walls were full of holes, the ground laced with tunnels.

'If you want to be on the moon,' said Baba Ram Dass, 'just be on the moon.'

Richard Alpert, academician and dope-fiend had just turned into Baba Ram Dass the guru. Although not my guru, I looked to Dass for wisdom anyway: 'What about my alimony and child support? I can't afford to go to the moon.'

'Money and truth have no relationship.' Dass stroked his unruly beard. There had been trouble at the door of the restaurant. Dass was not wearing a necktie. In fact he was not wearing what you might call a shirt. Dome-tipped, the head waiter had sneaked us to this obscure corner, where the future seemed equally obscure.

'What the fuck am I doing in the steel business?'

'There are many levels of business.'

I had once invested in Alpert the doper, who, along with Timothy Leary needed money to tune in, turn on and drop out the world. Noble charity. Now Guru Dass was paying me back in enlightenment: 'Buddha talks about "Right Livelihood". You've got to keep your body together somehow as long as you're in this place. There are, remember, shoemakers and shoemakers. It depends on your shoeliness. Just try and do what you do the Right way. Try to figure out "Right Livelihood".'

'I don't even know if I like music any more.'

'Perhaps you should not be plugged into any one channel. Do not exclude the others.'

'None of my channels are coming in. Maybe I need a new antenna.'

'You have to be free of attachment to any one reference group. When you are free of that you will know what to do. You must go beyond your attachment to being an American, a musician, an intellectual, a businessman, a journalist, a hipster . . .'

'Hip,' I smiled, 'may no longer be hip.'

'What do you mean?'

I told him about the square on the lawn.

'Not bad. Mind if I use that sometime?'

'Bless you.'

'Bless *you*.' Dass laughed over his mousse: 'You do not accept your alienation. That is a good sign. That is one level above the tape-playing level. Most people just rerun prerecorded tapes at each other. You are still not programmed. There is hope.'

'I'm lonely. Nothing gets me through the night. I'm scared.'

'How can you be scared watching God's design unfold before your eyes?'

'I fear his design may not include me.'

'The student learns by daily increment, but the way is gained by daily loss.'

'We lost $270,000 last year. Well, look . . . may I call you Baba? I'm enjoying this Baba but you probably have a lot of important work to do.'

Dass was now quite annoyed: 'If you want to leave, leave. Just don't hand me that "important" bullshit. I have nothing to do for the rest of my life.'

Nothing but count royalties. It was easy for *him* to talk. Along with Timothy Leary, Alpert/Ram Dass created the drug-culture of the sixties with his bare head. His conversion from Jewish scientist to professional doper to Hindu mystic had been extensively covered by the media and his book about it was a best-seller. It always came back to the same problem, you see. Alpert rejected his family's definition of success. (They owned a hunk of the New York Central Railroad.) He rejected his father's value system but managed to construct a viable one of his own. So he had his head and his wallet at the same time. Baba Ram Dass was a self-made bisocial. I was a Jewish businessman who had forgotten the changes to 'Stardust'. Just be on the moon indeed.

Another day, another dollar lost. 'What do your projections indicate for the third quarter?' Fred Mann asked me, cringing.

'A profit.' Things were getting so bad I was telling Solly's accountant jokes: 'But I've written it in red ink because if we bought black ink we'd be in the red.'

Fred let loose with a hearty guffaw. The worst thing about Fred is the good time he has being a dirty capitalist. He laughs with his entire body and it's contagious. When he plunges into hard facts, making tough decisions, soothing raw customers, placating beady-eyed bankers, he gives the impression that he is as much involved with the pure joy of honest work as with the making of good money. But there comes a time when Fred pulls his glasses down from the top of his head to the tip of his nose and looks sternly over them: 'Will we be able to clean up our loan from First National?'

'Not unless we clean up at the track.'

'What about our inventory position?'

'About a thousand tons heavy.' I had done my homework. Heavy.

The coffee waggon arrived. We ordered lights and prune danishes. We consulted every morning. There were sessions with lawyers and accountants every Thursday evening. Staff meetings had been switched to Saturday morning to save good time. Lunch at my desk with Uncle Morty digesting traffic. The banks were beefing. Suppliers screamed over extended lines. Dun and Bradstreet dropped our credit-rating a notch. The roof was collapsing, the fire approached the magazine.

Fred brushed off crumbs: 'Well nobody said the reinforcing bar business was a bed of roses.'

The cliché that broke the camel's back.

'I'm leaving,' I said. Or rather heard myself say. I had not intended saying it. It was just said.

'Sorry, Mike, didn't quite get you there.'

Louder this time: 'I'm leaving.'

'You mean for the day?' Fred looked at his watch. Ten-thirty, a little early even for Prez.

'I'm just leaving.'

It's easy. Just be on the moon.

Miles Davis bought a townhouse and disappeared again. Disappearing is something we have in common. 'I'm retired now because I don't do nothing unless I want to,' he said. I sold my townhouse.

I spent a lot of my Dome profit-sharing plan cheque in Dr Bent's office. I lost my leased car, my credit cards and about thirty pounds. People told me I looked like my own son. Buying blocks of Archie Shepp's shares left me lean and hard.

Miles reappeared for a short run in the Village Vanguard. Three months after the final prune danish with Fred Mann, I was set to leave for the Soviet Union with Earl 'Fatha' Hines. I lounged against a parked car in front at closing time, in thin glory. Miles slithered up and out of the Vanguard, looked me over, and passed right by without saying a word.

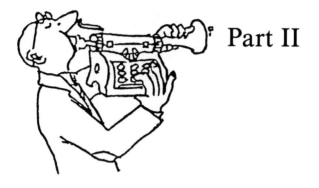 Part II

9
'Fatha' Hines and the Jazztronauts

They're Playing Our Song

The fact that Earl 'Fatha' Hines needed a white trombone-player had nothing to do either with social philosophy or musical texture. He was just one ofay short. Five of the six musicians already hired were black, and the US State Department – sponsors of this six-week tour of the Soviet Union – insisted on more than token integration to project an accurate picture of American life. I doubt that Fatha had ever hired a white musician before Bobby Donovan and me, who have good time for white cats.

So three months after deciding to be on the moon, I landed in Moscow feeling like a jazztronaut. Jazztronaut?! Is he kidding with that shit? Ever read anything so corny in your life? I'd go back and take it out but it's sort of catchy, the publisher might even use it in the title.

Our 'Gasconcert' road manager and interpreter ('What a gas they are,' would be one road joke), Vadim Petrovitch Belayev and Nina Morozova, were at Moscow airport to meet us, along with Alexei Batashev and Vadim Yushkenkoy. Batashev was president of the Moscow jazz club, Yushkenkoy described himself 'a retired musician' (he wrote his master's thesis on J.D. Salinger). How did we know these people were who they said they were?

We were invited to the Molodezhnoe youth café to meet the locals. Budd Johnson, musical director and tenorman who was close to sixty at the time, shook his head and said: 'Not me. I'm getting some sleep.' Our watches had moved ahead eight hours. Budd needed to cop some Zs.

We checked into an underwhelming hotel called the Warsaw, washed up and went to the American embassy for a cocktail party.

(A command performance, Budd had no choice.) The embassy people were friendly and complained about bad coffee and no air-conditioning in the USSR. Back at the Warsaw we found Batashev waiting with a red-head wearing Lee jeans who looked like he lived in Davenport, Iowa. Red was manager of the Molodezhnoe. Driving there, he told us in anguished English that there had been three jazz festivals in Moscow, which I found odd because jazz was supposedly banned here. I asked him about it. He said he did not understand my question.

Budd was dragging ass. We had had to appeal to his sense of patriotism to get him to come, but he perked up when we all got a round of applause just for walking through the door. Then his mouth hung open as he pointed to the combo on-stage: 'Listen, they're playing my song.'

Budd belongs to a 'school' of jazz called Texas Tenors, known for its prairie-sized sound. He had been musical director for the famous Earl Hines big band that had young Bird and Diz on it, and for Billy Eckstine's band which featured Dexter Gordon and Gene Ammons. Budd did some catalytic writing for Boyd Raeburn and Woody Herman and arranged the bebop vocal hit 'What's This?' for Gene Krupa. He'd toured the world with Quincy Jones's big band in the early sixties, gone to Asia with Benny Goodman in 1956. Like Gil Evans (with whom Budd also played), he was admired by young musicians for the way he kept up with new music. But he wasn't what could be called a 'star', so this Moscow band playing his not-so-famous tune 'Memories of Lester Young' floored him.

We sat around a formica table that had been reserved for us. It was a white, antiseptic room; third-degree lights burned the bandstand, which was in the lower left-hand corner of the L-shaped room. A doe-eyed blonde waitress put a couple of bottles of Armenian champagne on the table. I popped one open and listened.

Vladimir Sermokashev, short with tousled hair, a five o'clock shadow and a friendly slavic face played a silver-plated tenor saxophone in a mainstream style after Sonny Rollins. I said to Budd: 'Whatever he sounds like, let's encourage him.'

'Encourage, hell,' Budd answered. 'He's cooking his ass off.' Then he took a deep breath: 'Listen! He's playing my *solo* from the record.'

Sermokashev bowed to Budd when he'd finished. Budd bowed back, chuckling: 'I'll be damned. I thought there was a cold war.'

During the next number, a man in a trim beard danced with another man wearing rimless glasses. They turned out to be Yugoslavs, part of a group of twenty students who were soon snaking their way between tables, arms linked. The other car with Batashev, our drummer (and my roomie) Oliver Jackson and bassist Bill Pemberton arrived. Batashev asked me what I thought of the music. 'They're cooking their asses off,' I answered. He looked at me with disbelief: 'You appear to be putting me on.'

I tried not to smile: 'Who'd want to wear a Russian?'

He decided to let it go by and asked, without waiting for a response: 'You know how much they make here? Forty-five roubles a month. You cannot live on that.' The official exchange-rate was 1.1 roubles to the dollar: 'They could earn ten times that playing variety music with hotel bands. It is expensive to love jazz in this country.'

So you see there is such a thing as economic motivation in the Soviet Union. Or rather demotivation. Capitalist philosophy exists when it suits them. They do not have to ban what they do not trust, just make it a luxury, a deprivation, hard to find and a sacrifice to do. Batashev said that many of the officials of the Young Communist League, which ran this club, accused Soviet jazzmen of imitating Americans. 'They do not understand,' he sighed. 'It takes time to develop an idiom. But I think we will do it sooner or later.'

The next tune was a bebop version of 'Meadowlands'.

Between sets Budd inspected Sermokashev's tenor. He groaned and grunted trying to get a sound from it: 'Worst horn I ever played.' Nevertheless, he took it to the stand and played 'Bernie's Tune'. The Russians came in behind him. People pounded tables, big smiles on their faces. Oliver and Bill sat in. Batashev's eyes gleamed through his lush Fidelista beard as he exclaimed, as though announcing a diplomatic breakthrough: 'Jam session!'

Batashev asked me: 'Who's Bernie?'

They kept the place open after the customers left at eleven. Budd and Vitaly Kleinoff, another tenorman, hugged after having invented a riff together. Valery Ponomarev proudly displayed the engraving on his trumpet bell: 'Vincent Bach, Mt Vernon New York.'

Ten years later Valery would manage to emigrate to New York. One of his first nights in town, he went to the Village Gate to hear Art Blakey. He was introduced to Blakey, who said: 'A Russian trumpet-player?! Got your horn?' He had it, he sat in, he was hired. Now he lives in Queens and leads his own band.

But back in Moscow in 1966, Ponomarev was a jazzbug-bitten teenager transcribing Lee Morgan solos from black-market records. 'Do you know Lee Morgan?' he asked me.

'I blew with him once in Slugs.'

'Slugs.' He pronounced the name of that lower East Side insect-and dope-infested saloon like a *mullah* might pronounce 'Mecca'. I was finding such misplaced reverence hard to handle. He actually asked me for my autograph. 'Come on, man,' I said. 'I play a Bach horn just like you.'

'What does "Oop-bop-sh'bam" mean?' he asked.

'How the fuck should I know?' It came out instinctively, like a parent answering a child's 'stupid' question he did not know the answer to. 'It's a code, you have to know the password.'

I had not noticed Vadim our road manager behind me until I heard his knuckles popping after the word 'code'. How could he be sure I was who I said I was?

As Ponomarev started to play, note for note, Chet Baker's chorus on 'Darn that Dream', I remembered a story a guy named Jack McCullum once told me. During the Second World War, his infantry company was advancing single-file through a small Belgian town. The enemy could have been anywhere. It was the middle of the night, pitch-black and silent except for bombs bursting in air. Suddenly, he stopped short, he could not believe his ears. Behind one of those closed shutters, some saxophonist was playing Coleman Hawkins's solo on 'Body and Soul'. Was it a German or a Belgian? Should Jack shoot him or show him the right changes? The GI behind in line bumped into Jack, who said: 'Shhh.' The GI cocked his rifle: 'A sniper?' Jack laughed: 'Sort of.'

Bill Pemberton delivered a little speech when the music was over in the Molodezhnoe. Bespectacled, thin, dignified, Bill resembles a kindly schoolteacher. (Is he who he says he is?) He had written the Soviet musicians' names on a card and introduced them one by one: 'Valery, trumpet; Andrei, bass . . .' and so on. There was applause for each. Then Batashev called our names, followed by more applause.

Budd proposed a toast: 'Next time we play together, I hope it will be in Detroit.'

Vadim's knuckles just about popped right off his hands.

At the door, Batashev knocked himself out by his knowledge of the latest slang: 'Dig you later, alligator.'

Nothing Political

It was more like a Chekhov train than an Aeroflot jet. Three seats faced three others across a beat-up wooden table. The antique blue-shaded imitation oil lamp on it did not work. I watched the dirty commie family facing me.

The father was blond with no sideburns. Thirty-six, his short-sleeve plaid shirt revealed tattooed arms. He sat on the aisle, his five-year-old son beside him, twelve-year-old daughter by the window. I know their ages because I asked. Both my parents were born in the Ukraine, where we were now headed. I had taken a crash course in Russian with my mother before leaving and knew enough to read street signs and ask ages. The father tended to his children the entire flight – wiping noses, listening to secrets, gently disciplinarian when necessary. Both he and his wife, who was across the aisle, had extensive gold dental work. The little boy stared hard and long at Oliver Jackson and Clea Bradford, our vocalist; particularly Clea who was long and tall like an African queen. I guess he'd never seen black people before. When Clea offered him some candy, he blushed and ducked behind the lamp. Father teased him and offered Clea a Russian cigarette. She mimed a singer to explain her refusal. Then the little boy mimed her. Oliver said: 'I don't see any reason on earth why these people should be my enemies.'

If Oliver's observation is not the greatest insight you've encountered this week, it is however a reminder that we are all on Spaceship Earth. It's you *and* me, Charlie, not you *or* me. And if the State Department had told us before leaving that we are 'Good Will Ambassadors', it works the other way too. That Russian family radiated good will. People are good, life is good, let's all love each other. So much for cliche's.

Kiev. First lunch, Chicken Kiev. After sleeping all afternoon, Oliver and I went out for a walk. We just walked through the lobby, we had no guide and nobody appeared to be following us. (We kept looking.) Detroit black Oliver and this New York Jew had our curiosity in common. A pattern was already developing. Most of the other musicians would remain in the hotel playing pinochle, unless we were all taken on an official junket to some power station. This was once a city; the Russians adore power stations. Fatha did not approve of Oliver and I walking on the streets by ourselves. His philosophy was: 'If you don't go in the street, you can't get into trouble.'

We walked into one of those neon-lit, blue-and-white-tile underground passages that get you from one side of the street to another in Kiev. Women in knee boots, thick linen dresses and *babushkas* scrubbing. Strong sombre women. No dirt in Kiev's streets; trucks glide on the wide tree-shaded sidewalks flushing them down in the evening.

Nina the interpreter had told us: 'Other cities have parks in them, Kiev is a city in a park.' Trees and greenery everywhere, every apartment balcony with flowers or shrubs. We saw no hungry-looking people, no policemen, no lovers. One drunk weaved ahead of us for a few blocks before disappearing into a doorway.

The following evening, the Kiev Sports Palace was jammed to capacity, maybe 8,000 people, for the first of our four concerts there. We drank the flat brown beverage called beer here as Fatha Hines gave us a pre-concert pep talk in the dressing-room: 'When you're an entertainer, you've got to expect all kinds of things to happen. There are people out there who have toothaches, money problems, trouble with their wives. No matter what happens, remember we've got nothing to do with politics. We are here to entertain, to make people happy. From biblical times, that's been the function of entertainers. Jazz musicians sometimes forget that. When I hear a "boo" I always play harder.'

Fatha is considered the father of modern jazz piano. He was the first to play a line like a horn solo with the right hand and accompany himself like a brass section with the left. Fatha once had one of the best big bands in the business, with Bird, Diz and

Billy Eckstine in it. Now he had a septet. Why do I always play with shrunken bands and faded names? The critic Don Schlitten had recently written: 'Hines still thinks he is at the Grand Terrace in Chicago leading his sensational big band, only there is no band, only Hines playing the piano as though he was the band. He uses his left hand sometimes for accents and figures that would only come from a full trumpet section. Sometimes he will play chords that would have been written for and played by five saxophones in harmony. But he is always the virtuoso pianist with his arpeggios, his percussive attack, and his fantastic ability to modulate from one song to another as if they were all one song and he just created all those melodies during his own improvisations.'

I should qualify my reference to Fatha as a 'faded name'. True, he no longer made news but he was firmly implanted in legend. If not Louis Armstrong, he was about as close as you could still get in real life. But like Claude, he was a disappointed name. He was not King Cole. Fatha laughed telling us about the time he dived under the piano when a Mafia shoot-out started in the Chicago club where he was working . . . and found Louis already there. The mobsters used to give him half a hundred-dollar bill, the other half would come after he played their request. Dance, nigger, dance. Fatha had paid his dues in the white show-biz world and there were scars. Fatha did not want any trouble.

He went on in the dressing-room: 'And let's look like we're enjoying ourselves. Smile out there, talk to each other. Be loose. If we are happy, the audience will be happy too. It's like if you go to somebody's house with animosity in your heart, you're sure to have a bad time. People have told you your host is a bad guy, so you'll sulk and if he happens to be nice to you, you'll wonder if he's trying to put you on. But if you say "I'm going to see for myself," chances are you'll come out thinking "Well, hell, he was all right with *me*." So let's forget about politics and all of that, let's just go out and *play*.'

And the Ukrainian people were all right with us, exploding into applause and cheering in the middle of tuttis, they whistled on bridges of ballads, clapped when we broke into little riffs. It was obvious, they wanted swing. They were starved for it. We moved around on stage, sometimes looked at each other instead of the audience. During intermission the manager of the sports palace asked how we could play ensembles without written music. People in front rows nudged each other as the ex-Ellington trumpet-player Money Johnson grinned and catted. Swing, they gorged themselves on ours.

Back at the hotel we ate a late supper and Oliver and I stayed in the dining-room drinking sweet Armenian cognac after the others had gone to their rooms. The musicians from the hotel band introduced themselves. They had just finished a Beatle medley. One of them spoke English: 'How is Stan Kenton? We heard he was dead.'

'Last I heard Kent Standem was still alive,' I answered. This musicians' pejorative play on the not-so-universally-respected bandleader's name went undetected. Then there were other names, no context, just the names: 'Phil Woods Grant Green Ornette Coleman Cannonball Adderley Charlie Byrd . . .' They were so proud to know the names.

Oliver and I went out for another walk. We passed darkened shop windows with fat mannequins wearing garish print dresses in them. One window had cardboard notes, saxophones and violins in it, nestled in a thick green net of plants. Was it a music store with plants or a flower shop with music?

Three boys and one girl, all in their early twenties, were standing near a wooden bench in a park. One of them said: 'Good evening.' It was impossible to remain anonymous walking with Oliver, both because of his decidedly un-Russian skin colour and the shit-eating grin he almost never wipes off his face. Shit-eating grins are rare in this part of the world.

One young man was dressed in a black suit, the jacket tapered with high side vents. The pants were pressed and slightly pegged with no cuffs. The windsor knot of his red silk tie fitted into his continental spread collar, and his black shoes were pointed and shined. He could have played Alain Delon parts in pimp movies.

One of the other two boys, both in white shirts with rolled-up sleeves, asked us for a cigarette. Oliver distributed Parliaments. The girl admired hers for several minutes before lighting up. Black suit said that he and his male friends were all students. I asked about the girl: 'She's a who,' he said.

'A what?'

'A who. You know, women's work.'

Had we understood? She had close-cut naturally curly blonde hair with a nose that turned up, Nixon-like, at the end. Her knees looked too smart to go under such a dumb dress. The thought crossed my mind to take some comfort there but how did we know these people were what they said they were?

It was midnight. We suggested we all go for a vodka somewhere. Black suit said thanks, but shook his head: 'There is no place open. This is Russia, the USSR.'

A Walk in the Suburbs

Svetlana would have looked like a fat Elizabeth Taylor if she'd lost twenty pounds. She moved like a dainty tank in her spiked heels down the twisting, pitted path, speaking of Johnny Hallyday. 'He's a rocker,' she explained, mimicking his act which she had seen in Warsaw. Victor and I trailed behind, laughing at the good-natured fat rocking ass.

We had met that morning in a café. I'd been asking our guides to take me to a place they did not want me to see. They never said no. Victor recognized me from the previous night's concert. I asked him how to get to that place and he had said without hesitating: 'I know where it is. My girlfriend lives in the neighbourhood.'

He called Svetlana and we went by taxi to meet her. It was all so normal, just like any other city. I'm sure we were not followed and Victor did not look over his shoulder. However he looked amazed when I told him I was mailing my articles about the tour to the *Village Voice* in New York through normal post-office channels. (All five of them arrived in not more than ten days.) A great deal of innocence was involved here, perhaps some luck, and some sort of hole in the Soviet surveillance system. Either it has improved since then or perhaps that surveillance system is not as efficient as they would like.

White-hot. Svetlana sat down and fanned herself with her Cuban straw hat. Victor and I stood on the crest of a little hill looking into the gully where a woman overflowed her one-piece black bathing-suit. Her pale male friend was reading a magazine. Could they know where they were? These were no pilgrims in this neglected weedy gully in the suburbs of Kiev.

Babii Yar.

During the Second World War, the Germans massacred the Jews of Kiev here. Certain Ukrainians had not been all that sorry. Yevtushenko had recently written a poem about it, but it was circulating more or less clandestinely. At least in part out of guilt, the Soviets were hesitant to pay full homage. (Later a monument would be built.)

As a teenager I liked to say that my race was jazz musician. It was a master race. We were pacifists, outlaws, anarchists. Other people said: 'All politicians are crooked,' but went on trusting them. We knew better, we knew how to duck. Lenny Bruce once said it for us: 'If all politicians from the beginning of time were crooked, then there is no crooked.'

This probably explains my admiration for such wrecks as Allen Eager and Squirms. I admired them for the same reason a poor Italian kid, perfectly law-respecting, might have admired Al Capone. I admired their honesty. I, on the other hand, was trying to please all the people I did not respect but feared. I was living like an assimilated Indian, dressing like the white man. I was in the closet. A part of me was ashamed of my race, or frightened of what wrath belonging to that race might bring down on me.

There is room for many tribes within a race, I told myself. We are all family nevertheless. Not all jazz musicians had to be outlaws, and few of them are any more. It was an overly-romantic, unrealistic definition anyway. It has become a myth – like Mexican bandits or Far-West gunfighters. Take Don Ellis. He practised every afternoon in hotel rooms, he neither drank nor smoked anything. Everybody fought to get into the car he drove because he was serious and reliable. There is need for serious and reliable relatives. We would joke: 'Don may be a bore but he's a bitch of a driver.' That may sound like we were making fun of someone who was unlike us, or the way we preferred to see ourselves, but he was still family. Don once typed out a series of exercises for his avant-garde rehearsal band. One of them instructed the musicians to do the opposite of what the conductor indicated. If he requested a slow tempo we played fast, if he indicated piano we played loud, and so on. When Don thought it was time to go to the next exercise, he cut the band off. Obviously we continued to play. He laughed the first time but when he cut us off again, we still continued playing. He lost his already small sense of humour and stomped out of the rehearsal.

My race, my tribe: jazz musicians. Like the Welsh in Britain, the Bretons in France and American Mohawks, we have been assimilated. The assimilation went both ways. *Time* magazine picked up our language, advertising executives began using our drugs. On the other hand we began to be career-motivated, we wanted shiny machines like anyone else. We began to compromise to get them. But still I have more in common with a Russian jazz musician than with an American banker. Politics were easy to avoid; Fatha did not have to enforce his policy. It did not even take a conscious decision on our part.

In my experience cliques in integrated bands are rarely divided by race. The drinkers stay with the drinkers, the pinochle-players with the pinochle-players and so on. To this extent, the State Department *was* presenting an accurate view of American society. Miles Davis hired Bill Evans, Duke Ellington hired Louis Bellson, Benny Goodman hired Teddy Wilson. Of course there are racists everywhere, but rare, I think, in jazz. We are all of the same race.

Standing on the dirt hill overlooking Babii Yar, however, there were no riffs in my head. Only wailing. The chilling wail of another, more ancient blood-tie. I had not known it was so close to the surface. Was my adherence to the race of jazz musician just a hipper excuse for assimilation? The silver '1965 Moscow Jazz Festival' pin on Victor's lapel shimmered in the afternoon sun. I may have reeled. Victor asked me: 'Are you all right?'

He said: 'The earth was moving here for hours after the massacre. My mother told me about it. After they slaughtered a batch, a detail of other Jews shovelled dirt over the bodies. They thought this would save them in the end but they were shot too. Not all the buried people were dead. A man I know, the uncle of a friend of mine, was one of the few to survive. He still lives in Kiev. He's completely mad.'

The lady in the black bathing-suit shielded her eyes from the sun. Svetlana pointed to the rectangular concrete boxes in the distance: 'That is my home.' We walked back down the path to a wide and desolate modern street with stark precast concrete light-poles and only the occasional bus and us moving on it. Victor said: 'My mother and I were evacuated from Kiev in the middle of an air-raid. I couldn't even tell you whose side the planes were on. I don't think my mother ever mentioned it. Maybe she never knew. The train we were on was strafed but the engineer kept stopping and starting and changing speed. My mother lay on top of me to shield me from the bullets. It was very bad in Kiev during the war.'

While Victor was being strafed, I had been enjoying Lester Goldstein honking at the tennis-players in Forest Hills. Not once, not to this day, have I ever been in a position of serious physical danger. Am I lucky or a coward? Gerry Gilley beat the shit out of me in grammar school after I challenged him to a fight when he called me 'kike'. I made up my mind then and there, no more fights. I would take my own risks. I took them marrying at nineteen, improvising, writing risky things which revealed myself in not the best of lights, and they were real risks but not physical. I never put my life on the line. Am I like a gambler on a good run; when will my luck change?

By the time we reached Svetlana's door it was noticeably cooler. I shivered. They kissed. We left her and Victor laughed: 'I like heavy women.' He cupped his hands over two imaginary enormous breasts.

We walked on. 'What's it like living here?' I asked him. 'I mean, really, how does it go from day to day?'

'You don't have to ask,' he said. 'You know the answer.'

'No I don't. Come on, let's get a drink. I need a drink. Tell me about life here.'

It was so simple, the answer so obvious. I was ashamed to have forced him to say it: 'We're not free.'

We found a restaurant and ordered vodka. Victor asked me: 'Did you ever play with Charlie Parker?'

The Circus Comes to Town
On July 28 1966, the *New York Times* carried a story with the headline: 'US PROTESTS CHANGES OF CITIES ON HINES TOUR!'. The story read in part: 'American officials said the Soviet Union gave no reason in informing the United States last Friday that it was changing the schedule of the Earl Hines band. But there was no doubt in the minds of United States officials that the Soviet action was intended as a protest against American policy in Vietnam . . .

92

It appears to United States officials that the Soviet Union is deliberately attempting to minimize the cultural exchange program, particularly by reducing the attention paid to the more popular attractions from America. This was illustrated . . . in the changed schedule for the Hines group . . . The Soviet Union appears to be taking steps to ensure that the Hines band does not receive a warm reception in the larger Soviet cities.'

So we would not play Moscow or Leningrad. Ambassador Kohler was complaining. We were pawns in the cold war, political whether we liked it or not. The North Vietnamese were threatening to put our flyers on trial for war-crimes. How could I explain to the Soviets that they were not 'my' pilots, that I had less in common with them than with Valery Ponomarev. It would serve nothing other than to put Valery in jail perhaps. You can duck only so far. We were being exiled to the Caucasus, Armenia and Georgia. Oliver said: 'Georgia is the same everywhere.'

Resigned to piddling around the provinces, Vadim Petrovitch Belayev, road manager, Nina Morozova, interpreter, Sasha Ukolicheff, master of ceremonies, Bill Dixon, USIA escort, Clea Bradford, vocalist, and the Earl Hines Septet boarded the midnight sleeper for Mahatch-Kala, a fishing port on the Caspian Sea.

Four in a musty compartment. In my upper berth I read a newspaper, our first in three weeks, which Bill had brought from Moscow, where he had gone for an unsuccessful consultation over the scheduling crisis. An item caught my eye: 'Vancouver – The Bolshoi Ballet, stranded here because of a United Airlines strike, finally got a plane Monday night and flew eastward . . .'

Having just read the same thing, Bobby Donovan poked his head in our compartment and said how sorry he was that the Bolshoi had been stranded way out there in the sticks in Vancouver. We charted their next tour of the States: the largest town they play is Big Spring, Texas.

We had not met before the tour and we would rarely see each other after it was over, but the experience of this faraway obscure road was pulling us together. We were playing straight-ahead mainstream jazz that was at least ten years behind the times but Budd Johnson had arranged it cleanly, we were playing it every night and better and better and it was all something special so our spirits were high.

As the train rolled along, Budd and I shared a pint of vodka and he talked about other roads: 'I left home in 1926 when Holloway and his Merrymakers came through Dallas. Holloway had what we thought was the most beautiful tone in the world on alto saxophone. He had this deep vibrato, kind of like Carmen Lombardo. Most of the guys in the band were from Little Rock, Arkansas. Holloway used to play with Alphonso Trent's band. Back in those days, Trent was like Duke Ellington. They called his band the "Orchestra of Gold", and they played all the big-time white hotels all through the south. The sidemen were making a hundred and a quarter a week. That was an awful lot of money in those days. You got to remember that with $125 a week you could support a family with two or three kids, put them through school and everything.

'We all looked up to those guys. So when Holloway formed his own band and came into Dallas with it, it was a big deal. I felt pretty proud when I got on that band. I was only sixteen. I eventually joined a band called Eugene Coe and his Happy Black Aces. Coe played drums and his wife was on piano. She wasn't bad either. We played some little town in Oklahoma, I forget the name now – it's where the Blackfoot Indians come from. I got in on the tail-end of that job. When it was over a week later, Coe didn't have any more work but he wanted to keep the band together. So he decided to take everybody to Amarillo and feed and sleep us until he could get something.

'That was some trip. Coe had this touring car. Everybody was in this one car, and it was a twelve-piece band. We kept having blowouts. We were all over the fenders, standing on the running boards. It took us three days to get to Amarillo. We were all broke. Coe put us in this little hotel a friend of his had. It was right next door to a theatre. That's when I met Ben Webster; he was playing piano for the silent movies in the theatre.

'Ben wanted to learn saxophone. At the time Frankie Trumbauer was the baddest cat around. Everybody dug Frankie Trumbauer. He had recorded a solo on a tune called "Singin' the Blues" and everybody memorized the solo. Ben said to me, "Hey man, I sure would like to learn to play that solo on the saxophone." I said, "First you got to learn to hold the thing."

'Then I went to Tulsa with a guy named T. Holder, who had

once played trumpet with Alphonso Trent. When we got there the place we were supposed to work at had a padlock on it. So there we were, stranded in Tulsa. Being infuriated with T. Holder, we decided to fire him. We elected Jesse Stone, who was the piano-player, leader and told T. Holder: "Man, for the money you owe us you can drive us to St Jo, Missouri," which was Jesse's home town.

'That was some ride, the same situation as before, everybody in one car, hanging all over it. I remember two of us got on top of the car. Can you imagine that? It was a fourteen-piece band. We were like immigrants. Jesse went down to a hotel and put us in two rooms, seven to a room. The first four that got to the beds slept in them. Everybody else was on the floor or in chairs. Sometimes a guy would stay in bed all day not to lose his place.

'Jesse hustled around but we would only get a little gig now and then, something like three dollars a man. We rehearsed all day every day and we were getting pretty good. People were talking about us. Whatever money we earned went into a pool. We used that money to pay rent, buy food and uniforms. We just worked for the survival of the whole fourteen, not as an individual. Even if somebody got hold of a dime or something and bought crackers he had to share them. It was one big family. What a beautiful band that was. This was 1929. Oh, did we have a band . . .'

I woke up a little after sunrise and looked through the window, lying on my stomach. The train was passing through stark primitive countryside which reminded me of Budd Johnson's 1929 Missouri. Ducks, cows, sickly corn, high-tension poles strung out over the brown land. Burgundy-coloured stone houses appeared with increasing frequency alongside the tracks. A work-gang laying rails watched us pass – one strong figure, large back, black cap and knee boots, bushy Stalin moustache.

A small delegation holding eight bouquets of flowers waited for us on the tiny concrete platform. Among them, the director of the Mahatch-Kala Philharmonic Society. He was short, fat, bald, myopic and extremely nervous about the capitalists who would be his responsibility.

He led us to the Caucasus Hotel. Rural types smelling of monthly baths trooped through the peeling lobby dominated by a larger-than-life socially realistic painting of Karl Marx. My room overlooked a small produce market. Two women in oriental robes sliced up a watermelon in back of a shed, looking furtive. I figured I'd better report them to the proper authorities. There's something about this country . . .

Everybody stared at us. We were used to it by now. Getting further into the boondocks, larger and more brazen crowds inspected us with unabashed curiosity. On the train, a policeman had parked himself at the door of the compartment in which Fatha, Budd, Bobby Donovan and Bill Pemberton were continuing their marathon pinochle game and just stared at them. Sasha, our master of ceremonies, chic, in his forties, chivalrous and protective of us, came up to the policeman and said: 'Don't stare, it isn't polite.' The policeman scowled: 'Don't talk to me like that. I could have you put away for fifteen days.' Sasha's habitual ear-wrinkling smile vanished: 'I could have you taken off the force for fifteen years.'

Central versus local power. Sasha would never have been trusted to travel with us had he not been considered reliable. He must have had a power-base somewhere. He could have been KGB; any or every one of our Soviet hosts could have been, just as Bill Dixon may well have been CIA. Bill certainly looked suspicious carrying his enormous short-wave radio that seemed to have enough room for radar in it. But we were so harmless, going to bed early, playing pinochle. Except for me, maybe, and my dispatches to Greenwich Village, there was not a hint of a threat among us and our hosts could see that. They relaxed their guard, leaving Oliver and me, and occasionally Bobby Donovan, free to roam at will.

No trouble, no sir, not from Fatha Hines. Vadim, who took pride in being a good road manager, would fight for better-quality pianos, only to hear Fatha say it was OK, he did not want to cause any trouble. You could see Vadim's respect for Fatha fade. Poor Fatha had been conditioned to submission for too long. He was respected here, a first-class world-quality pianist, and classical musicians were invariably part of our audience. In any case, Fatha could make any old beat-up provincial piano sound like a Bosendorfer concert grand. His large hands covered the keys like tender tarantulas and somehow, within the confines of a fixed and dated style, he would manage to sound totally modern almost despite himself. We all had a lot of respect for Fatha's historic past and lively present. We, particularly some of the other black members of the band, could not understand why he did not have more respect for himself. We were embarrassed by his definition of entertainment. Our show-stopper was 'St Louis Blues', featuring Fatha's six-chorus right hand octave trill. There would be inevitable cheers, after which he'd pull out a white handkerchief and, to prove how effortless the trill was for him, dust off the piano with his left hand. This may have been entertainment for Fatha but black men blushed over the assumption that the menial role usually reserved for their race was something to laugh about and entertain people with.

If there were political operatives in our Soviet entourage, they were soon lulled by what they must have seen as our naïveté. We were people who only thought about pinochle and jazz (and drinking). The fact that I had no typewriter and was hand-writing the articles to the *Voice* in letter-form may have had something to do with their getting through. And then both sides began to see each other as people rather than representatives of one system or another. Dealing with most people, you sooner or later come to the point where common human denominators dominate. So much for geopolitics.

We had become used to being stared at. Standing outside the hotel in Mahatch-Kala, waiting for the bus to take us to the concert, Money Johnson observed the gathering crowd and said: 'Looks like the circus has come to town.'

Every eye in the early evening street was focused our way. These people may never have seen anybody from the other side of the Caucasus before, let alone non-Caucasians. A little old man looking as though he had been born in the tall brown fur cossack hat he wore despite the extreme heat came up to six-foot Clea and stared at her eyeball-to-Adams apple in Barnum and Bailey juxtaposition.

The concert was held in an outdoor amphitheatre in 'Green Park' by the Caspian Sea. Backstage, long tables covered with red velour cloths held cookies, mineral water, black bread and caviar. This was the land of caviar. I was king here. It was served with every meal. These other Americans considered caviar too salty.

'Pass it this way,' I kept saying. There was always a mountain of caviar on my plate.

It was also the land of vodka. When I asked Herr Philharmonic director to get three bottles before the concert he went into what resembled a *petit-mal* epileptic fit explaining that drinking was forbidden before a concert. I told him this was a special occasion, which it was. He was probably feeling like a New York cop when Castro is in town. He wasn't taking any chances. When I insisted, he spoke to Vadim Petrovitch. Used to us by now, liking us, Vadim shrugged his fat shoulders with a smile, extended thumbs up and arranged for the vodka.

'We're celebrating a wedding,' I announced, pouring it around. We toasted the happy couple. Nobody asked who they were. Maybe they thought I was kidding, or looking for an excuse to get bombed, but the wedding was real enough. Bill Dixon had brought me a telegram from Eleanor in Miami, announcing her marriage, which meant no more alimony payments. Glasses were raised: 'To the bride.'

Fatha played his opening solo number, 'Lover Come back to Me'. In Kiev this had been substituted, by Soviet request, for the original opener, 'I've Got the World on a String', which somebody apparently thought subversive. I peeked through a small hole in the wooden barrier to look at the audience. Student faces mostly, intelligent; total concentration. A girl in large round glasses like Janis Joplin was wearing at the time looked just as pseudo-serious as American girls wearing such glasses. The faces were mystified rather than hostile, but distant just the same. The response was mild; they were thinking too hard to applaud. Our first mild reception. The radio, Bill Dixon had told us, was bombarding them with news of evil Americans bombarding Hanoi; they have heard and read the official view of jazz as 'decadent capitalist' music and were too busy trying to figure us out in relation to all of that to swing.

Tiredgrad

They did not have enough swing in their lives and I was learning not to take mine for granted.

I have not been back to the Soviet Union since that summer,

though I visited Eastern Europe several times. Each time I returned just that much more of a capitalist. A trip to Eastern Europe can make a capitalist even out of an anarchist. People complained about my *Voice* articles, saying they were full of clichés about 'Communist oppression'. But this seems to be one of those unfortunate cases where clichés are true.

Recently I interviewed Leo Feigin, a Russian emigré living in London who is releasing albums by Russian jazz groups from unauthorized tapes. When I questioned his statement that: 'Russian jazz will be *the* jazz of the eighties and nineties,' he asked me: 'OK, tell me. Under what condition was jazz born?'

I hesitated: 'Slavery?'

He shrugged his shoulders: '*Voilà!*'

'Many listeners perceive this music as a cry for freedom,' the critic Joachim Berendt said about the Russian Vyacheslav Ganelin trio; 'they ask themselves how much suffering you must endure before your rebellious cry assumes such proportions.' Though the word 'slavery' is not to be taken literally, it is true that creativity has less options in Russia and that Russian jazz musicians in general and the Ganelin trio specifically have begun to express what has been called their 'Slavic spirit' with an intensity they would not have in a more open society.

So the process I heard begin with a bebop Meadowlands in Moscow in 1966 was well on the way to maturity in 1983. Feigin sees the Ganelin trio – which bears a superficial resemblance to the Art Ensemble of Chicago, Anthony Braxton and Ganelin himself to Herbie Hancock – as the continuation of the great Russian musical tradition, following Scriabin, Tchaikovsky and Stravinsky: 'Before free jazz, Russians were good copiers but they were playing somebody else's music. Free jazz discarded harmony, tonality and the strict rhythm of traditional jazz. With the appearance of the new music, Russian jazz began to develop its own identity.

'The reason this is so significant is that improvised music is the only art-form that cannot be censored. Censorship permeates every level of Soviet life, but improvisation by definition is happening right in front of people at the very moment. The Soviets have not been able to define an official attitude towards improvised music. They can see possible political capital in the fact that jazz was started by oppressed blacks in the United States. But on the other hand it comes from the West and that makes it immediately bad – whatever comes from the West is bourgeois propaganda. They don't know what to do with it.

'When I released the first Ganelin album in 1981 and told people it was Russian jazz, all I got was pity and smiles. People thought I was mad. "What is this loony talking about, jazz from Russia?" But now I can tell you nobody thinks I'm mad any more.'

Since the Hines tour I have heard from several sources and read several times that many of the emerging generation of Russian jazz musicians with their 'Slavic Cry' refer to our tour as a turning-point in their lives.

10
The Sound of Flat Feet Flapping

When faced with a tough decision, my father wrote down the pros and cons in two columns and added them up. The *Village Voice* had offered to send me to London as their European Editor. If I could tell a pro from a con I would have added them up, but I can't so I took a walk.

It's a tough place, New York. I had written for *Esquire* and *Playboy* and others and had written a book, I was beginning to make my mark in that tough place. It would be tough to leave. I'd already thrown privilege away once, leaving Dome. I found myself in front of the hospital where I was born.

The week before I had had an argument with Claudia in front of the same building. Claudia had long streaked hair and bangs, and her rings and chains were always bouncing and clanging. She was a stylist for a fashion photographer and could rent a camel on four hours' notice. She thought the fashion business was fashionable; boy she could twist and shout. I had yelled at her in front of the hospital: 'For Chrissakes don't you realize there's more to life than fun and games? Pick up a book sometimes. Read something beside the fashion page.'

'Thinking too much is bad for you!' She thought I was kidding. She never really believed people could be angry with her. She tried to kiss me: 'Thinking gives you a headache.'

'*You* give me a headache,' I shouted. 'You dumb broad, the whole world is falling apart, massacres everywhere, famine, we're all about to blow fucking up and you're not even interested. Fucking shit!' You have to admit, I have a way with words.

The New York pace was taking its toll. I was running hard and fast to prove I'd done the right thing leaving Dome. Never, it seemed, hard or fast enough. Not playing music every day, not having written for a living before the age of thirty-four, I was at a double disadvantage under my two hats and between stools. I faced every day with fear. Claudia faced the day with a smile, the bitch. She made me tea when I had a cold; I never even had to ask her. She sat down on a bench in the concrete park across the street to cry.

My mind wandered back to a warm May night in 1930. I had just been born on the top floor of this very hospital. There was a nurses' dance on the roof and the window was open. My mother could hear the jazz come down. Her nurse pointed to little new me and said: 'He's going to be a jazz baby.' Two old drunks sat down on Claudia's bench.

Walking north on Second Avenue towards 19th Street, I remembered playing stickball in Queens. Having moved to the first street of a tract in Jamaica, building dust was our lot. We turned uninstalled boiler tanks into rafts which we floated on foundation ponds after heavy rain. We climbed all over split-level framework. Our stickball games were interrupted almost every time at bat by passing vehicles. We made faces at the drivers. If somebody hit the ball on Mr Glass's newly seeded lawn, it would be confiscated and a parent would have to see Mr Glass about getting it back.

I travelled two and a half hours back and forth by subway to the High School of Music and Art in upper Manhattan, doing my homework on the way. The school was largely Jewish and on Jewish holidays nobody would be there but the blacks and heretics like me. We could jam all day long.

The verb 'to jam'. A jam is a fix, an awkward position; or jam can be a treat. Improvising involves a series of jams, how to get out of them is the real treat. Other people climb Mount Everest, I jam. Trouble was I tried to carry improvisational techniques into journalism, which was resulting in too many rejections from serious journals. I was jamming my own communications. Only the *Voice* seemed to want my verbal jams and perhaps it is smart to stay where you are wanted.

Flat feet flapping on foul pavement, I reached 34th Street thinking that there is absolutely no way I will ever be able to get there from here. The wind blew dust and old newspapers. My eyes ached from the ugliness of New York – physically ached like being too close to a rock band can make your ears ache. Just below the heart of the city, $5-a-day hotels peeled over patched bars with people talking to themselves in them. Barbering supplies, medical trusses ('wholesale only'), Eddie's Bowling Lanes. A black man on a chair tipped back against an oily garage stared at me.

In the elegant residential neighbourhood squeezed between shiny glass towers a few blocks south of the railroad station, uniformed doormen hailed cabs for painted matrons. A filthy dogwalker with frightened hair jogged by with six of them on leashes.

I looked through the spotless windows of the Advertising Club to watch the big grey gentlemen reading long lines of figures, swallowed by easy chairs. I attended business lunches here, where a visiting executive once asked: 'How can you folks live in New York? Nothing but Jews and niggers here.' I said nothing; he was still giving me credit. Besides, my race was jazz musician, right?

Half-hour north I passed the place where I had lived with a wife twice removed and three daughters removed now in Miami. We were already removed by the East Coast of America; in Europe there would also be the Atlantic Ocean. My daughters might become totally removed. I remembered my youngest, four at the time, waking to middle-of-the-night prowl-car screams and crawling into our bed crying. She thought the screams were a nightmare.

But I'd miss the interesting people, the people pushing themselves to the limit. People pushing themselves make life interesting. So many interesting people – I was on speaking terms with Norman Mailer, Murry Schisgal, Rip Torn and Francis Ford Coppolla, to drop a few names. Why then was I waking with fear? Perhaps I was not interesting enough for all my interesting acquaintances. And too much interesting, like too much anything, becomes boring. Enough interesting already.

I passed Elaine's Restaurant, a place that was more a hospital for me than a hangout. The writer Christopher Hitchins in *Mother Jones* magazine described Elaine's as a 'gruesome media restaurant . . . the perfect spot for an evening of social ironies'. I did not find it gruesome, and loved the ironies. My dictionary defines irony: 'Incongruity between the actual result of a sequence of events and the normal or expected result.' Before I got in a jam by improvising in their pages, I used to have a restaurant column in *Playbill* magazine, the programme that is given away in Broadway theatres. I wrote in praise of Elaine's and it was ironic that for weeks Elaine had to stand at the door turning away customers who did not fit her orchestration. I liked Elaine because she could laugh at that; she understood the irony of it. She even bought me a bottle of Dom Perignon champagne.

Elaine's was closed the afternoon of my pro-con walk. I sat on a garbage can, lit a cigarette, and thought about wonderful ironic Paul Desmond the night he became bored by an interesting philosophy professor. Paul usually wore a suit and a tie and looked quite professorial himself. This is one jazz type, a sort of ironic hip hype being run down, a boss duck – Jimmy Knepper and Lee Konitz also come to mind. You would never guess by looking at them that these men earn their living taking risks. Ironic. After listening to the professor pontificate, Paul Desmond slowly lifted his glass of J&B and water and poured it over the professor's head. The professor stopped talking, achieving Paul's immediate purpose, and slowly, like a Laurel and Hardy number with inevitable, predictable escalating violence, took off Paul's glasses, placed them on the floor, stamped on them and stalked out. Paul put on his smashed lenses and said with the ironic English accent he could affect: 'I thought he'd never leave.'

A bit further north, two cops dragged a black drunk off the curb into their patrol car and drove off, roof light flashing. A Rolls-Royce took their parking-space. People can get really mean about parking-spaces in Manhattan. I know a guy who goes out and sits in his car just to give false hope to circling motorists. He takes a taxi even when he needs his car to be mean about it.

Further north still, where the park ends, I bought a hot dog from a Puerto Rican with a bad habit. Earlier the same year, I had written a book about a halfway house for Harlem dope-fiends. It was on 123rd Street and I headed in that direction. I spent days there for months, slept over often. Iron cots with lumpy mattresses and unpainted walls covered by sinister shadows. A garbage can fell over, a pack of dogs barked in the alley. Brushing the gnats from my face, I stood at the window and watched an elderly black woman bend over her ironing-board in Bea's Laundry. Up too late, a young boy helped her. I wondered where the rats were.

Everybody knows there are rats in Harlem; we've all seen the pictures of bitten children. 'Oh, isn't that terrible,' we say, thinking thank God it's not our child. But being right in it is another matter. I heard the patter of small feet in the wall.

Seventh Avenue swings uptown. Smiling men rap and finger-pop on the sidewalks, slap each other's backs. It's called 'hanging out', which can be defined as 'doing something doing nothing'. In suburbia men mow their lawns, trim hedges, wash their cars or have a catch with their kids on weekends. During the week they work somewhere else. In Harlem the men are there every day – leaning on parked cars, drinking from bottles in brown paper bags. Here's one now smoking a long cigar on the top step of his stoop. He's wearing a sharp beige camel-hair coat and a fedora to match. He is clean, manicured; his brown shoes have a high shine. What can a black man do to be dressed like that hanging out on a weekday? Maybe he works at night. In that case, he is not using his leisure-time creatively. There's another one, washing his car in a sea of garbage between two stripped wrecks. It is a shiny American car and he seems very proud of it. There is something un-American about a man washing his shiny car parked in garbage on a weekday.

On a business day in the fashionable east 60s, you see women with Saks shopping bags, nannies escorting children and overbred dogs, delivery boys, uniformed chauffeurs. On Seventh Avenue and 123rd Street there is no such thing as a business day.

Rocky from the rehabilitation centre, detoxified only a month at the time, helped me paint my loft. Rocky had been a junky for the worst part of fifteen years. All his friends were dead or in jail. I lived in a loft because it was one way to get cheap space in Manhattan, not because I preferred living in a manufacturing zone with an airshaft for a view. It was no penthouse, but Rocky was impressed. 'It's so beautiful here, Mike,' he kept repeating. He stood staring out my front window, a sight I did my best to avoid; the Apex Technical School across the street. That cross-section of functional classrooms containing the working class trying to get ahead on their own time reminded me of packed subways, lines of stuck traffic, of all the interesting people I was not interesting enough for, of the pushy masses in general. Start thinking about all that in New York and you're in trouble. You remember it is a skinny island with limited access. If something should go wrong and everybody wanted to leave at once, forget it. You remember the fierce competition and the hustling, scheming hordes ready to overtake you should you falter. Rocky had another perspective: 'That's nice over there, people trying to improve themselves.'

I decided I could not take rehabilitating dope-fiends at that moment and took a cab downtown to Dr Bent's office. I left impressed by how good I felt.

I put Feelgood in my pro-leaving column and called Claudia to invite her to dinner in the Russian Tea Room from a phone booth in the lobby of the Great Northern Hotel. Busy. Waiting for the line to clear, I heard music coming from 'Fine Sound' Studio A just off the lobby. I pushed through the door.

It was a mirage, certainly a sign of some kind. Duke Ellington and his orchestra were recording in there. Only in New York can you look for a phone booth and find Duke Ellington.

He had added a chorus for one of his religious works. After some briefing by Duke and a slate from the engineer, the chorus began to chant slowly, a-capella: 'FREE-DOM FREE-DOM.'

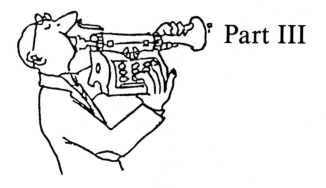 Part III

Part III

11
Scoop

Although a fan of American culture, Timothy the barrister was appalled by the rise to power of Richard Milhous Nixon, about whom he said: 'The only positive aspect seems to be his middle name.'

Handing me the London *Times* of 21 January 1969, Timothy said: 'I guess he didn't know about you,' indicating an article which read in part: 'There were a good many people early last year who would not believe that Mr Richard Nixon could become President because they felt that his election would be a national disaster. There is still not much enthusiasm, but also no reports of heavy emigration . . .'

It had been heavy enough for me. Packing my bags to leave for Europe on 20 January 1969, Nixon's inauguration day, I knew somehow I would not soon return to live in a country that could inaugurate such a President. I leafed through that other *Times*, now my home-town paper, stopping to study a photograph. Somebody, Timothy I presumed, had drawn a thick black circle around Spiro Agnew, and a mighty exclamation mark above him. Standing between Chief Justice Warren and Milhous, Agnew had his right hand up, swearing. Behind Milhous, framed in his right shoulder, was the sullen head of defeated Hubert Humphrey. Lyndon Johnson was at the extreme left, almost out of the picture. You may remember it.

They looked so foreign, all those down lines on grey faces, like masks. After six hours' jet-lag and with 5,000 miles between us, they seemed a bunch of kids playing grown-ups who had somehow managed to talk themselves on to the front page. Milhous and Hubert are trying to make us believe they have made up after a fight, but are goosing each other off-camera. Gawky Spiro is having a hard time suppressing the giggles, though the lower half of his face does succeed in a pretty good imitation of vice-presidential solemnity. Hubert is the ugly kid on the block, the one who continues hiding in Ringolevio while the others have quit to go for a soda without telling him. Meanwhile Lyndon keeps smiling, hoping they'll still let him play too. Milhous of course has all the marbles.

Who were these jokers and what did they have to do with me? Lifeless actors in an endless play with tacky scenery and a predictable plot; how have they become such a hit? How could I know then that Milhous was a villain of Shakespearian proportions? Anyway my reservations were cancelled.

I also cancelled out my mistress again, mistress music. I had not even bothered to pack my horn. At the age of thirty-nine, I found still another stool, one more hat.

Scoop's the name, news is my game.

Scoop wrote about the Beatles and the Stones, about student protest in Paris, the Living Theatre in Berlin, a dissident East German poet, about the Cannes Film Festival, Jewish anti-Zionist Israelis, the world's first porn film festival in Amsterdam, and there was one genuine scoop. Having just broken out of a California jail, Timothy Leary was taking refuge in Algiers. Scoop called and he said: 'Come down, we'll talk.' He was not at the airport as promised. A black voice answered Leary's phone, refusing to identify himself, and told Scoop to stay put until picked up. Taken to Leary, Scoop asked what was going on. Leary said: 'We're under arrest, and now presumably so are you.' The Black Panthers had an 'embassy' in Algiers, Eldridge Cleaver felt threatened by Leary. He took action, calling it 'a revolutionary bust'. Sixties underground politics no longer interest me, and anyway the matter can be summed up by simply saying the town was too small for the two of them. Scoop interviewed Leary and Cleaver together and broke the story. When he walked into the Coupole, crowded with photographers and models for *prêt-à-porter* week in Paris, Penelope Tree shouted over several tables: 'You're a star.' A UPI reporter called it: 'The biggest story since Jerry Garcia first dropped acid.'

But most of the time Scoop wrote about his friends, and the

small adventures they had together. He wrote about his daughter Rikka's visit to Europe. Above all, he wrote about himself. The *Village Voice* began to send distress signals: 'Send hard news.' He jammed them. He developed a theory about 'soft news'. He considered each article a jam. There were plenty of clinkers. He sent stuff like the following, and they printed it, every last one of these soft news tidbits.

No Substitutes

The lady and I strained failure. It was a lady I'd been wooing, who now wooed left me limp. Coaxing too long, I went down. There's always that. She pushed me away and said: 'No substitutes.'

This is rather painful to write, not sure why I'm trying. It's sort of a dare, an exploration, pushing the boundaries. It might be useful to demystify this unfortunate male trait. Or is it to assert my masculinity by being 'man enough' to write about when it failed me? Perhaps I'm proving something to Richard Neville.

Neville's hair had been cut short in prison where he'd spent two weeks after being convicted of publishing obscenity in his magazine *Oz*. Without his long hair, Richard looks like a medical student, or, with his beautiful battered face, like an Australian sailor who reads a lot. He was going to Cornwall to recharge batteries before more trials and appeals. Richard is the king of the 'swinging London' underground, a true presider, and he is usually surrounded by his court. This was the first time we'd ever talked one-on-one. He told me he was going to fight the English censor who wanted to send him back to his native Australia. I wondered what was so great about England to make him want to fight to stay here. He said he felt at home here, and with all its faults London was still one of the more civilized cities in the world. One thing he would most hate to leave, he said with an embarrassed smile, is the BBC.

Then somehow we were talking about whores. I don't recall the transition. He'd gone to a whorehouse in Australia with the wise-ass idea of writing up the experience for his school paper. Which he did, described everything in detail with only one omission. He could not get an erection. We laughed over the Hemingway/Miller/Mailer myth about the literary stud with his stiff cock forever at attention which was in fact as much of a lie as the full-breasted *Playboy* spread who never has pimples or bags under her eyes. We are all sold to measure up to these lies. And perhaps I too have been guilty of this lie.

Having written in this column about some of my successes with women, I am lying by omission unless I also document the failures. 'Would you leave it out if you were writing that story now?' I asked Richard.

He thought for a short while: 'No. I would include it now.'

'You mean you'd even write it in the *Evening Standard*?' Richard has been offered a column in that London paper.

'Yes. I think so.'

Basic life truths are often hidden behind the who, when, what, where and why of hard news. I had been scribbling notes for a short story about my bout with impotency, having instinctively assumed it too dangerous, perhaps bad taste, for the first person in newsprint. 'Do you think that's copping out?' I asked Richard.

'Yes,' he said, 'I do.'

So let me tell you about the spell I've been under, an evil spell that began with the lady who would allow no substitutes. Sex was a kind of combat for her, and it was not cricket to substitute lobs for hard ground strokes. It should have been clear to me that she was involved with something other than the joy of sport, but it was the first time my masculinity failed (except for a college gang-bang and I've always been rather proud of that failure). It would not be the last. I turned unreliable for almost a year. I considered preparing a wake to lament my departed virility. Though the failure was selective – only with new women and not always then – doubt seeded. Even when everything went well it was no longer taken for granted. I found myself pushing for entry sooner, striking while the iron was hot as it were. I practised erections on the street, testing at the most inopportune times. Failing, even knowing the experiment's control system was faulty, confirmed future failure.

For several months I 'solved' the problem by managing to turn myself off, smothering desire. If I didn't try I couldn't fail.

It might have had something to do with passing forty; beginning to feel over some kind of hill. With good female friends I would wonder why it works now and not then, intellectualizing passion away. With a new woman, I might drop acid for reinforcement – something like blowing up a wall safe with a nuclear bomb.

Then last spring, *Newsweek* came out with a cover story on hot-pants, illustrating it with a perfect pair of slender female legs. At the same time the weather broke in London. Slender female legs were all over the place. I sat on my terrace one afternoon watching those lovely, pale English beauties walk by; what a pity I could no longer afford to lust after them. Was it really all over? Already? Maybe I ought to find one woman fast before it gets worse. I went inside and looked at *Newsweek* again.

Then I decided to give it another try. I would work hard to turn myself *on*, build a foundation of desire. I swallowed handfuls of Vitamin E, studied volumes of Danish porn, tacked the *Newsweek* cover to my wall. I leered at every attractive passing woman, consciously reducing them to objects so that I might once more be able to relate to them as people. During the worst of it there had been women who had attracted me; interesting, lively, intelligent women, but I feared stagefright with women who might broadcast my failure, not realizing in my temporary insanity that she might consider it *her* failure and thus have as much interest in secrecy as I would. Or that any such failure might be her *fault*, if fault can be assigned at all in such touchy testimony.

One thought kept cropping up in my fever . . . I'll bet this doesn't happen to Neville. Richard has the pick of the London birds. Those legs on the *Newsweek* cover could easily have belonged to one of Neville's birds. I never approached one particularly strong friend of his; though there was mutual attraction, I was afraid of her. So you can imagine my reaction when he told me: 'The first time I fucked her I was really nervous. I thought, what happens if I can't get it up? You'd read about it in *Oz*, for Chrissakes.'

Like waking up with fear in the morning, everybody feels it but nobody wants to talk about it. Richard and I agreed that it was a valid journalistic subject, and that the first person was essential to its telling. It's now three in the morning and I've been struggling with it since dinner. I was just interrupted by Odile, a cheeky visitor from across the Channel, who had been asleep upstairs. 'Stop working so hard,' she said, 'come to bed.'

Soft news. With Northern Ireland going up in flames and the Continent terrorized by terrorists, Scoop ran after soft news. He was soft, there had been no time to harden. Scoop sprung full-grown from his previous incarnation Doctor Jazz. Doc was living in the Village, he read the *Village Voice*, saw they had no jazz column and decided to write one. Bang like that. A flash. Six months later he was in there every week. He had never written anything but letters before. Doc started to become a fairly good writer but he had no nose for hard news to bequeath Scoop.

Time to define soft news: news is not necessarily what happened to happen today, or yesterday. News is anything that makes the reader say: 'Well that's news to me!' Soft news can be anywhere in time or space; what happened to me or you today, for example, or what we happened to think about.

After a year in London, Scoop asked *Voice* editor Dan Wolf what he thought of his stuff. Wolf replied, enigmatically: 'It's not exactly what I expected.' Scoop took this as a compliment, he liked surprising people. Later, too late, he recognized the warning this should have been. Enough soft news, Scoop baby!

Scoop moved to Paris to live with Odile in Victor's place.

Victor's place is somewhere between a telephone exchange . . .

'Hello is Victor there?'

'Victor is in Rome.'

'Say Yoko called.'

. . . and an oasis on the trade routes. While Brian passes through from Delhi to New York – from Paul Haines (who has recorded his opera) to Steve Lerner (back in New York from Victor's place via around the world) by way of Copenhagen. Victor (in town for about seventeen minutes) drives two girls from Tucson to Orly en route for Bombay.

Victor's place is spread over two and a half rambling floors in a

Montparnasse courtyard, one of those hidden Parisian marvels. Bells ring continually upstairs and down and they are loud: 'Hello is Victor there?'

'Victor is in Geneva.'

Victor made several million dollars selling IOS stock and got out in time, before IOS crashed around Bernie Cornfield's greed. He is conferring with his Swiss broker.

Bells ring at five in the fucking morning: 'Pierre Biner please.'

'Who's calling?'

'Brazil on the line.'

They ring six months late: 'I'd like to speak to Steve Ben-Israel.'

'Steve lives in New York now.'

An emergency: 'I'm a friend of Samantha's and she said I should call Victor because I don't have any bread and I need a place to crash tonight.'

'This white bag belongs to Samantha who says she will come by for it in a few days.'

Samantha's stuffed laundry bag is brown by now, and the note has faded along with other echoes of crashers-past. Well-browsed copies of *Commentary*, *Suck* and the *Village Voice* are spread over benches around a pillow pit that was once the first water bed in Paris before it sprung a leak.

The doorbell rings loud as the phone: 'I am in the production company of Claude Chabrol. I wonder if we might have permission to shoot our film here next week.' (Victor's place can be seen in François Truffaut's *Woman in Black*.)

'Sorry, Victor is in London.'

Late, mixing with the soft sighs of lovemaking, rain pours down. The phone is silent next to expired itineraries: 'Gideon Bachman will be in Crakow through 6/6 . . .' and current petitions: 'We demand of the Brazilian government the immediate release of all the members of the Living Theatre.'

'Hello Nicholas De Jongh of the *Guardian* here. Can you give me any information about the Living Theatre?'

The entire Living Theatre lived in Victor's place before going to Brazil where they got busted for subversion and where they are now languishing in jail. Living with the entire Living Theatre is *living*.

'Sorry Pierre Biner is in Avignon and won't be back till tomorrow.'

Pierre has a gentle face, a bit emaciated like you remember drawings of John Keats. He sleeps on the balcony with his lover named Frankie. It is dark up there and, sure Pierre is in Avignon, Odile and I clang cooking supper. But then there are groans and the low murmur of conversation and Pierre descends the spiral staircase followed by Frankie. We apologize for our noise. Pierre smiles: 'It's okay. I was making noise too.'

If you need help with petitions and raising money to get friends out of jail, contact Pierre. He telephones around the world all day and half the night. He called John and Yoko. They sent $2,000 to fly a lawyer to Rio. He called Keith Richard on the Riviera. ('Keith doesn't want to hear any bad news today. Sorry.')

'Hello, where can I find Steve Lacy?'

Steve once stayed at Victor's too, he was a sort of caretaker like we are now, but he moved around the corner with his soprano sax. Sometimes he falls by to hear new jazz releases on Victor's expensive stereo, lying in the hammock staring at the thirty-foot-high skylight. (There's a Steve Lacy poster on the wall next to the *Oz* poster and all the others.) Tonight Gil Evans is listening with him. Gil has one ear clogged from swimming in Portugal and is temporarily hearing mono. Gil Evans listening to music is a work of art in itself. *Merde!* The doorbell.

A spaced-out dark beauty of a woman married to an actor currently languishing in an Italian jail wants to know how 'my friends' are but nobody can figure out just which friends she means.

'Hello, is Victor in? My name is Robin Kenyatta.'

Victor is in London again. Might as well go for a coffee in the corner *tabac*, can't write with all the bells anyhow. Look in at the Tarantula bookshop down the street on the way. In a back copy of *Oz* magazine, Richard Neville describes Victor's place as: 'one of the nastiest environments I have ever endured. Guests included a poet who came for a weekend two years ago and won't budge, a pair of video heads, remnants from the Living Theatre and several nameless others. The atmosphere created by most of these superhip freeloaders manages to be simultaneously hostile, slovenly and as exclusive as White's Club. Membership to the inner sanctum revolves around facility with drugs and, as the pleasant Victor himself is rather slow on the draw, he is excluded in spirit from his own house.'

True perhaps once, it is a cooler more communal sanctum now. Just in time. The phone.

'Hi, this is Thom Keyes.' Thom Keyes is calling from the Café Flore. You can hear his ghetto blaster blasting a tape from LA: 'Hello all you beautiful freaks this is station KOLA bringing you the outta sight sounds of . . .' commercials and all which is really wild at the Flore.

Thom discusses Alistair Crowley with Pierre in the pillow pit and spends the night in Victor's bed since Victor is still in London.

The bed is busy for the week – Jeffrey Robinson, a lady named Brigitte and Gil Evans, one after the other all on the same sheets whether they knew it or not.

'Hello. This is Vanessa Redgrave's secretary calling about The Living . . .'

Good news. The Living is out of jail in Belo Horizonte. Pierre will leave immediately to join them in New York.

'Hello.' The financial genius on the line: 'How would you like to drive to Iran this week? Hello hello . . .'

A disconnect.

'Hello, Scoop? There's a soft story in the south of France. Get down here right away.'

Scoop died a hideous untimely death in February 1971, in Switzerland. I'd rather not talk about it if you don't mind. He was reincarnated as a plant.

12

The French California

Whack!

I just killed two flies with one swat. That's an occasion in a rockpile. Sometimes I miss going only for one.

It is night and mine is the only light in the village. Hearing an airplane, I imagine passengers looking down like I used to when I flew a lot, wondering about those lights down there in the middle of nowhere. Such tiny lights so far down. Who lives there? What is life like there? Would I be happy living there? Probably just a bunch of hicks.

City folk warned us we'd become hicks in the sticks. They said we were leaving because we could not cut the big time. Our move upset them. They were forced to think about what they run around all day and half the night trying to forget. We ran to a place where we hoped to forget about running forever. We did not miss all those 'what do *you* do?' conversations shouted to strangers over nightly dinner out.

It was inevitable. Normal. Our own fault for leaving. They forgot us. There are no more visits from city people. Mail has dried up with the weather this summer. My credit cards have all expired. Our phone does not ring. (We have no phone.) I have nothing to say at parties. (There are no parties.) Not that I consider myself above all that, *better* than anybody or anything. I just have nothing to say. Tall buildings overwhelm me. I am really overwhelmed. People I have never met before upset me. I am however fairly comfortable with several hundred trees I know. I speak less now, not to imply I necessarily think more. I probably think less. I'm not even sure I think better.

A happy ending. What begins after a happy ending?

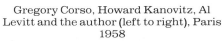

Gregory Corso, Howard Kanovitz, Al Levitt and the author (left to right), Paris 1958

Claude Thornhill (left) and Squirms, Oklahoma 1958

Miles Davis, New York 1961

Elvin Jones, 1959

Orchestra USA: (top) Phil Woods (left) and
Eric Dolphy, 1962 (bottom) John Lewis, 1962

Everybody's only president, 1963

The author with Larry Rivers, 1958

Dick Katz, the author, Richard Davis and Joe Chambers (left to right) playing with the Upper Bohemia Six at the Five Spot

Official State Department photo of 'Money' Johnson, the author, Earl
Hines, Bobby Donovan, Budd Johnson, Oliver Jackson, Bill Pemberton
(left to right), 1966

Budd Johnson

On the set of <u>Steppenwolf</u>: (dancing) Max von Sidow and Dominique Sanda, (playing saxophone) Pierre Clementi, and the author

Timothy Leary in Algiers

The author and Odile getting married in French California

Marcel in French California

Tony Petrucciani carrying Michel. Next to them are Kenny Clarke and Louis Petrucciani

Marcel with Michel Petrucciani, French California 1978

'Mike's got the best job in the world'— the author with Bill Graham

The author with Jimmy Knepper

MC at the Bombay Jazz Yatra Festival

Telephone on tour: Starcruiser — Jean Louis, Corine, Richard and Louis (left to right) singing 'I am the Walrus'

Telephone on stage

John Cage

Elvin Jones

This is a message in a bottle tossed on a lost sea of wine. A cry for help from the vegetable kingdom. If it doesn't reach a sea lane soon we're sunk. They'll never think of looking for us *here*.

It will be difficult to write with a stalk. We have taken root. This is plant life. Please don't say so to her petal, but look at Odile – she's even plantier than me.

Would you mind removing that snail? Snails give me the creeps.

I have eaten snails with presidents. Critics asked my opinion. I am listed in professional encyclopaedias. My credits take up pages. I was on the *Playboy* party list. I have slept with the wives of our foremost creative people. There are plenty of notches on my pistil.

Sorry. Name-dropping irrigates you? I was hoping it might prune my drought. Now I feel soiled. It stems from insecurity. I'll try and branch out.

(*Sotto voce*) Pssstt. Hey Pops. You holdin' any fertilizer? Sure could use a line of fertilizer.

Strange, we *wanted* to be plants. We took root on purpose. It wasn't easy.

One final favour, these weeds are choking me. Please weed me.

Order! Order in the greenhouse! Any more of this plant shit will be held in contempt. The image has been driven into the ground. It doesn't even get to the root of the problem. I'll nip it in the bud and leaf through my notes.

It has been raining for days; the fields around the village are too muddy to work and when José doesn't work he does not get paid. Practising longtones, I watch José drain a bottle of wine in the one dry room of the ruin his boss lets him live in free. Longtones build muscles, not brains; they are boring. My first trombone teacher suggested I practise them listening to the ball-game. Now I watch José, who comes out, feels the rain with his palm, mumbles '*Miedra!*' and trudges off.

I slur painful sixths (pain is a part of it) and hold each interval for the length of my breath. Longtones can be a sort of mantra if you relate to them properly. I close my eyes on a series of fourths. Opening them, I see José returning with a wriggling rabbit by the tail. He bangs the rabbit's head against the wall until it is dead.

I eat rabbit. Somebody has to kill them. They are no different from chickens. The idea does not torture me in the abstract and I am shocked by the unexpectedness of it rather than disgusted on principle. It is casual, innocent, organic, even loving in a caveman sort of way. Nature went like this for millennia. Hungry? Catch a rabbit and bang its head against the wall. The way life once was, possibly the way it ought to be, the way it still is with Spanish immigrant farm labour in the south of France, and the way it might be again everywhere at the end of the petroleum age. The blood is on the product, no silver-wrapped slices disguising the murder.

The rain turns to mist. José plucks the rabbit and starts a fire in his chimney, which draws poorly. Smoke fills his ruin and the lane between us. As the animal cooks, he wails Arabesque chants under his bare lightbulb; ancient chants of despair passed down through generations with short life-expectancy float up on the mist and mix with my longtones like two animals groaning in a zoo.

'José's peeing outside again.' Odile came as close to bounding up the stairs as her condition allows. Her stomach is growing up-front like it will be a boy.

'This is France. Everybody pees outside.'

'You've got to speak to him about it.'

'Not me. Poor bugger doesn't even have a pisser. You talk to him.'

'I can't do that.'

'Why not?'

'I'm a woman.'

I was waiting for that: 'I thought you were liberated.'

'I am. He's not.'

'Liberate him.'

'Bullshit!' Her English has been improving lately: 'It's part of give and take. I sew your buttons.'

'With plenty of string apparently. I thought we agreed the one the problem bothers most deals with it.'

This is a seventeenth-century village in what has come to be known as the French California. There are gentle green mountains, virgin canyons, fertile valleys growing fruit. Electricity and indoor toilets do not pervade, however, and if you can't stand the heat get out of the kitchen. I lecture Odile on the ecological virtue of peeing outside.

She sticks out her tongue at me: 'I just don't like somebody peeing two metres from my face at teatime.'

'Teatime!? Boy are you bourgeois.' I try to grab her tongue but she takes my hand and puts it between her thighs.

The sun begins to burn the mist away. Closing the shutters for sexier light, I spot José coming out of his ruin with an old newspaper under his arm. Rounding the corner, he lowers his pants.

'*Oui, comme ca.*' Odile rubs her belly against mine from on top, which no longer takes much leaning. I cup her breasts, swollen with arriving milk. As a force-one Mistral wind begins to howl, José strikes up a conversation with Isabelle below. Their rough peasant voices bounce off the ruins, all '*eingh*' and '*ontza*' endings punctuated by toothless cackles. Isabelle is the only local who talks to José. The locals do not like the Spaniards. Neither the locals nor the Spaniards like the hippies. Anyone who does not work in the physical sense of the word is a hippy. People from north of a line drawn horizontally through the centre of France are 'them' (*ils*). We are them.

Only hippies make love in the afternoon. '*Doucement . . .*' Easy. Odile comes down and rolls over on her back, careful not to disturb Marcel, a provisional name for our foetus, better than 'It'. I have begun to imagine Marcel emerging with a greasy moustache and a yellow Gitane hanging from his mouth, carrying a *baguette* and smelling of garlic. I have also begun to imagine the Alpine pile of shitty nappies in my future. How did I ever let her talk me into this? A Frog Sprog. Doting papa is one of the most demanding roles in movie history. I've already played it, thank you.

'This baby trip is getting to me,' I'd said at breakfast. 'Maybe I'll go to LA for about fifteen years.'

Before lunch I caught her caressing her stomach: 'Well, Marcel, looks like it's you and me all alone in the world.'

Marcel is so close to being born and has been so present in our lives that it is like a *ménage à trois*. She motions me over her. Aah. A happy family, our child warm and safe between us.

121

Odile squats on top, tickles my scrotum behind her back and like that we shout a provisional truce.

José has been saying that even though hippies smell bad, he does not think they should all be sent to jail like Mrs Juval says. He stopped talking.

'Did we make a lot of noise?' I whisper.

'*Oui.*' Odile stifles a giggle.

I kiss her neck: 'Friends?'

'Friends.'

The main square of the village of Villars is not very main as squares go but it is on the other hand quite square. Cool in the afternoon shade, I sip a beer on the terrace of the Friendly Café. The one parked car across the way seems more sculpted than parked, a car in a Keinholz. Frozen. A frieze. A picturesque Provençal frieze, harmonious but no major attraction.

In three years here I have written and published two books. Not bad, but they came and went fast leaving no wake. We pay $60 a month rent for the house and there's nothing to spend money on, no sweat there. But I cannot get published on toilet paper and I miss my interesting acquaintances. This is not exactly a big time corner.

Town hall looks closed. It looks closed even when it's open, which isn't often. The first 'i' of '*Mairie*' has fallen off, leaving only '*Marie*'. We were married in the *Marie*, Odile five months pregnant, under an official portrait of Georges Pompidou who had died in office half a year earlier.

'That's the wrong President,' I said to Serge the mayor who is young and a Socialist and sports a sense of humour about such things.

'De Gaulle fell down and broke his frame,' he smiled.

'What about Valéry Giscard d'Estaing?' You'd be impressed hearing how that name rolls off my tongue by now. *Je suis très cultivé, mon cher.*

'Oh, he hasn't arrived yet,' said Serge. Official presidential portraits arrive six months late in this small-change seat. Babies arrive right on time.

A Mama-Papa Rap

PAPA: I just had this tape machine fixed but there's already a rubber band around it – my whole life has a rubber band around it because of this kid who was born because I have a wife who doesn't know what she wants to be in life so she had a baby. She was in trouble before and I told her she'd be in even more trouble after having a kid and now that she's in more trouble she's making all sorts of rationalizations, one of which is that having a child is a generous act.

MAMA: It's more than generous. It's the gift of yourself, of your own body and life.

PAPA: You gave Marcel the gift of death not life. How generous is it to bring someone into this world who's just going to die eventually? That's selfish. It's a mistake of youth, having a kid. Everybody makes mistakes in youth, like cracking up the car or getting sick drunk or kicked out of school but I'm supposed to be old enough to know better. As you get older you realize that having kids has less to do with human nature than with finding some phony meaning in life. It's kind of like joining the Communist Party.

MAMA: What's wrong with that? You belong to nothing. That doesn't seem to make you so happy. And that business about death is not even worthy of discussion. If you think about the fact that he's going to die when you bring a kid into this world, that's a pretty good insight about how you relate to life. Kids are life, not death.

PAPA: Kids are a way of avoiding being lonely for a few years.

MAMA: You can be very lonely with a kid.

PAPA: Kids are like legos, dolls; toys for women to have fun with.

MAMA: Fun?! Everybody knows how hard it is to have a child. You, for example, never stopped telling me how hard it was going to be. 'You won't be able to sleep late, go out at night,' etcetera etcetera.

PAPA: You never believed me.

MAMA: No, I had a different idea about it and what our relationship was going to be like. Having a child is better than I expected. Our relationship is worse. Sometimes I get angry or depressed and I can't really call it 'fun' but having a child is the

123

most emotionally fulfilling, most satisfying experience I have ever had, it's . . . clean. A kid has no bullshit.

PAPA: Marcel shits more than any person I know.

MAMA: Very funny. If you spent more time with him, you'd realize how beautiful his shit is.

PAPA: He's all we talk about any more. Having a kid immediately locks you into the kid cliché. Couples talk about their kids because they've got nothing else to talk about. 'Isn't he cute?' They start defining themselves in kid terms. Pretty soon we're going to be calling each other Mama and Papa.

MAMA: We know some extremely bright people who talk about their children. That seems to be an acceptable topic of conversation for everyone but you.

PAPA: Let's talk about Marcel's shit. It was kind of loose this morning.

MAMA: Having a child is just part of nature.

PAPA: Would you feel the same way about him if he were adopted?

MAMA: If I couldn't have a child I would adopt one. It's important that he comes from my womb, I won't deny that, but the essential thing is to be around a growing human being. It's an affirmation of the future. I think your writing is much more of an ego trip than having a child. You want to communicate, to be understood, admired. You're selfish, that's why you can't relate to Marcel. If you want my opinion, one reason you are having so much trouble accepting Marcel is that you're competing with him.

PAPA: I love him, you know that. I love *who* he is, I just can't relate to *what* he is. Mae West said when she was asked if she had any advice for today's kids: 'Yeah, grow up.'

MAMA: You don't know what you are, who you are, you can't relate to yourself properly, how can you expect to relate to your child?

PAPA: Look, this world is just not a place I want to bring a child of mine into. Dying is only part of it, living is worse. I'm already here so I try and make the best of it. What right do we have to inflict it on someone else? It's the ultimate control trip.

MAMA: I know that's the way you feel about this world. It's a miracle I still enjoy life after all these years with you, after hearing about how lousy everything is seven days a week. Fortunately, not everyone is as pessimistic as you are.

PAPA: A pessimist is somebody with some idea of what is actually going on.

MAMA: My main worry is to avoid your pessimism destroying me. I worry about that all the time. I worry about that so much my stomach hurts. I think I'm pregnant again.

PAPA: Maybe you should have another child at that. You can avoid thinking about your future for another few years.

MAMA: No, my brain will go on thinking about what I'm wasting.

PAPA: Aha! Having a child is a waste?

MAMA: I won't have another child unless I can afford to hire somebody to help take care of it. I want my own life too.

PAPA: It's all about money, then? See, you have a baby and immediately you have to start worrying about money and maids and good schools and how to get away on weekends. The bourgeois life begins with the birth of a baby.

MAMA: Worrying about money is not bourgeois.

PAPA: Preoccupation with security and comfort is my definition of bourgeois. We're becoming slaves to security.

MAMA: If having a baby was a happy experience for you, you wouldn't always be complaining about having no freedom.

PAPA: Why don't we have twins? Then I can get a job copywriting for J. Walter Thompson and we'll have lots of little insurance policies and die happily ever after. You can play bridge in the afternoon.

MAMA: May I remind you that during all those years when we didn't have a child I always heard complaints about no money, no job, no security. Having a child has not made that any worse. You're just using a new vocabulary now. Marcel has changed your vocabulary. He's given you new material, which is good for a writer. You ought to thank him.

There are many divisions between human beings. Man and woman, old and young, black and white, rich and poor, left and right, square and hip. But the most basic division is between country and city. Time is different, and space.

Hamburger was out of focus in the French California, and out of sync in so much space and silence after an all-night drive from his habitual jumble of jangling telephones and big days.

'Boy oh boy, Mike,' he said, with admiration. 'Where is everybody?'

I hoped to impress him further: 'There are less people living here now than there were in the eighteenth century.'

He blinked for a minute: 'Why did they leave?'

I turned testy: 'How the hell should I know? It's empty, I like it like that.'

'I don't like it, Joe,' Hamburger said with a black-and-white American war movie accent, 'it's too quiet.'

I drove him around the French California pointing to the vineyards and cherry orchards, to the fairy-tale hilltop villages, between which, even in August when half of Europe descends on the south of France, it is possible to drive without passing another motor car.

'Why do you suppose they all left?' he asked, and I knew then that I too would leave.

You say you can't find us? Look down. No no no . . . a bit to your right. That's it. Now up a little. Right. Here we are. HERE . . . WE . . . ARE . . . YOO-HOO . . .

13

The Last of the California Hippies Meets the Prince Mishkin of the Provinces

Dick Scott was living in the mountains near an obscure village in the remote Ardeche, he wasn't living at home any more, he had no phone; when he's living at home he's hardly ever there anyway and his name isn't even Dick Scott.

Playing drums with the white *Who's Who* of fifties jazz – Marian McPartland, Bobby Brookmeyer, Warne Marshe, Zoot Sims, Bobby Hackett, Lee Konitz and so on – Scott supported a wife and five children before he was busted with a lid of grass and lost it all, plus one year of his life.

When he came out of prison he no longer felt like Dick Scott. He was funkier for one thing, for another he'd lost his zest for jazz. He went down to the North Carolina mountains and lived with the Indians for two years. Later, tripping on acid in California, he decided to bury Dick Scott for good and took the vague anagram Tox Drohar.

Tox disappeared into the Santa Cruz mountains, building his own tree-houses, back-to-nature with a friend Tox calls 'a legend in his own time' who had taken the name Charlie Nothing. They formed the Charlie Nothing Band which improvised on home-made axes: welded copper harps, bamboo flutes, barrel-drums. Sometimes it would be a duo, or there could be ten on stage. They played in the Haight, Santa Cruz, Big Sur and became a sort of under-underground Grateful Dead.

After the Manson affair, it seemed time to move on. Tox was with a lady named Anita, and her two children. She had just sold 'The Pleasure Dome', her boutique on Sunset Strip. Tox played a bit part in *Alex in Wonderland*, a film by his friend Paul Mazursky. They had cash and took it to Europe.

It was love at first sight with the Ardeche. They rented a ten-room farmhouse for $35 a month. South-west of Valence, the Ardeche is hard mountain country with cold winters and hot summers and in 1972 it was one place you could still find cheap real estate. There was no lease or anything, this was the Midi, the south, farm country; nothing but honest country folk down here. A man's word still means something here, people are 'sympa', not like people in LA or Paris. The farm was not much more than a ruin. Tox rebuilt the roof, installed a chimney and plumbing, built a barbecue pit, dug out and replanted the garden. The rent went up to $70 a month.

The house was beginning to look like a set for a modern-lifestyle magazine spread about Monterey. It represented a bisocial concept of paradise the locals had never known before. Tox calls it 'American funk'. Ecological pollution, modern primitivism, quality deprivation – it means living in a ruin out of choice, knowing there is adequate water pressure and electrical wiring waiting for you in California should you get fed up roughing it.

Each autumn Tox picked grapes for the landlord as part of the rent. This was okay with him, another facet of American Funk. But the landlord's family had sold wet coal – it weighs more wet – during the war; he figured he had a rich American pigeon here. He sent Tox a registered letter saying buy or move. The price was right up there. He sent the letter after the grape harvest of course.

No matter. Tox found another ruin. He made hand-drums out of 400-year-old olive trees and sold them to local burghers as lamps. Once a year he'd help somebody build a house. He met a flautist who used to play with the St Etienne opera, a PR man for the Communist Party who played some saxophone, a folk singer who played guitar and before long he was behind a drum-kit again. They worked cultural centres, parties and small festivals. Tox was the only person he knew other than peasants who could manage to live in the Ardeche year-round. Everybody else had to leave for Lyon or Paris sooner or later to make a living. Summer people would shake their heads with grudging admiration: 'You see? It takes an American to figure out how to do it.'

Then Tox met the Petrucciani family, who were living in a Mussolini-modern concrete house right out of some Fellini industrial zone, between the Paris–Marseille railway line and the six-lane Autoroute du Soleil. Not on the wrong side of the tracks, *on* the tracks. These two main arteries are maybe 500 yards apart south of Montpelier where the Petruccianis lived. You could put the neighbourhood in a how-to-ruin-the-environment manual.

Readers should be warned here that they are being blatantly exploited. This is in fact being written with only one reader in mind, a movie producer looking to invest seed money. What a property! The life of Tox, the last hippy. The credits come over Gerry Mulligan blowing in a chic east side *boite* in fifties New York. Then some exciting, violent prison footage, with dialogue about unjust marijuana laws. Cut to psychedelia in California with special guest star Timothy Leary. Followed by American Funk in the picturesque south of France. Kris Kristofferson plays Tox.

Now we come to the second lead, Michel Petrucciani, a big part for a small man. Michel is small, very small, you won't believe how small Michel is. He must have been out to lunch when they were handing out bodies. Physically he was more five than fifteen when Tox met him. Chunky hunchbacked trunk, withered legs, emaciated arms; he was nothing but heart, mind and hands – such agile and beautiful hands. Mentally he was more like thirty. Michel plays piano, you won't believe how good this little fifteen-year-old from Montelimar could play piano. The only English he knew was 'Hey baby' and 'Fuck you'. Michel Petrucciani plays himself in the movie.

Tox attended a Kenny Clarke drum clinic in Montelimar. Klook was Tox's main man. There was a concert afterwards and Tox was backstage when in walked the Petruccianis. It's a heavy Corsican family number, Tony the father is a Godfather type. He plays guitar sort of like Wes Montgomery, not bad at all. Michel's brother Louis, seventeen then, plays bass. They had a whole crowd following them around wherever they played in the south of France. Although he had to take variety-music gigs to do it, Tony supported the family by playing guitar which isn't easy to do down there and there was a lot of macho pride involved. The three of them were backstage before the concert all dressed in suits and ties. Michel was wearing a tiny little suit and tie. Tony carried him like a doll. Tox said to his old lady, as if about some sort of carny hustle: 'They must be the opening act.'

They were but it was no hustle. Tox was not really listening when Klook poked him, his mouth hanging open: 'Listen to *that* shit!'

Clark Terry passed through and played with Michel as guest soloist, Joe Pass heard him at a festival; they both said more or less the same thing as Klook. Bluesman Sugar Blue played after the Petruccianis at the St Rémy de Provence festival and said: 'That's the best French jazz I ever heard.' Drummer Daniel Humair wanted to take Michel to Paris to record with Ron Carter which would have made a good album cover with little Michel next to Ron who looks like a Harlem Globetrotter. It would also have made a good album. Already at fifteen, Michel's voicings were rich, ballsy, innovative, his solos were derivative but more than interesting. He could have played with anyone anywhere. The rare bone disease that was the cause of his shrunken size was, in a musical sense, a blessing in the form of a handicap – like being blind. He invested his total energy in music, there was nothing else left to him. He practised all day long throughout childhood, but it's more than practice. It is the Gift. God has chosen to give the Gift to tiny Michel Petrucciani.

When Tox took me to jam with Michel in Cliusclat, a village in the Drome where the mayor, a fan, put on jazz concerts once a month, he just said: 'Wait till you hear this piano-player.' No details. You can imagine my surprise as we were sitting on the terrace of a café on the narrow, unpaved, main street and this Citroen 2CV (those sardine-can cars which run on rubber bands) pulled up with a hunchbacked doll wearing a yachting cap like Count Basie's waist-high at the window, exclaiming: 'Hey baby!'

I wrote the first article ever written about Michel Petrucciani; you could say I discovered him. I also wrote the first article about the Soft Machine. People say I discovered them too, although it is presumptuous to claim to 'discover' something that already exists. The comedian Dick Gregory used to have a routine debunking the idea that Columbus could 'discover' a populated country: 'It's like I'm walking down the street and I see a Cadillac and I say, "That's really a sharp car; I think I'll discover it." '

Michel was an important discovery for me personally. I had not thought it possible to be pushed musically in the French California, that temple of mediocrity. The term is all wrong, by the way. California infers a forward-looking vibrant lifestyle; whatever its faults, it is a happening place. Nothing ever happens in the French California, which is why the people all left. We played together often, on the same bill as Steve Lacy at the Grand Motte Festival, in the Hot Brass club in Aix-en-Provence. We made a record in the French California towards the end of my plant life. I joined the élite club – we considered it an honour – who carried Michel around. When Michel visited New York later, Lee Konitz became part of that club. They toured France as a duo. Now Michel works with Charles Lloyd, lives in Big Sur and is married to an American woman. He no longer speaks to his father.

Even after Michel reached the age of eighteen, Tony wanted to keep him home for 'more seasoning'. It might be that Tony was jealous. Before Michel left home for good (there always seemed to be at least one person available to carry him to wherever he needed to go), Tony said: 'People cry listening to Michel.' Yes of course, so much force and beauty in such a helpless frame. Michel looks embarrassed being carried around like a doll, but somehow amused at the same time – do you believe this happened to *me*? – and often frightened of being dropped. He is fragile. He could not take too many drops. Of course people cry – Michel perched on his special stool enabling him to look down on the keys, withered legs pumping a specially-built pedal extension, can bring tears. Tears of joy mixed with the pity, though. Think of Dostoyevsky's Prince Mishkin, the 'wholly beautiful man', the so-called 'Idiot' whose function it was to disseminate the aura of a new state of being; somebody who makes us re-evaluate our definitions of ugly and beautiful, bad and good luck, a sort of redeemer.

Tox Drohar left the Ardeche to go back to California for some fast bucks. He had what he considered a boss fast-buck idea; an all-girl band. Frances Davis, Miles's ex-wife, would dance, Pera Brent, Bud Shank's ex-wife (and Ravi Shankar's ex-assistant) was a good percussionist. Tox had a couple of 'heavy chicks' from Watts lined up, and he knew a singer named Lilly who could dance on her hands.

14

The Bermuda Triangle in the Lowlands

Daybreak. Gare du Nord. Wearing a Lester Young-style porkpie hat and a Dizzy Gillespie goatee, I'm sitting on my horn case, like that famous picture of Bird, waiting for the 3 a.m. mail train to the Lowlands. It's cold and foggy and I've been on the road so long I don't remember what off is like. I'm sick and tired of waking up tired and sick. My mouth feels as though there are dinosaurs in it. I have to jerk off to get my heart started. My eyes look like road maps.

Actually it was a sunny day and I had the foresight to book in advance, first class of course. I caught an 11 a.m. train, a sensible hour, and I'd slept eight hours last night in my comfortable apartment in a bourgeois section of Paris. Before that I had lived a sedentary life in the same country house for five years. I was wearing a Swiss suede jacket and a Brooks Brothers turtleneck. I'm told I resemble the French actor Michel Piccoli, a bit kinky around the edges but not enough to scare anybody.

I've always wanted to live like the jazz greats of yore; fearless outlaws travelling the less travelled road, tragic, uncompromising trail-blazers, psychic anarchists with no thought of tomorrow, pulling slick chicks, vomiting in taxicabs, going to sleep at nine in the morning. But I have this awful sensible streak ('Hi there, officer, nice day isn't it?') which is one reason I am not as great a jazz musician as I would otherwise be. It is not really a sensible thing to do, you have to be crazy to play jazz for a living. Excess is essential, you've got to be eager to spew it out every night, to follow the poet William Blake who said: 'The road of excess leads to the palace of wisdom.'

Our band came to be called the Bermuda Triangle after some

132

mysterious disappearances. Four drummers for example. Beats and measures could get lost, entire tunes went out of sync and the leader once faded with neither warning nor explanation into a bebop time-warp, shouting: 'Donna Lee . . . one two three four.'

Actually, the leader is a rather down-to-earth Taurus, not unlike myself, trying to live out his fantasies, only he works at it more seriously that I do. He was always late. Everybody knows how hip it is to show up late for the gig. Charlie Parker did it, it must be hip. Starting an hour late after an argument with the promoter creates aggressive energy. Miles Davis did it, it must be hip. Miles is said to believe that if the guys are mad at each other or at him they play more aggressively. Let us examine the American amelioration of the pejorative verb 'to aggress'. To be called an 'aggressive salesman' or an 'aggressive linebacker' is a compliment. They are winners, go-getters, good Americans. Yet aggression involves violence against the bodies and/or minds of others. Hitler was branded 'the aggressor' and thus automatically the bad guy, along with the Japanese who bombed Pearl Harbor with unprovoked aggression. 'Remember, whatever you do, always play aggressively,' I once heard a teacher of jazz instruct his pupils. A lot of saxophone players play more like Adolf Hitler than Adolphe Sax. They say they represent the times, and there is something to that. They consider it survival, aggress or be aggressed. They relate to the art of music as though it was undeclared war. Fuck or get fucked. Come to think of it 'fuck you' as an aggressive expletive misses the same point. Miles sometimes aggressed his personnel by neglecting to list their names on record jackets. Remember who's boss, buddy. To foster aggression within the Bermuda Triangle (he called it 'just keeping you on your toes'), our leader called out hard up-tempo lines like 'Donna Lee', which we had never rehearsed.

For up-front aggression he had hired a front line consisting of a bebop tenorman who wanted to play free jazz, a free jazz altoman who wanted to play bebop and me, making one more comeback, who was grateful to get through a solo of any kind without disaster.

The Bermuda Triangle played in clean towns all over the Lowlands, which reminds me of Greater Los Angeles. Uniform urban centres spread between freeways and patches of greenery you can drive to in two hours. Lowlanders were generous with applause and free booze. Genever gin followed by beer, a combination called in their language 'a hammer on the head', disappeared inside the Bermuda Triangle by the case.

Some optional folklore. Bud Powell walked into his favourite café on Rue du Seine just in time to see this elderly Parisian wreck raise a glass to his lips, drain it, and immediately pass out cold. Bud pointed to the stiff on the floor and said to the bartender: 'I'll have one of *those*.' Now alcoholics are nothing to make fun of, certainly someone as talented and tortured as Bud Powell. But the story does illustrate the ambience and alienation involved in this *metier*. Somebody who decides to play jazz for a living knows he will struggle for the rest of his life, unless he opts for predictable and soothing compromise. Honest jazz involves public exploration. It takes guts to make mistakes in public, and mistakes are inherent. If there are no mistakes it's a mistake. In Keith Jarrett's solo improvisations you can hear him hesitate, turn in circles for a while, struggle to find the next idea. Bird used to start a phrase two or three times before figuring out how to continue it. The heart and soul of improvisation is turning mistakes into discovery. On the spot. Now. No second draft. It can take a toll night after night in front of an audience that just might be considering you shallow.

The Bermuda Triangle had been hammering itself on the head for three hours in a packed, insanely friendly joint in Den Bosch when a tune called 'Potts's Paradise' began to disappear into an alcoholic mist reinforced by the inexorable eclecticism of the front line. The drummer fell madly in love with his tom-toms, the pianist banged the keyboard with his elbows, the bassist rolled his eyes *à la* Steppin Fetchit. I stopped in the middle of a cold lick and hid behind a speaker. Suddenly an infantryman climbed out of the trenches and charged towards certain death. It was Steve Potts, whose tune it is, volunteering with alto sax fixed. Everybody else had deserted, the entire company, to a man. Potts was a one-man front – hopeless, suicidal. But the tide began to turn as he wielded his axe fast, slow, sweet, hot, in and out of time. We fell in behind him. 'Potts's Paradise' came out of limbo, beyond rhythm and notes into music, something they tell me used to happen regularly on Duke Ellington's band.

Nights off on the road are a nightmare. Too much to think about with nothing to do hung out there motionless on this

obscure voyage. If you're a nice guy, the leader's wife might invite
you to dinner, in return for which you could be asked to write a
complimentary arrangement. Happy to be occupied, I transcribed
the tune the leader liked from a cassette. When we rehearsed it the
drummer and the horns kept coming in a beat apart after a break.
He said we were a beat late, I said he was a beat early (it was a
unison break for the three horns). It felt right, he was sure.
Although good time is not determined by race, whites sometimes
have less faith in the invincibility of theirs. The drummer was
black; we played it his way. A few days later I thought to check
back with the cassette and found the break in question to be three
bars of three rather than two of four.

Larry Rivers said that his relationship to jazz is so intertwined
with his relationship with blacks and his response to their place in
American society that it is almost impossible for him to talk about
one without the other. Me and the black drummer for example.
The tune involved was by Wayne Shorter, who mixes metres. It
had been recorded by the sophisticated Brazilian singer Milton
Nascimento. I should never have assumed obligatory 4/4. Afraid
of being too intellectual in this instinctive medium, I had not
followed my intellect far enough. I squeezed one beat out of it. In
effect turning the time around was the correct thing to do in this
case, but I was so concerned with avoiding ridicule I couldn't hear
straight.

Listen to this from Art Pepper's book *Straight Life*. Some of
Pepper's friends told him that bassist Curtis Counce and drummer
Lawrence Marable, both black, were making fun of Pepper, who is
white, behind his back on the bandstand. (Marable has since
denied this entire incident happened.) He asked Marable about it.

Marable said: 'Oh fuck you! You know what I think of you, you
white motherfucker? You can't play. None of you white punks can
play,' and spat on the ground.

'You lousy, stinking, black motherfucker!' Pepper said: 'Why
the fuck do you work for me if you feel like that?'

Marable answered: 'Oh, we're just taking advantage of you
white punk motherfuckers.'

After that, every time Pepper would run into Ray Brown, Sonny
Stitt or Benny Carter, he'd find himself shying away from them
because: 'I'd be wondering, do they think: "Oh there's that white

asshole, that Art Pepper; that white punk can't play . . ." '

Writer Gene Lees comments on Pepper's passage: 'White motherfucker . . . that nigger . . . the damage spreads from there. What makes this ironic is that the jazz world, both artists and audience, was the first stratum of American society in which an extensive integration occurred.'

During the sixties when jazz was about as political as art could get, a manifestation of the growing 'black is beautiful' consciousness, Archie Shepp was often quoted as saying it was black music and only blacks could play it. Yet Roswell Rudd was his steady trombone-player and he engaged me for an album (*The Magic of Ju-Ju*). I interviewed Shepp for several articles and while he went on record still again about jazz being black music, never once did I feel any personal racism. Either Shepp says that because it makes good copy, or maybe he made me an honorary brother. Once I asked Gil Evans to tell Miles Davis that I would like to write his biography. Some time later, Gil brought me Miles's answer: 'If anybody writes my biography it's going to be a black chick.' So much for ethnomusicology.

The Bermuda Triangle was integrated both by nationality – Dutch, French, American – and race. If there was any segregation at all it was the Dutch together speaking Dutch, though even that was no major fixture. Perhaps we were all so busy struggling against treacherous currents threatening to pull us under that we had no energy left for colour-coding. The relationship between black and white American jazz musicians takes on a different character in the European context, but more about that later.

In The Hague, the Bermuda Triangle was recorded by Lowland radio. Having messed up a blues, I was not exactly eager to hear the playback. So simple, the blues. How can anybody mess up the blues? I substituted speed for swing, range for content and once went into the wrong key because I was so absorbed with audience response that I lost contact with the music. Then I stopped trying, gave up a lost cause like a tennis-player, who, having lost his service one game away from losing the set, decides to concentrate on the following set.

When I heard the tape, though, in all modesty, I sounded like the best forty-eight year old trombone-player in the Lowlands. Even the wrong key sounded polytonal on purpose. It was a bitch! That is, it was a bitch until the point where I decided to give up. Instead of leaving the past where it belongs, the mistake deformed the present. In the process of worrying about why I had messed it up and what does that imply and what a fool I had made of myself, I worried myself down the drain.

Later I talked about all this to the bass-player, who was reading, *Pyramid Power*. He stroked his bushy beard and smiled sagely: 'Got to keep the faith, baby.'

15
Jazz in China

Hans Dulfer sells Opels during the day, plays jazz at night and wrote a book called *Jazz in China* (in Dutch) which has nothing to do with China. Hans is known as the Dutch Archie Shepp, who says: 'Hans plays more like me than me.' The story goes that every Opel Dulfer sells includes a Shepp cassette as standard equipment.

Hans hired me for three Lowland gigs because I recorded with Shepp. Although he never said so in so many words, that credential goes a long way with Hans.

The later Hans stays up the better he feels and mornings are lousy no matter what. Even after playing late he's out there selling early. He can laugh saying this: 'I may not be a good musician but I'm a bitch of a car salesman.'

Another bisocial. Hans plays rock, funk jazz; he has several musical personalities – a double bisocial – but I can describe the music we played together by the following story. He asked me if I knew 'Little Willie Leaps', a fast-moving line written by Miles Davis based on the chords of the standard 'All God's Chillun Got Rhythm'. I said I know the line (practise it all the time) but not the changes. He smiled: 'Oh, I don't play the changes.' So here's what free jazz is all about. One big copout. Play the line of a tune with difficult chords and then forget all about the chords. Anything goes. The composer Paul Hindemith said: 'Where anything goes nothing counts.' Go outside, keep the time, not even all the time and stick somewhere vaguely near some tonality or other. Just about anything goes.

Hans plays like that other bisocial tenorman Larry Rivers, the Caribbean revolution syndrome. Born in 1940, self-taught, he started on valve trombone in his high school brass band. He fell in love with saxophone honkers like Illinois Jacquet and identified to the point where he told people he could play the instrument. One Wednesday somebody offered him a job. 'I'm in trouble,' he told his father. Wednesday night Hans played tenor sax.

He formed a quartet with that genial Dutch madman of the drums, Han Bennink. They played easy bebop tunes like 'Walkin' ', with a lot of feeling but paid no attention to the chords. They had never learned chords. Bennink is more theatre than music. He makes music with an ashtray, garden shears, a washboard, Korean drums, a Tibetan trumpet, an African Balafon, giant drumsticks, feathers, flags, accordion and just about anything else including the kitchen sink. Perhaps I should qualify my smart-ass write-off of free jazz. Yes, this music disregards tradition, but on the other hand the idea is to find new forms or frameworks to replace the old. Trouble is ninety per cent of the free players disregard period. It is much harder to invent new forms than improvise over old ones. The Art Ensemble of Chicago succeeds, Steve Lacy, Carla Bley, Keith Jarrett, Sun Ra, Han Bennink – not too many others. When Hans and Han began to play together back in the early sixties, they were playing free jazz before the term. One day they worked with a pianist who did know chords and everything sounded funny. Hans turned around and said: 'Man, you can't play the piano.'

He laughs thinking back: 'I found out of course it was me who couldn't play not the pianist, but by the time I learned chords everyone else stopped playing them when free jazz arrived. I learned everything backwards.'

Jazz musicians are not supposed to be hotshot car salesmen, let alone unabashed about it: 'I liked the job from the beginning. It was sixty-three, the car market was going up, it was easy to sell cars if you were willing to work hard. I sat down with the phone book and started from the A's: "Hello, are you in the market for a car?" It also gave me the freedom to play at night and, strange to tell, one of the reasons I learned music so fast was because better musicians would agree to play with me since I had a car and could bring them to the gig and back.'

When the youth club Paradiso opened in the late sixties, Dulfer saw that jazz was going out of fashion and rock was coming in. He saw a thousand kids in there every night and decided that if the audience no longer came to jazz he would bring jazz to where the audience was. He sold the Paradiso on the idea of jazz Wednesdays, which, to everyone's surprise, were just as packed as the rest of the week. He booked his own quartet regularly and once more was working with better musicians, this time because he had the gigs rather than the car.

The song 'My Way' could have been written about Dulfer, who analysed his talent, made a game plan and stuck to it: 'I realized very fast that I'll never be another Coltrane. I decided not to go for international fame. I just like to play. I wanted to play in local clubs and be a local musician. When I go to France, for instance, they don't know about me as a media figure, running clubs, writing a book or selling cars and they judge me just as a musician. That's not enough, let's be frank. I can tell the difference between me and Shepp. I may not be a great musician but I know how to listen.'

After woodshedding his prose technique through hundreds of letters to editors, he started a column for a jazz magazine and *Jazz in China* collected them. The title comes from a chapter which copies a published discussion between China experts, changing the names from Mao to Charlie Parker and so on: 'They were talking nonsense and if you changed the names it was the same nonsense.' The book sold more than 4,000 copies: 'I'm good at publicity.'

People accuse Dulfer of being on a power trip, of always wanting to be the leader: 'I've got to be careful, if I let other people pick the tunes they might pick some I don't know. But the audience hears that I always give everything I've got, I always put a lot of energy in my playing because I have no real technical resources. Yeah, you could call me intense.

'Sometimes it gets me into trouble. I was recently on Amsterdam radio with a panel of serious journalists discussing the squatter situation. I figured these guys really needed a joker like me and I said that I didn't see anything wrong with throwing rocks – people have been throwing rocks in Amsterdam since the sixteenth century so what's the big deal? My co-workers in the Opel office didn't talk to me for awhile. Maybe it's better to keep my intensity for jazz.'

16
The Critic Blues

I'm a frustrated sneeze, a pimple that won't pop, an orgasm that can't come. I would like to come all day long but my father, who has been dead for years, would not approve. Be mature, son, take care of business. Not monkey business, business business. Show up on time, do your homework, take your elbows off the table if you want to be a success. I waste a lot of good time ('time is money, son') worrying about failure, never having been able to figure out what constitutes success. When I try to explain to friends how confused and anguished these questions leave me, they exclaim impatiently: 'At *your* age?' I suspect their response may be due to an inadequate verbal exposition of the problem. Trouble with words is why I started to write in the first place. Often I do not know what I am writing about until it is written. This sort of therapy does not make editors confident, and I have found that if I want to publish what I write I cannot write what I want. Editors scratch their heads and ask: 'But what's it *about?*'

I wrote a long article about a serious subject for a serious monthly. Rejecting it, absolutely insulted by having had it handed to her, shredding more than rejecting it, the editor said it was sloppy, not profound enough, and the style was 'breezy', light-weight by her definition. But I search hard for breezy frameworks. If only she could know how hard I worked to be breezy, how many years of experience it took to get the courage and the chops to treat a serious subject in breezy terms. Perhaps there was a bit of hot air in with the breeze, but not enough to insult anybody. Like most journalists, however, I have learned to survive by writing to order in several house-styles. That way I manage to get quite a bit of approval from everyone but myself.

A series of coincidental adventures involving a hooker named Sophie, a VW mini-bus and Roswell Rudd gave me strength to continue the good fight. This is not about Sophie, bless her dope-sotted head. There is no space for her here, or perhaps anywhere. The mini-bus is sort of interesting, but let's drop it more or less arbitrarily. That leaves Roswell. Now we know what this is about.

Writing for me is a process of discovery, not all that different from blowing a horn. My ambition is to have musicians play about my writing rather than the other way around.

There are reasons for the general low quality of jazz journalism. For one thing it's badly paid, so you get three kinds of writers. 1: Bad writers. 2: Writers who make their living doing something else and write in their spare time. They are tired writing after a hard day's work and have not had the professional experience to express themselves with style and accuracy. 3: Good writers often forced to write too fast in order to make a living at existing price-levels.

Part of the problem with criticism is the name. 'To criticize' implies negativity. To look smart, critics find fault; clever irrelevant nitpicking bolsters credentials. They invent fancy philosophies, missing the music in the process. The critic should be a commentator, an enhancer, provide positive feedback, add another instrument to the choir. At the least he or she should be like a weatherman, help the listener know which way the wind is blowing. They should be able to write as well as the people they write about can play.

Most jazz journalism is boring, a worse sin than excess ego or inaccuracy. Writers are either forced or choose to go by journalistic rules, the sort of rules Charlie Parker and Louis Armstrong broke to create the music that is the subject-matter. Why is the journalist the only cat on the scene expected to play the melody all night long?

The Riverbop, a damp and smoky cave, late at night. Customers are arguing with the waitress over the price of a bottle of champagne at a table next to the bandstand, on which a rumpled, no-longer-a-kid trombonist is playing seated. Worth noting. The trombone is a formal instrument that is generally played standing at attention to breathe correctly, to have elbow and slide room – to project. Also odd, you can hardly hear him. He does not seem to be trying very hard to be heard, playing with a mute in the lower register. Sometimes he does not even play at all. He chants and moans: 'Oye oye oye . . .'

Not to imply he's Jewish. Roswell Rudd comes out of WASP Connecticut stock via finishing schools, where he played ice hockey, and Yale frathouse dixieland bands. But then somehow he went beyond the pale of his peers' definition of 'respectable'.

Aggressive creativity threatens respectable peers. He went outside with Carla Bley, Steve Lacy and Archie Shepp and, unwilling to set up shop even only that far from the shopping centre, now it's hard to tell whether he's playing 'King Porter Stomp', 'Klactoveedosteen' or some post-Albert Ayler lament too incredibly sad and brittle to be named let alone sold. He's telling us what's on his mind tonight. He seems content that only me and three other misfits are listening.

J.J. Johnson ruined a generation of trombonists by learning how to articulate the slide like valves, no mean feat, which gave birth to the 'machine-gun' school. It wasn't his fault because that just happened to be the way he told you what was on *his* mind. But J.J. was just about inescapable for a trombonist playing bebop, similar to Charlie Parker on the alto sax. Everybody became so preoccupied with overcoming the slide they forgot how to *use* it. They developed false position to fly all over the place, triple-tonguing at unbelievable tempos up to double high B-flats – louder, faster, higher; the musical equivalent of yellow journalism. A few organic loners like Jimmy Knepper and Roswell followed forgotten old-timers Dickie Wells and Vic Dickenson, slipping and sliding in a normal tone of voice. And you're not listening.

Jazz deals with the moment: say your piece, whatever comes into your mind and hope someone's touched. How many times have you touched someone? Changed them, even for a moment? How many times have you been touched? Am I touching you? Roswell was teaching, which he detests, at the University of Maine at the time and he paid another teacher to replace him so he could have the pleasure of sitting in a damp and smoky cave, a losing proposition, trying to touch someone accompanying an argument over the price of a bottle of champagne.

And though it doesn't seem to bother Ros, Jean-François Jenny-Clarke and Aldo Romano, bass and drums, are engaged in their own private conversation about how hip it is to be playing in a left-bank cave; laying down a copy of what they have heard Jimmy Garrison and Elvin Jones lay down behind Trane, a stale conversation about cheese or getting laid or something while Roswell is trying to tell you that he is a frustrated sneeze, a pimple that won't pop, an orgasm that can't come.

Jeezus! Does anybody ever listen? Do you know how to fucking read? I splat this anguish on the page anyhow, trying to break through accepted forms, tearing up page after page hoping to make passion coherent, to touch at least three misfits, to convince myself and them that it is necessary and possible to be neither Leonard Feather nor J.J. Johnson, trying to find a way to be Michael Zwerin, to reach out of the frustration and loneliness that just seems to get worse all the time, wondering who cares, begging Roswell Rudd never to stop and maybe just maybe to give him something to play about.

It was nothing to take seriously when I started to write about jazz for the *Village Voice* in 1964. I wanted to communicate a little passion, the free records and concert passes were nice and it feels good to see your name in print. It wasn't for the money: $10 a column.

It began to get less frivolous when my phone rang at 4 a.m. one Tuesday morning. I had just got home after a gig with the Upper Bohemia Six at the Five Spot. The Five Spot paid $10 a night. 'Hello is this Zwerin the bigtime critic?'

The female voice was not sober: 'I think you stink. That review you wrote about Brew Moore . . .'

I knew what she was going to say. There had been second thoughts: 'You mean the part about Brew sounding like he was playing through a keg of beer? But you've got to understand; I *love* that sound. Do I know you?'

'No. Don't you realize what one stupid statement like that can do to a guy's career? Brew's a fine musician, now everybody's going to think he's a drunk. You don't seem to care about anything except being clever. Goodnight.'

I never slept that night. There were responsibilities after all. Was I superficial? A parasite? Even worse – destructive? From now on I would take more care to express myself with precision.

But I neither can nor want to stay serious writing about jazz, which should be above all fun. Breezy swing interests me more than accuracy. Not that I don't try to be accurate, but who cares about accurate unreadable prose. 'You can't beat fun,' someone said.

My memorial piece about Birdland when that jazz landmark closed included amusing Pee Wee Marquette anecdotes. This black midget master of ceremonies had processed hair, wore a cummerbund, walked with a fancy cane and his tiny fingers were covered by diamond rings, one of which was a present from Dinah Washington. Pee Wee would be sure to announce a musician's name at the end of a set for a fiver a week. For ten he'd pronounce it correctly. Doug Watkins was 'Grub Hawkins' until he wised up. When Irving Levy, the best-liked Birdland partner, was stabbed to death, Pee Wee wept in a corner. Irving had treated him like a big man, a normal human being, dinner with the family for example. On crowded weekends, Pee Wee would grope through the forest of standees' legs with a lit flashlight looking for loose change on the floor. Just before dawn after the customers were gone and the naked cleaning lights had been turned on, he sat on the bandstand with a microphone in one sparkling mini-hand singing 'South of the Border (Down Mexico Way)' all by himself. Lester Young once responded negatively to Pee Wee's request for a tip: 'Leave me alone you half a motherfucker.'

Pee Wee sued the *Voice*. Our lawyer, Ed Koch, later mayor of New York, asked for testimonials from musicians verifying my Pee Wee stories. Everybody said of course everybody knew they were true, but nobody but Pepper Adams and Patti Bown would sign their name to anything because they were afraid of being blackballed. Koch thought it was very funny being sued by a black midget. The case was settled out of court.

This taught me a lesson. You *can* beat fun.

A certain Marilynn K. McAusland wrote to my editor complaining: 'According to Michael Zwerin, "People who like jazz generally also like to drink and hang out." My high school music teacher, Sister Mary Norine, RSM, was the one who evoked my earliest interest in jazz and she rarely drinks and hardly ever "hangs out" . . . Charlie Mingus quite often leaves the stand in the middle of a tune rather than put up with "boozing friends". Mr Zwerin states: "Also, there are many young players who do not work since there are few places which can afford, or are willing, to take chances with unknowns." This is unfortunately true, but if clubs will not hire "unknowns", then it is up to Mr Zwerin to make them "known" by mentioning them in his weekly column . . . It seems to me that rather than helping jazz, Mr Zwerin is doing it a great disservice both by perpetuating the false association of jazz with "booze" . . . as well as by devoting valuable *Voice* space to such well-established people as Miles Davis and John Coltrane.'

Squirms had died prior to the publication of the questioned passages. What would Sister Mary Norine RSM have thought about that chemical garbage-can? Obviously all jazz musicians do not drink. I'm the last one to push boozing, but it is part of the inside story. Ms McAusland started me wondering if such inside stuff isn't bad publicity, and maybe she was right about the known *v.* unknown part. I wrote a profile of Billy Rubenstein, an unknown pianist of some talent, leaving out the junk habit that would soon kill him.

Now skip to Paris, November 1977. 'Gerry Mulligan,' I wrote in the *International Herald Tribune*, 'is one of those rare jazz musicians with interest in and ties to other branches of the arts. As he put it: "I couldn't function being in contact only with musicians." '

Music is a hard mistress who does not encourage competition. Concert pianists practise ten hours a day, John Coltrane and Eric Dolphy spent every waking hour playing, writing or thinking about music. But Mulligan, like the late Paul Desmond (literature) and French percussionist Daniel Humair (painting), uses energy that others reserve totally for music in bisocial involvements. There are 'other things in life besides killing yourself to become somebody else's definition of success'.

A combination of talent, panache and luck brought early success to Mulligan. Just after the Second World War, not yet twenty, he scored with a hit single, 'Disc Jockey Jump' for Gene Krupa. He played baritone sax with and wrote for Miles Davis's 'Birth of the Cool' tentet. In 1952, he moved to Los Angeles and formed a pianoless quartet, featuring Chet Baker's trumpet, and created open, horizontal music the implications of which led to free jazz. The quartet was photogenic, quiet, communicative. Its sensitive handling of melody made Mulligan at once famous and respected. He has appeared in films (*I Want to Live*), played on soundtracks (*The Subterraneans*), scored them (*La Menace*, starring Yves Montand). His friendship with actress Sandy Denis put him in touch with the theatre. He has felt increasing affinity for Europe: 'Even though Europe is more and more Americanized, values are still not as mercenary here. More attention is paid to the quality of life. In America, for example, they sell music as though it were a can of peas.' But his lifestyle has been described by one of his peers as 'dilettante'.

The actual way it was put to me, and the peer shall remain anonymous, was: 'If Gerry spent less time fooling around with all them bitches and more with his horn he'd play a whole lot better.' I just put 'dilettante'.

Mulligan telephoned yelling: 'Yellow journalist'. He yelled for quite some time until we hung up. Guess I'll never play with Gerry's big band. Too bad, always liked that band.

Remember that the events herein described happened over a period of some seventeen years. I'm obviously leaving out the good news, but good news does not make headlines and I don't see why I should be an exception.

You could have called me on that one. I keep saying I want to find new stools and create my own forms and all that crap and here I go spewing out somebody else's bullshit about good news not making headlines. Let's throw in some good news for the fun of it.

I reviewed an obscure Beatle track called 'Old Brown Shoe', analysing Paul McCartney's bass-line, which I found outrageously hip, in my *Voice* column. Some jazz people were not happy about wasting column inches on the Beatles. There were nasty letters. But it was good I knew it was good and I wanted to open a few ears. A year or so later, Steve Swallow told me: 'I listened to "Old Brown Shoe" and you were right about that bass-line.'

Reviewing a Dave Brubeck album, I said it looks like they'd lost something. I compared them to Citizen Kane losing Rosebud. The next time I saw Paul Desmond in Elaine's, he laughed: 'Rosebud?!' and bought me a drink.

Bill Graham, the rock impresario, introduced me to Mick Jagger. It was a press conference, no private dinner or anything, but still it felt good when Bill singled me out of the journalistic crowd and I went with him to the private place where Jagger was sitting. Bill said to Jagger: 'Mike's really lucky. He's got the best job in the world. Writing about music for the *Herald Tribune* in Paris.'

My first thought was: if they only knew how little money I was making. But he just might be right. He seemed really to mean it. Rarefied company, people who make a living doing something they like to do. Doing it in Paris for a paper read in 140 countries could be worse. Right Livelihood.

George Orwell wrote in *The Road to Wigan Pier*: 'What is work and what is not work: is it work to dig, to carpenter, to plant trees, to fell trees, to ride, to fish, to hunt, to feed chickens, to play the piano, to take photographs, to build a house, to cook, to sew, to trim hats, to mend motor-cycles? All of these things are work to somebody. There are in fact very few activities which cannot be classed either as work or play according as you choose to regard them.'

I do not really regard writing about jazz as bad news but so long as I've started let's get it out of my system.

An article on Charles Mingus included the insight: 'Mingus was not a great bass-player. His genius consisted of . . .' I thought it read pretty well until I bumped into Sugar Blue, who growled: 'Just who do you think is a great bass-player?'

Always happy to explain: 'Scotty LaFaro, for example. He really revolutionized . . .'

Sugar's finger poked my chest: 'Are you kidding? LaFaro wasn't in the same class as Mingus. Now you might mention Oscar Pettiford, Percy Heath, Ron Carter . . .'

It dawned on me that my example had been white and Sugar's were all black: 'Hey are you trying to call me racist?'

'Well let me put it this way. If you think Mingus was not a great bass-player you've got no business writing about jazz. Deal with *that*.'

Clark Terry told me how hard it was to find good young black players for his big band. There was a piece there. I wrote 'Why Young Blacks Don't Play Jazz' for a small magazine. The editor was pleased, it made the cover. I was walking on air. People I didn't know said hello. There was a letter of praise from the

University of Massachusetts Afro-American Studies Department. Then another letter, scribbled on graph paper: 'I think jazz is full of shit and the reason it's full of shit is Crow Jim. The first Black Nationalist thing happened in jazz when mediocre black assholes took over and frightened the shit out of everybody with their constant references to "our music". I say – OK then, shove it up your ass. I think jazz is dead, murdered by the creator of jazz – the Spade. And the critics fell for it. Why don't you cats lighten up and let jazz be free? (signed) an ex-jazz freak.'

By this time I had another family and was writing for money as well as passion. Straight ahead.

My article about an unknown singer helped her get a good gig in Mexico. I like discovering people. Unknown people are generally more interesting subjects than stars. I had in fact written the first article about Sugar Blue, while he was still busking in the metro, and this led to his record-dates playing harp with the Stones. But I found the singer's pianist Ham Jonas waiting to ambush me in a bar. Ham was fuming: 'I don't see how you can write a three-column story about a singer and not even mention her accompanist once.'

'I did mention you but my editor cut that paragraph out, said he needed the space for a perfume ad and it wasn't essential to the story.'

I could see Ham didn't believe me. People do not understand how low on the totem-pole journalists are. We cannot write our own titles, our leads, syntax and tenses are subject to change without notice, we are cut without being consulted and sometimes even the point of view is altered.

His rage had passed. Ham was folding up before my eyes: 'I know what it is. You don't take me seriously because I'm Swiss.'

I played the Nice festival and reviewed it, saying how remarkable it is that jazz is no longer merely a young man's art. I mentioned how wonderful Vic Dickenson and Budd Johnson still played at their advanced ages. Promoter George Wein pulled me aside and asked: 'What do you want to be doing when you're an old man?' I said: 'I always want to play jazz.' He said: 'Then why did you write that?' Wein never hired me for Nice again. Am I here all alone?

Recently I stumbled on this statement by Chick Corea: 'I'm all for just completely ignoring critics. They have no use.' Erik Satie, one of my heroes, once said: 'Last year I gave several lectures on "Intelligence and the Appreciation of Music among Animals". Today I am going to speak to you about "Intelligence and the Appreciation of Music among Critics". The subject is very similar.'

Picking through a pile of albums waiting to be reviewed, I spotted Sugar Blue's latest release. The thought crossed my mind – that motherfucker, I'll get him, he asked for it. I'm going to give Sugar a bad review.

17

The Warsaw Rag

The only passenger in the last car of a train that crossed northern France, West Germany, East Germany, over the Wall twice in and out of Berlin and into Poland after five customs, I was thinking about Napoleon, Von Rundstadt, Humphrey Bogart and Eddie Rosner.

Flat, foggy country, lights along the tracks grew dimmer and far between. Streets were unpaved and muddy, even in the middle of towns, the names of which sound like striped pyjamas and tattooed numbers. The train had been standing still for something like twenty minutes now, in the middle of nowhere. Somebody's nowhere is somewhere for somebody else, but this was really nowhere. Maybe they had unhitched the car. Why was I the only passenger in it? The windows were fogged over. Gas? Squinting tough like Richard Burton, I drained my pocket flask, tugged up my trenchcoat collar, pulled the brim of my Borsalino down and stepped on to the platform to look around.

There was no platform, only a gravel bed in the middle of nowhere. The car was, however, still attached to a train. Maybe they'd unhitched the train. After marching footsteps in the fog, and barking, a husky voice attached to a police dog emerged: '*Verboten*. Forbidden. Get back on board, please.'

How did he know I speak English?

The Man. The Man is always the Man, regardless of race, creed or political preference. The Man is to be avoided at all costs. They are very bad Men. Alone in the middle of somebody else's nowhere, even the Man was welcome. He was sweating despite the chilly air, and his unpressed fat-man suit looked like a Sidney Greenstreet costume. Inspecting my visa, he commented pleasantly: 'So you're the music man?'

Nothing in my passport said anything about music. I flashed my best mild-mannered reporter smile: 'How did you know?'

'Oh, I know everything.' He gave the impression that he was not so pleasant as he tried to appear. He tipped his hat: 'Sir.'

SHOCK CUT. A noisy bar packed with journalists of many persuasions, festival officials, scouts from other festivals, musicians, media moguls, miscellaneous capitalist parasites and Men in brown shoes backstage during the twentieth annual Warsaw International Jazz Jamboree. Whatever they name that one-two punch in this country, I had already raised a couple of hammers on the head.

'Pssst . . .' A Polish hipster whispered in my ear: 'I heard a rumour that . . .'

'I can't hear, sorry.' The Yosuke Yamashita kamikaze trio on stage had hijacked conversation.

He moved closer: 'I heard a rumour that there will be an uprising at Christmas time.'

'Jeezus!' This was several years before Solidarity. 'Are you sure? How did you find out?'

He led me into the courtyard for greater security ('I've been tipped off, backstage is lousy with secret men') and lit a joint ('Krakow home-grown'). 'Well, see, this trombone-player from Posnan has a friend who said . . .'

How did I get into this bebop spy flick?

The atmosphere was palpably sullen. Poles referred to 'Socialism' in a tone of voice westerners usually reserve for 'inflation' and 'unemployment'. There had been demonstrations against short supplies. There was currently no coffee. Earlier there had been no sugar. Coal would be rationed that winter. Bus services were getting worse and you had to wait in line for everything except meat. There was no meat. (Krakow home-grown appeared to be plentiful.)

A Polish Polish joke. An eighteenth-century castle outside Warsaw is being restored as a museum. One room will be hung totally with beef. Asked why by a visitor, the architect responds: 'To preserve our past.'

Another Polish Polish joke: 'Q: What's the difference between the American dollar and the Polish zloty? A: There is no difference. In America the dollar buys everything and the zloty buys nothing. In Poland the dollar buys everything and the zloty buys nothing.'

Dollar stores in tourist hotels were packed with Poles buying Kleenex. They could have blown their noses in zloty bills, but the ink bleeds. This is a land of soft currency and hard toilet paper.

The Forum Hotel is twenty-six storeys high, a cross between a Hilton and a warehouse. Casimir, who looks like a Polish Woody Allen, was tossed out of the Forum Bar for asking for a screwdriver with grapefruit and orange juice in English. The waitress said that was not possible. Casimir explained that instead of just orange juice you mix it half and half with. . . The waitress called over one of the secret men who are always secreting in there. Casimir was asked to leave. Casimir also speaks Russian and he tried to make the secret man believe he was a visitor from that country but the secret man only said: 'Poles are not allowed in the Forum Bar.'

A Polish Russian joke. A Russian dog tells a Polish dog how marvellous everything is in the Soviet Union. Happy workers, lively arts, great medical care, advanced space programme, plenty of sports; such a large and beautiful country, such lovely bitches. The Polish dog asks why, if everything is so great there, his friend spends six months a year in Poland. The Russian dog replies: 'Because here I can go "arf arf".'

A Polish journalist complained that his magazine was three weeks behind schedule because of the printer. 'Why don't you change printers?' I asked him.

He looked at me like I was nuts.

Meanwhile back at the twentieth annual Jazz Jamboree, Zbigniew Namyslowski was, as they say in my country, cooking his ass off. Ornette Coleman filtered through a lonely Slavic Cry, his playing touched the Universal Funk. Extended haunting melodic lines were carried on a sublime tone, but he was alone. The rhythm section behind him was way behind. They were like children struggling to catch up with a striding parent. What they did was correct but they were not doing much. Casimir says there is only one good Polish rhythm section, and they live in Los Angeles.

But Polish jazz is integrated into the cultural life of the country. The Polish Jazz Society is the largest such national organization in the world. Poland has produced players of international standing, including Namyslowski, Michal Urbaniak and Adam Makowicz. They were all influenced by pianist, composer and bandleader Krzystof Komeda, who wrote the music for Roman Polanski's film *Rosemary's Baby*. When you admit you never heard of Komeda, Poles look shocked. You apologize and say it must be a hole in your education. The hole in your Swiss cheese is their Swiss cheese. Your nowhere is their somewhere.

Eddie Rosner, a German Jew who played trumpet, came to Warsaw to escape Hitler in 1933. He was soon thought of as Polish. The Belgian critic André Ache described him in *Melody Maker* as the 'Polish Louis Armstrong'. Rosner's popular big band played dances and nightclubs until Goebbels banned what he called 'plutocratic capitalist music' and Rosner vanished.

Post-war Polish jazz first appeared in Krakow, the university town which remained relatively intact. The film *Sun Valley Serenade*, featuring Glenn Miller and his orchestra, spawned Miller spin-offs all over the country. Every big band had a few soloists who improvised. The Warsaw YMCA was the first real jazz club until a Stalinist regime banned it again.

Musicians were not put in jail but Andrzej Kurylewicz was thrown out of conservatory for playing jazz. It was played by students in private apartments and if an official arrived to question it, everybody suddenly broke into 'Happy Birthday'.

A bass-player named Witold Kujawskie functioned as a sort of switchboard in the early fifties. He knew who the best players were, who had a drum-kit and a piano, and he organized a lot of jam sessions in his one-room apartment on Stradom Street, Krakow. The Fersters – two doctors with children – sponsored jam sessions in their apartment on Retoryka Street, Krakow. Young musicians copied American arrangements and solos. Saxophonist Jan Ptaszyn Wroblewski, a member of the International Youth Band that played the 1958 Newport Festival, describes this period: 'We would sit with Krzystof (Komeda) by the radio and have a prearranged pattern: "You take down the first two bars, I'll take down the third and fourth and so on." We were doing everything blind.'

Under Gumulka, after 1956, culture-control loosened up and Gerry Mulligan could be heard on Polish radio. The birth of Polish jazz as a creative force is given as August 1956, when the first Polish jazz festival was held in Sopot, a seaside resort near Gdansk. There was a New Orleans-style parade and the beach was dense with campers. Mostly Poles played, plus obscure groups from Czechoslovakia and Britain, but next year Sopot featured clarinettist Albert Nicholas and Albert Mangelsdorff, the West German trombonist. Writer Leopolod Tyrmand noted: 'The 1957 Sopot Jazz Festival signified the first true cultural relationship between Germany and Poland since 1938.' Ray McKinley and the Glenn Miller Orchestra toured in 1957, Dave Brubeck in 1958, the year of the first Jazz Jamboree.

Twenty years later, I listened to two Polish student big bands ignore their funk. The Poles are a funky people but have not learned to be proud of it. They believe foreigners consider funk plain dirt, one facet of a backward nation. This may be so for foreign bankers or bureaucrats but jazz comes out of bodily fluids, it is based on the uninhibited flow of mental and physical sweat and these big bands wore too much perfume. Few surprises in the voicings, no astonishment to the solos. To survive in the reality of East European Socialism you learn to do what others expect of you even when you think you're doing what you want. Jazz was born here after the death of Stalin, whose ghost still hovered. Hitler and Stalin stifled a generation of swing. The Poles lost the habit of keeping good time.

When ageing Woody Herman kicked his young Herd into 'Blue Flame', the difference was first of all visual. The brass section stood up, fierce and loose. The drummer dropped his jacket when it got hot. Technical proficiency was not noticeably higher than the Poles they followed, but the difference was a killer – psychological, cultural, political in the broadest sense. They considered playing jazz a right rather than a privilege. You can't beat fun.

My paternal grandfather packed up his family and emigrated from Kharkov just before the First World War. My name remains Russian (means 'beastly') and when the Russian pianist Leonid Czizik saw my identification badge, he asked how come. I explained it all to him.

His eyes lit up: 'Me too.' He spread his arms and shouted with joy: 'I'm from Kharkov too.'

'Cousin!' we exclaimed simultaneously, hugging right in public backstage in front of all the secret men. But then, as though yanked by the same puppeteer, we disengaged quickly and stayed out of each other's way for the remainder of the festival. He could get into trouble for spending time with someone like me. If not for my grandfather, I too might be someone who could get in trouble for spending time with someone like me.

The following night it was Czizik's turn to play. Czizik means 'little bird' in Russian and he looks like one. He was meant to chirp more. As he was introduced, the name of his country induced boos and hisses. (The Culture Palace holds 3,500 people and was sold out the entire five-night festival.) Imagine being a jazz musician in Russia. Czizik makes records that do not get distributed, plays concerts that are not reviewed; this may well be the only time in his life he will be allowed to play outside his borders. Poland is the West to him, maybe there will be a critic from *Down Beat* here. Here he can hear Johnny Griffin and Art Taylor live. He was obviously so excited to be here and before one note he gets booed. His playing was free in the freest sense, free even of dependence on freedom. He made his own space using elements from East and West, shuffled them to his taste, and at the end the audience cheered the musician just as it had booed his nationality.

This was a hole in the Wall. We were all aware of something special, similar intensity must pervade during international sporting events. The atmosphere was charged. These holes can be closed without notice. We felt privileged. There were toasts. Rounds followed rounds. Drinking was compulsive, necessary rather than social.

It picked up momentum during afterhour jams in the Aquarium across the street from the Culture Palace. This two-storey jazz club smack in the middle of romantic downtown Warsaw serves sandwiches and records downstairs, and live jazz in the café theatre upstairs. Sound was levelled for listening. A conversation shouted over two of Woody's hot young tenor-players racing through 'Giant Steps' would seem to be relatively tap-proof. Not that we were saying anything subversive, mind you, but this dirty

Commie, a Russian I'd seen around, had already showed me his Party card. Now he was calling me 'wishy washy liberal'.

This Bolshy bastard with a red beard down to his 'Bird Lives' button and Ivan the Terrible eyes – why was I laying the story of my life on him? How did I know there wasn't a microphone in his 'Bird Lives' button?

'Not me.' I denied his charge, being not quite blotto enough to avoid the suspicion that something was backwards here. We had been kissing each other on the mouth, as drunken Russians do, for some time now; calling each other 'brother' (in French for some reason) and I drank to it when he raised his glass: 'To Jelly Roll Menshikov who invented jazz in Odessa.'

'Yeah baby, dig it.' I gave him some skin.

'Ah, you know,' he said, 'that is an old folk habit from the Caucasus, giving skin.' He gave some back.

I put it in my pocket and told him that my mother, who remembers life under the Czars, thinks things were so terrible then that whatever the present system's faults, it must be an improvement.

He looked over his shoulder and then whistled:

(IT AIN'T NEC-ES-SAR-I-LY SO)

I don't know how we got into politics but something I said about Santiago Carillo, the Spanish Communist Party and the Basques got his back up. This Pinko punk actually said to me: 'You know what you are? You're a fucking Marxist.'

'I've never been so insulted in my life.' We looked at each other across our grand guignol Iron Curtain – me from my over-motivated, me-generation, violent, money-first society (I had told him how alienated it makes me), and he had already said: 'Socialism works pretty well until you start to think.' We looked at each other from our mutual alienation, alike in intensity if not kind, trying to hold on to the moment like soldiers in opposing armies exchanging a cigarette during a truce. 'And you know what *you* are?' I said, poking him in the chest, 'a bourgeois reactionary, that's what.'

He called the waitress: 'Darlink. Wodka. Doobels.'

Then a fat fellow traveller joined us, smiling, even more cockeyed than we were. Commie translated for Fellow Traveller, who was giving me the once-over and frankly I was getting a bit nervous. How did I know these people were who they said they were? They had not even said. Why was he smiling?

'Who's he?' I asked Commie.

'Don't worry,' he answered. 'Only KGB, a nice agent.'

Going along with what I chose to consider a joke, I extended a hand: 'How do you do. CIA.'

'I told you . . .' Fellow Traveller shook his finger at Commie. The thought had crossed their minds, and probably would again one day. But for the time being we were lost in the hole in the Wall, protected from systems that divide us by the music that unites us. Commie pulled a record out of his large shoulder-bag and handed it to me as though made of uranium. No, he did not 'hand' it, he slipped it under the table, saying: 'The first jazz record ever made in Lithuania. The Vyacheslav Ganelin trio. They are so beautiful, so excellent . . .' He started crying: 'Please have it played on the radio, review it, write about it; tell people.' Tears were streaming down his cheeks now, and mine.

We kissed one last time in front of the Aquarium, hugging in a stumbling huddle. Commie pointed to the moon, which was almost full and hung low in a sky beginning to be streaked with red-eyed dawn: 'Just think. The same moon shines over New Orleans.'

18
The Bombay Raga

Earning a reputation in the jazz business does not necessarily equal high earnings as in other businesses. When Niranjan Jhaveri invited me to be unpaid master of ceremonies for the 1980 Bombay 'Jazz Yatra' festival, I drove a hard bargain. I insisted on being an unpaid musician too.

Using India, the mecca of improvisation, as bait, Jhaveri managed not to pay anybody (some were subsidized by their country's cultural establishment). He called the festival: 'a nightmare more than a miracle'. One musician called him: 'a hustler more than a promoter'.

Rang Bhavan, an outdoor arena seating 6,000 people, was sold out the entire week. Transportation and hotel costs were picked up by states and private industry. Which left lots of rupees unaccounted for. Where did all the rupees go? When a promoter's risk makes a return, bravo. But there was no risk here, though unctuous officials mouthed presumptuous pieties. Never mind. The temple remains despite the money-changers.

Yatra means 'pilgrimage' and there were pilgrims from Bulgaria, Hungary, Poland, the United States, West Germany, France, Italy, Portugal, Finland, Sweden, Britain, Soviet Russia, Australia, Japan, Brazil, Yugoslavia and of course India. Jazz is relatively unsophisticated next to ancient complex Indian classical improvisation, so Indian jazz musicians can be considered pilgrims too.

A red face. Except for morning Indian classical music concerts and the evening festival, I barely left my modern air-conditioned hotel. We could charge any of its five restaurants (or sandwiches by the pool) to our bill, picked up by Air India. Why pay to eat out? A head bowed in shame. Frenchmen reproached me: 'You mean you went to India and never left your hotel? Fucking Americans. You're all the same.' However I have one air-tight alibi (plus several less air-tight): Jimmy Knepper.

There are few things I would rather do anywhere than play duets with Knepper, boss trombone as far as I'm concerned. We'd already done it in his Staten Island home, in Paris and in Basel when we were both on tour with the George Gruntz Concert Jazz Band. We passed entire afternoons in his thirty-third-floor room overlooking the Indian Ocean reading Telemann flute duets (put a tenor clef in front and add two flats for trombone) and Bach two-part piano inventions.

Melvin Fishman, may he rest in peace, once booked a suite in Hamburg's Atlantic Hotel after having put together his first big-budget Hollywood package – a film of Hermann Hesse's novel *Steppenwolf*. He was ecstatic, as much for the chance to play mogul as make the movie. Fishman is the author of memorable lines, such as 'A movie without Marlon Brando isn't a movie,' 'The holes in your Swiss cheese are somebody else's Swiss cheese,' and, in the Atlantic, unable to find a room for a visiting journalist: 'Let's order a room from room service.' The Atlantic rooms are furnished with solid good taste – period furniture on thick carpets, a fridge stocked with goodies, there are sewing-kits, shoe-shine kits, packets of bath foam, a swimming-pool, nine-channel colour video. Fishman lit a long cigar, ordered a steak (and flowers for his star, Dominique Sanda) from room service, put his Italian boots up on the *Louis Seize* coffee table and cackled: 'This is a fucking fat hotel.'

All of which is to explain what I mean by saying that Jimmy Knepper has a fat sound. Not overweight, slow-moving, out of shape. More like a bulging pay envelope, rich, rewarding, happy; it surrounds you luxuriantly.

It is essential to remember that Knepper's name begins with a silent letter. People's names affect their behaviour. We live up to the implications of our names. There's a football coach named Charlie Winner. The Hocq family runs the luxury product company Cartier. Mick Jagger cultivates a jagged image. Rollie Fingers pitches a baseball. A lifetime of spelling a name that begins 'Zw' can make a recluse of anyone. Knepper has won the *Down*

Beat poll, he could double his fame and income if he stopped hiding behind his silent 'K' and promoted himself. He is perfectly suited for Staten Island, a hideout if ever there was one, which also has a silent letter and on which he owns three small houses on obscure streets. During the sixties, he covered his expenses playing Playboy Clubs and Broadway shows. Knepper's stock went up after Charles Mingus died, partly because he was by then, along with Albert Mangelsdorff, one of the only undeniable monsters on the instrument and partly because the Mingus legacy was marketable. He twisted his mouth into a smile that made him look like a cynical Abe Lincoln and mumbled: 'I made more money playing Mingus's music in the first nine months after he died than I did in twenty years when he was alive.'

Their relationship was not always smooth, but even after Mingus punched him in the mouth and knocked out a tooth, Knepper eventually came back to play with him again: 'That motherfucker kept calling it "my tooth". It didn't hurt, no blood or anything, but I lost a tooth along with about an octave of my range. Friends of mine said I should have him offed, but wiser heads prevailed and I just sued him. Nothing ever came of that. I rebuilt my embouchure working the entire Broadway run of *Funny Girl*, three years and three months. It was like retiring. Maybe Mingus did me a favour by putting me out of the jazz business in the sixties. Nothing much was happening anyway and I came out of it fresher than a lot of guys.'

Playing duets with Knepper is one intense learning experience. Out of the corner of my eye, I watched him articulate out in the fourth, fifth and sixth positions, false positions, difficult to ring and play in tune, but you can play faster out there because the notes are higher up in the overtone series and thus closer together. You can play fast like a fast trombone rather than machine-gun triple-tonguing imitation trumpet. He showed me the scales out where the slide must only move fractions of inches between notes. Most trombone-players are aware of those positions and can read in that fashion but Knepper uses them improvising. You wouldn't hear that just listening and it's not really essential knowledge, it is however the hidden truth behind the virtuoso, his musical silent 'K'.

Knepper is a mine of Mingus folklore: 'We were driving from

New York to LA for a gig. When I got to his house I found out that he and I were going alone in his Cadillac limousine. "You're driving," he told me. "But Mingus," I said, "I don't have a driver's licence." He didn't mind at all: "That's cool. Nobody ever stops a Cadillac limousine." He was right.

'Mingus was unavoidable for me, I used to get very depressed. Good God, I'd say to myself, I'm stuck with this guy for the rest of my life. His music was so difficult, with all those time-changes and different sequences. You had to concentrate real hard just to get through the lines. They seemed to be purposely written to trip you up. I wanted to relax and play "All the Things You Are". But Mingus had an innate musical instinct that could come up with something coherent by putting little bits and fragments together. He took snatches of different little melodies he sketched out here and there and hooked them together. Some of them he might have written years ago and not known what to do with at the time. He didn't call it "free" but he used to talk to us about "peaks of intensity". And he could make a whole tune out of a vamp-till-ready. A lot of rock is based on that – the introduction becomes the entire piece. Outwardly he came on like "this is my music and don't you dare mess with it", but privately I don't think he had that much respect for the stuff. He once told me: "I realize I'm only writing ditties." '

One night off when we were on tour in Germany with Gruntz, I said to Knepper: 'Hey let's hang out and get drunk.' He moped and said: 'Naah. I think I'll go to my room and mope.' He knows how to mope all right. We were playing with one of the best drummers in the world (this guy would be on anybody's five-best drummers list), but Knepper abhorred his abstract time. The drummer likes to come off a long roll crescendoing right to the second beat for example. Hearing this one night, Knepper got up and looked under his chair: 'Seem to have lost one.' This was during a gig, we were on the bandstand. He looked under my chair, then behind the saxophones: 'Hey, I'm looking for one. Anybody know where one is?'

Knepper leaves as little as possible to chance. One silent 'K' is enough. He knows where he's going and how to get there. The slide never moves more than the minimum distance necessary to get from one note to the next. If that means G in the sixth position, so be it. He improvises like he dresses, rather rumpled. There's a certain amount of disorder which, given his flawless technique, serves to humanize what otherwise might come out cold. You keep wondering . . . is he going to make it? Suspenseful, dramatic, he straddles the beat like a loping halfback in the clear, running only as fast as he has to. You shouldn't really hand the ball to Knepper for short yardage. This is no bone-shattering fullback, it takes time to get in the clear and finesse to stay there. He's brittle, avoid power-plays to avoid injury. Enough of this stupid football analogy. The season is over anyway.

One month before the Bombay festival, the Soviet consul visited Niranjan Jhaveri, secretary-general of the Jazz India Club, to plead with him: 'Jazz Yatra must include Soviet jazz musicians. Please. See what you can do.' The programme was already completed, but Jhaveri had been in his family's electronics business long enough to have learned the importance of practising the art of the possible. India and the Soviet Union were strengthening ties at that moment. Why not make everybody happy? Jazz Yatra '80 was being billed as a 'festival of Indo-Euro-Afro-American music'. Surely there was a place within that concept for Russians.

And so it happened that on the same day that the Carter administration issued a statement affirming its boycott of the Moscow Olympics, Melodia, a group of Soviet musicians, was playing Thelonious Monk's 'Straight No Chaser' in Bombay. These Russians had arrived with their equipment erroneously documented. Festival officials feared it would take at least a week to clear through customs. It took the Soviet consulate four hours. The police had clamped a 12.30 a.m. curfew on the festival, but Melodia was still going strong at one. One festival official was overheard to say: 'Don't worry, an Indian policeman will never tell Russians to stop.' So much for music not being political.

Jhaveri did not consider me a masterful master of ceremonies. He wanted jokes and speeches. I've got nothing against that sort of thing, only I can't do it. Actually I do have something against that sort of thing. MC speak with forked tongue. An MC should introduce the musicians and that's it. With all those musicians from so many different countries, East and West, introducing the musicians was no easy verbal exercise. Jhaveri's wife tried giving me elocution lessons and told me to stand up straighter in front of the mike. Since I was the only one who could be depended on to be near the stage at all times, I found myself scheduling and organizing as well as announcing for free. Wondering where all those rupees were going, I stopped announcing after Steve Lacy said: 'There's only one thing wrong with this festival. They aren't paying the musicians.'

There were concerts of Indian classical music each morning. Few jazz musicians attended because it meant getting up early. We regulars – Knepper, *Down Beat* correspondent Lee Jeske, *Melody Maker* staff writer Brian Case, Mingus Dynasty bassist Mike Richmond and a few others – soon began to feel a bond. It was the reason we had come, an important reason in any case. After listening to vina-player Ustad Asad Ali Khan, Richmond said: 'It's like seeing a movie that takes place in 1900 with a Boeing 747 in it.' Indian musicians have been improvising for many centuries, in time signatures like 15 and (literally) 10 $\frac{1}{2}$. But classical Indian music has become élitist, stagnant, removed from its old functions. Music was once completely integrated into daily life here – there were morning *ragas*, wedding *ragas*, etc. Now it has become concert-hall music, only the upper class can afford to listen, and some Indian intellectuals are looking to jazz as a possible revitalizing catalyst.

Ravi Shankar composed, arranged and conducted a fusion effort based on the fact that 'one doesn't listen to jazz, one digs it'. He dug for precious material. 'Jazz is mine as well as yours,' he also reasoned, and called his composition 'Jazz Mine', which closed the festival at 3 a.m. Sunday morning. (The police will never tell Ravi Shankar to stop.)

Shankar was at one time or another the teacher of George Harrison, John Coltrane and Yehudi Menuhin. He is basically responsible for teaching Indian music to the West. It is hard not to call him a guru, though he says the word with hesitation, as though afraid to distort it as his music was once distorted: 'Being George Harrison's – you might say – guru was good and bad at the same time. Good because Indian music was discovered by young people, and bad because most of these people did not realize the seriousness of our music.'

He came to the West for the first time in 1932, at the age of twelve, with his brother Uday's folklore troupe. He danced and played bowed instruments, flute and sitar. They came again in 1934, 1936 and 1938. Shankar went on to perform in the great Western concert halls. He had met Casals, Segovia, Heifetz, Paderewski and Toscanini before being introduced to George Harrison at a London party in the late sixties, and he would like once and for all to erase his hippy image: 'It must be made very clear that the music I play is Indian classical music. It goes back 2,500 years. It is serious music.'

When Shankar met Harrison he did not know who the Beatles were. He had been told they were very popular, but he had not heard Harrison's sitar playing on their hit 'Norwegian Wood'. Harrison took three lessons in London and then studied with Shankar for six weeks in India until 'he saw how difficult it is. You know, he meant well.'

Shankar speaks slowly, repeating key phrases for greater precision: 'All of those young people did not understand the seriousness of our music. They thought that to go and hear Ravi Shankar you must be high as a kite. It is a superficial approach. It does not go with our music. You must listen with a clear mind and respectful attitude. "Attitude" is the word I am stressing. Freaks were freaking out and dancing in the audience. The things I have seen, the things I could tell you. I made speeches asking people to sit properly and not to smoke, neck with their girlfriends or sip beer. That does not go with our music. You don't do that with Bach. Some of them listened to me but most – what's the word you use? – copped out.'

Yet no other Indian musician could reach such a wide and young audience, he felt cultural responsibility, while at home he was being, as he puts it, 'put down' for commercialism and sacrilege. Often he stopped in mid-concert and walked off the stage. He told rock audiences that Indian music should be a spiritual experience: 'We have to be clean in mind and body while we play and we can only improvise when our minds are happy and under control.'

Indian classical music is based on *ragas* and *talas*. There are thousands of *ragas*, melodic forms that relate to seasons, times of day, festivals of one kind or another. *Talas* are rhythmic cycles, from three to 108 beats in length. The music is handed down orally and keeps developing. After years of training, the musician begins to improvise, the amount of improvisation depending on his ability. Shankar improvises up to ninety-five per cent of the time. The Indian scale has twelve semitones, like the Western octave, but there are ten extra microtones, used as a pulse and bent much like blue notes in jazz and rock. One *raga* can go on for hours without modulations, monotonous to Western ears. One reason for Shankar's success in the West, but drawing criticism at home, is that he played three or four shortened *ragas* during a two-hour concert. Now that he has accustomed audiences to the Indian sound he plays here almost the way he does at home. Traditional and spontaneous at the same time, Indian music has a unique mixture of spiritual peace and physical excitement. Largely thanks to Shankar, it has had an enormous impact on Western music, particularly jazz.

He was exposed to jazz on his European tours in the thirties. He loved Cab Calloway and Duke Ellington and jazz still moves him but he denies being influenced by it: 'We have an improvisational form called *thumri* which has certain qualities quite close to jazz. I use these often in the West and people tell me I am influenced by jazz. I do not blame them but *thumri* existed long before.'

He taught Don Ellis, Budd Shank, John Handy, Tom Scott, and, just before his death, John Coltrane: 'Coltrane was so serious, studying yoga, a vegetarian, such a gentleman. I taught him the *raga* system, a few ascending and descending structures, the scales, some elemental rhythmic patterns. He came for six days and listened to me play and talk for four hours at a time. Do you know he named his son Ravi?

'But I would like you to mention the fact that I also taught Yehudi Menuhin and Jean-Pierre Rampal; our music is classical music and it is taken seriously by your classical musicians. You know I've gone through three phases. First I brought my country's classical music to the Western classical audience. Then came the second period, the hippies and the guitar explosion. Now that is all over and I have come back to a classical phase, where I really belong. I don't want people to have a preconceived idea that Indian music is like jazz or rock. I want it to be appreciated for what it is.'

So it was surprising to hear Shankar's 'Jazz Mine' fusion, which did not work at all. Comparable to the failure of Third Stream music, it compromised both its sources. More modest morning fusions mined richer veins, John Handy's alto saxophone duet with Kadri Gopalnath for example. Gopalnath discovered the alto sax by accident. He plays compositions meant for *nadaswaran*, an oboe-like double-reed instrument. He had never heard Johnny Hodges or Charlie Parker before pairing with Handy. Born in 1950 in a southern Indian village sixteen miles from Mangalore, he does not even speak Hindi. John Handy was born in Dallas and lives in San Francisco. Their lifestyles are about as different as possible. Yet they 'spoke' to each other through collective improvisation, made each other laugh, communicated.

India. I have neither the desire nor the space to describe the place, and as I said I rarely left my hotel. Trumpeter Ted Curzon (like Handy, with Mingus Dynasty), who grew up in Harlem, literally ran away from the maimed, begging children in the streets. He wanted to go back home to New Jersey right away; only contractual obligations stopped him. His panic was real enough, so much extreme poverty threw him back into remembered personal misery and he could not handle it. He worried so much about dysentery that he once seriously asked a waiter if the chocolate cake had been boiled.

Indians seem to accept their misery with a contentment that makes you wonder about the wisdom of acceptance. Believing in reincarnation, they probably figure they got a bad ticket this time around and can afford to wait for the next. I was driving to the festival with Ted when a man with no legs lying on the sidewalk waved to us with a broad smile that only a millionaire would wear in America. I said to Ted: 'Look at that guy. He isn't freaking out about poverty.'

Ted was not convinced: 'Oh, yeah? He's got no legs. Probably got brain damage too.' So much for mysticism.

The undisputed hit of the festival was Aladar Pege (pronounced Paygay), a Hungarian who can do anything with the bass except eat it. He even resembles a bass. Knepper, the sourpuss moper who approves of so little, had to admit: 'Masters are rare. When you discover a master, it is important to acknowledge him.' Four days in India, and Knepper was talking like a guru's disciple. Knepper and I fronted a rhythm section for my set. I tried getting Pege but he did not have his bass that night and would not play a borrowed one. One hour before hitting time I still had no band. Then Stan Getz's fine young rhythm section arrived, their plane had landed not two hours earlier. I grabbed them and we all decided on a basic, common-denominator repertoire. Knepper insisted on including the 'St Louis Blues', which I thought a bit too common but he insisted. It brought the house down. 'Told you,' Knepper said. 'People love them old favourites.'

A journalist friend of Jhaveri wrote in the *Times* of India: 'Zwerin was a failure as master of ceremonies.'

19
The Festival Shuffle

Olé! Hear the cats kill the aficionados folks. Corridas with soul food. Funky picadors riffing horns. Musician matadors in blood-less bullfights with licks as bulls. Dig that Pass. Give them all ears. *Olé!*

'We cannot get away from the critic's tempers,' wrote George Bernard Shaw, who was a music critic for six years: 'his impatience, his soreness, his friendships, his spite, his enthusiasms, nay his very politics and religion, if they are touched by what he criticizes . . . It should be his point of honour not to conceal them.'

So you should know that I look gift-horses in the mouth. I rarely take yes for an answer. I argue with success. I bite hands that feed me. I have a ray with words. I try to figure out 'what does it all mean?' and 'where are we going?' all the time. You could call me an élitist.

Jazz is élitist music in the sense that it assumes a certain amount of, if not sophistication, intellectual involvement on the part of the listener. The unfortunate fact is that when it gets a mass audience it becomes popular music rather than jazz. No! Please don't. Don't ask me to define jazz. If you insist, Louis Armstrong's famous definition may bear repeating: 'If you have to ask what it is, you'll never understand it.' Jazz is swinging improvisation. (Swing is funky time. Funk is healthy dirt.) *New Yorker* critic Whitney Balliett called it 'The sound of surprise'.

The natural tendency is to play it safe with a mass audience. Next year's gigs are at stake. Lay your sure-fire licks on the masses. Save those slick new sequences you've been woodshedding for some Monday night in the Village. Audiences now applaud after every solo, soloists have come to expect applause. The emperor may put thumbs-down if there is none – off with their heads.

The marriage of jazz with the European tourist industry (and with industry in general) which took place in the seventies is a curious match. The kid just grew up, it happened so quickly we did not even notice, the kid left home and started gigging in the wide wide world. Not to say he got rich. Rich*er* perhaps, but he's out there in any case. Cities and states started to subsidize jazz festivals, national networks shot them, airlines and hotel chains subsidized them. The season grew more crowded, successful and longer. Jazz festivals spread to such places as Warsaw, Bombay, Tokyo and Sydney. But it was born as outlaw music, the secret language of slaves, and though it has become more respectable, its outlaw side is still central, or should be. As Dylan says, 'To live outside the law you must be honest.' Yet there is something about this 'low-brow' music (a Nazi edict proclaimed: 'In places of entertainment in some areas of the Reich, the spread of music pervaded by the Jewish Bolshevik plutocratic infection of nigger jazz has been noticeable') that prompts hundreds of thousands of people to travel thousands of kilometres on their holidays to hear it . . . ordinary people of all ages, including family groups. Part of the appeal is that it is honest, individual expression in an impersonal and cynical time; and it has just the right combination of intellectual content combined with contemporary zap to serve as a bridge between classes, cultures and generations. Am I arguing with success when I question the structural soundness of such a bridge?

Probably, but I'll question it anyway. That famous picture of Jimmy Carter scat-singing 'Salt Peanuts' with Dizzy Gillespie was enough to make an old bebopper throw up. I once saw Charlie Parker throw up, in 1946 on 52nd Street in front of the Onyx Club where he was working. A young trumpet-player named Paul Cohen (who later played lead with Basie) sat down on the curb next to him and delivered a stern lecture on the evils of what had made him throw up. Who did Paul think he was, lecturing *Bird*? I was sixteen, anything Bird did was all right with me.

I grew up on bebop, it was the first intellectual food I found on my own – before Hemingway. It was the first real secret I had from my parents. I never recovered from its anarchism. I still love bebop, I still play it sometimes. I'll never escape its influence.

Barry Harris knocks me out, Pepper Adams thrills me; I love Jimmy Raney, Art Blakey, James Moody. The same night I saw Bird throw up, he played a solo on 'Slow Boat to China' which, in the sense of creating a warm corner that otherwise would not be there, probably changed my life. Bebop remains one of my fondest memories in an otherwise sombre adolescence.

The first thing I liked about bebop was the fact that my father did not like it. He considered it noise, which is what another generation of fathers could consider rock. Such explosions threaten professional grown-ups. Bird and Dizzy transformed standards like 'Indiana' into their most ambitious implications ('Donna Lee'), and studied musicians were forced to study again or be left behind. It was a new order, a revolution. Beboppers screamed at the establishment in furious tempos and were pleased when serious critics belittled such dadaist flagwavers as 'Salt Peanuts'.

History is marked by arbitrary milestones. That photo of Jimmy Carter and Dizzy scatting 'Salt Peanuts' marked the end of certain illusions some of us may have retained about bebop, just as the one of Nixon shaking hands with Mao ended certain illusions about Maoism. I once wrote under the pen-name 'Doctor Jazz' and some readers may think that here is one doctor who does not know how to deal with good health. How can a bebopper complain about a scat-singing President of the United States? If there was such a thing as a bebop lobby, this would mark its finest hour.

Re-examining that photograph, I tuned into a radio programme during which a French bebop purist who considers all subsequent styles heresy introduced an early Miles Davis record by speculating that had Bird lived longer he might have saved Miles from the dreadful electric fate that befell him. It seems clear to me that had Bird lived longer, he would probably have plugged into every electric toy he could lay his hands on when he realized how much it annoyed grown-ups.

Jazz is subversive, or should be. Swing symbolizes individuality. Governments by definition do not swing. Swing is a dance to the unexpected. The unexpected ruins federal programmes and five-year plans.

I played a Stockhausen piece with Alan Silva in Beaubourg

(Centre Georges Pompidou) several years ago. Silva settled in Paris in 1972, intending to stay a season, but one season ran into another and by now he considers himself 'on permanent loan' to Paris. Silva's thirty-piece Celestial Communication Orchestra creates music, which, while formal in the loosest sense of the word – modes, moods, short themes – can explode its boundaries at any time. Anything can happen, the same explosion rarely twice. There are regular last-minute instructions to play themes backwards, upside down, twice as slow or fast, or Alan may just shout: 'Chord!' Any chord, no key, no register, just: 'Chord!' This can lead to confusion, clusters somewhat funkier than normal.

The Stockhausen piece was part of 'Improvisation Week', under the auspicies of IRCAM, a musical research organization run by Pierre Boulez subsidized handsomely by the French Ministry of Culture. It consisted of four sentences which instructed the musicians to find a sound, follow the sound wherever it takes them, and then return to the sound. The same piece was played by a synthesizer group, a contemporary music ensemble, and by us jazzers; one after the other. The idea was to show how different musical backgrounds would handle the same problem.

The other two groups handled it seriously, they were 'good boys'. We had rehearsed it seriously ourselves. When shape was slow in coming, Alan began to panic. He talked about 'my reputation' being at stake. What would Boulez say? At stake were more gigs, perhaps subsidies. But when the concert arrived, instinct surfaced. To hell with your fucking rules. Alan jumped all over the stage screaming at the audience and at us, not in anger but to heighten drama. The piece became extremely theatrical all of a sudden and what we played had very little to do with Stockhausen's rules, which, it must be admitted, were not all that constricting to begin with. We brought down the house with our anarchism, and like it or not nobody walked out on us as they had with the 'good boys'. (An unfavourable review in *Le Monde* said something about rules being made to be followed.) Ron Pittner the drummer shook his head after it was over: 'I had a ball but I guess we can forget about any more gigs from Boulez.' I gave Alan some skin: 'You had me worried for a while.'

Bebop has become institutionalized; expected, formalized. There are no longer too many surprises there. It is too young to be called 'classical' and too old to be contemporary. Looking back, I suppose bebop's terminal coma began with Coltrane's 'Giant Steps', which took chord changes to their ultimate complexity, after which there was no place else to go inside that structure. I can hear screams of outrage. Let me insist. I love Charlie Parker. (Why am I so defensive?) I play his records all the time. I go out of my way to hear Chet Baker and Red Rodney. But when the President of the United States lets his picture be taken singing 'Salt Peanuts', it's time to focus our energy some other place.

Increased institutional attention to jazz is generally considered encouraging. 'More and more funding bodies now regard jazz as a legitimate art-form,' says Charles Alexander of Britain's Jazz Centre Society. The Arts Council of Great Britain earmarks hundreds of thousands for jazz. The respected West German Goethe Institute subsidized the Globe Unity Orchestra concert in Bombay. The Dutch government and municipal authorities in France and Switzerland help out. The Swedish government set up subsidies to provide the country's leading players with life-long stipends. The Moscow Experimental Jazz Studio (Alexei Batashev is one teacher) has more than 200 students, and a waiting-list. Trombonist and educator Jiggs Wigham teaches jazz in the tradition-bound Cologne Conservatory, the first university-level jazz studies chair in West Germany. There are hundreds of university-level jazz degrees offered in the United States. What's going to happen to all these people studying jazz? There's no more bloody work. When Elvin Jones told me there were over 100 students in a drum-clinic he gave in Japan, I asked him about that and he said: 'You don't have to enter the *Tour de France* to enjoy riding a bicycle.'

The Nice festival is (sorry) nice. One nice thing about festivals in general is that a whole bunch of musicians accumulate in one place and a journalist can make a lot of deposits in his bank with a minimum of legwork. Going to the roof-top bar of the Frantel Hotel to interview Zoot Sims, the elevator door opened and I tried to appear nonchalant seeing Cab Calloway and Count Basie in there: 'Going up?'

Zoot had just checked in, downed a few doubles and would soon be moving on to the next town without waiting for a 'thank you masked man'. This particular western hero (born in LA) looked like William Holden in *The Wild Bunch*, a craggy vagabond sticking to his guns despite the fact that pea-shooters are supposed to be out of style. He rides out alone, no fancy waggons to carry his band. He has no band. He hires local hands and chops. Steady bands ask for draws. They have to be fed, the chief must ride herd on them. Too much responsibility for an old cowhand.

'Let's get this thing over with,' he began. Words are not Zoot's medium. There were silences. To fill one up I said something about Herbie Hancock and Donald Byrd going commercial. It was worth not much more than a shrug, and Zoot shrugged: 'I don't know, they do what they want to do. I just go to the club, unpack and nobody says anything. I never had anybody say anything about how I should or shouldn't play.'

He looks dusty, kind of like a bowl of Familia, Alpen, Country Store – one of those health-food cereals that seem dull until you add milk which brings out the taste of the raisins and nuts. Zoot's flavour is brought out by a saxophone. He has broken no stylistic or harmonic barriers, never had a big hit, but fads come and go and he remains more tasty than ever. He just does one thing unpretentiously, fills his own joyful space, his music is underwhelmingly comfortable. Interviewing him was overwhelmingly uncomfortable. I squeezed out a quote: 'I don't make a hell of a lot of money, probably never will. But I don't need anything. If you start wanting Cadillacs and swimming-pools, you're going to have to pay for that shit somehow. I have a nice place in Nyack, it's beautiful up there, only seventeen miles from the George Washington Bridge, and my wife's got a good job.'

Wife's got a job – way to go, Zoot. He likes to keep his days small. He makes perfect structure and goose-pimpled swing seem like small achievements, like he learned them whiling away afternoons in pool parlours. He may have at that; Zoot plays easy like a pool champion makes a triple rebound look easy. Later that night, with a limping rhythm section, this Lone Ranger made 'Tangerine' into a riding demonstration even without his faithful servant Tonto.

After midnight he was back in the bar on the roof of the Frantel. He had just come from two weeks in New Orleans followed by a tour of Japan and would open in Chicago in three days. He hunched over the bar playing dice with the bartender. Imagine all the bartenders he's played dice with. We were supposed to finish the interview but 'Tangerine' was all the information I needed about Zoot Sims. Thank you masked man.

I'd rather play notes than take them. I was in Nice with the New York Jazz Repertory Company (NYJRC), and here I go again looking one more gift horse in the mouth. This band was driving strong men to drink.

George Wein is a fast horse who likes fast tracks. He started the Newport Festival, then 'Kool' Festivals all over America and the Nice Festival in France. The amount of work he generates can be estimated into the millions. Why, then, do you not hear more cats purring over him? Perhaps they resent the fact that he profits from the Concorde while they ride slow jets to a nightly wage. Wein takes risks. He's a smart better but the risks are real; he has taken losses. Jazz musicians take far greater risks in the psychic sense, but our society rewards financial risks with lifetime security, psychological risks are far down the Risker Scale. Wein lives better than most players he hires. He has not made the odds, it's not his fault. A musician (pianist) himself, Wein loves jazz with undeniable passion and he is hip enough to know exactly what was driving strong men to drink.

He called a meeting backstage. Have fun, he said, don't play old notes make new music. Exactly what we'd been saying, but it was lost on our dedicated leader, Dick Hyman. Hyman is a hell of a pianist, a credit to a variety of schools, but no inspirational leader of strong men. His respect for tradition does not include an interest in creating tomorrow's tradition today. Wein founded the NYJRC to preserve classic jazz like symphony orchestras preserve what 'serious' people call 'serious music'. ('Do you play jazz or serious music?') So we played Louis Armstrong, Duke Ellington, Erskine Hawkins, Benny Goodman and early Dizzy Gillespie arrangements as though they were the three Bs. It was a good idea but, as bureaucracies will, form won out over content. A great deal

175

of attention was paid to proper order. We questioned the premise that the music had to be played the way it *was* played, we wanted to play it the way it would have been played had the creators been playing it today. It was a repeat in another context of Gunther Schuller instructing Jerome Richardson to play Darius Milhaud's saxophone solo in 'Creation of the World' with a 'classical sound'. And once more there was no suggestion box, or if there was nobody knew where to find it and in any case it was never opened. This resulted in strong men taking secret nips from pocket flasks. Wein's lecture had tried to change the frame of reference that produced the following rehearsal incident back in New York.

Running down a fifties Ellington classic, trombonist Britt Woodman had trouble sight-reading the written transcription of the original improvised solo. That's right, you got it, we read what had originally been improvised. This is neither swinging nor funky nor Right Respect. After the first read-through, during a moment of silence, Woodman leaned close to the music, inspected it again, and exclaimed: 'Hey! That's *my* solo.' Dig it. He had trouble reading what he had improvised easy as rolling off a B-flat seventh chord. There was a good all-round laugh and after that reading improvised solos was no longer mandatory, but the stance towards old arrangements remained fixed. Wein did not like that mind-set any more than we did. He wanted us to respect the past without being enslaved by it. But lecture or no lecture the slaves remained rowing to a slow cadence down in the galley.

As Guru Knepper said in India, 'People love them old favourites' and the nice people in Nice loved jazz that sounds popular (thus not jazz at all, but let's not quibble). One hundred and thirty thousand people swarmed over the Cimiez Gardens overlooking the city for an eleven-day picnic featuring cotton candy, baby prams, pets, soul food, silver balloons and a choice of three simultaneously running bandstands. Wandering between them, I asked myself who are all these people and why are they having such a good time? Whatever happened to our tight little band? When I started playing jazz in the late forties we were like the Resistance, the Underground. We'd blow up your complacency when you weren't looking. You had to get security clearance before we'd lay our code on you. Digging our redoubts required serious effort. We were proud to be minority music, and our alienation was a badge of courage.

Conducting my own little poll, I wondered what had happened to my music that it could now attract the manager of a Renault agency in Limoges and his computer-programmer son, a Frankfurt stock-jock with his secretary, two female phys-ed teachers from Brussels, three American women who 'simply adore Count Basie', an English rocker casing the broads keeping time with his pocket comb and a bikini-clad golden girl who thinks 'Dizzy Gillespie is sexy blowing out his cheeks like that'. There's not enough suffering here, I thought. It's all too pleasant. Is it possible to play the blues looking at a palm tree? Yet over 200 musicians were being put to work, staying in clean hotels and travelling like businessmen. Isn't that wonderful? Was I being a spoilsport to ask if personal music for the masses wasn't a contradiction? Another spoilsport put it this way: 'Jazz is supposed to be more than some kind of package tour.'

On our first night off I ran into Budd Johnson alone in the hotel bar. This was the first time I'd played with him since the Fatha Hines tour of Russia, fourteen years earlier. He was by now, as Henry James would say: 'of a certain age'. Budd was the 'judge'. Every band has its judge. Budd levelled fines: 'You're late. That'll cost you a jug of vodka for the saxophone section.' Budd had earned his seat on the bench. He studied music with Booker T. Washington's daughter, played with Louis Armstrong and was still strong; slowing down a little, but he drank, smoked and had not lost desire. He's an easy-going man but the road can get to him; this band was getting to him bad and as I arrived he shook a warning finger at me: 'Don't mess with me today. I'm *mean* today.'

Where there's a judge there must be an 'outlaw', and here the role fell to Joe Newman. When there was some music Joe did not like to play, he somehow found a good reason not to be needed: 'But I thought you told me there were only four trumpets.' He tended to disappear just when the bus was about to leave. We once pooled a bet on how close Joe would come to missing the plane. Eleven minutes won. Joe loved to tell about the time he arrived in Japan without a work-permit. They put him on the next plane out, to Seoul, South Korea. He called Tokyo, delighted: 'You'll never guess where I am; in a place called Soul.'

Joe chanted a daily mantra with prayer beads. It's hard to chant prayers with guys passing a jug in the front of the bus, a Clifford Brown cassette blaring two rows behind you and a conversation about the old days in Detroit across the aisle. 'Try it sometime,' he chuckled. His grey-tinged hair and fine features made him look more like a skinny guru than one of the best jazz trumpet-players in the world. Buddhism found him rather than the other way around.

In Japan with Benny Carter's band, he drank quite a bit of champagne one night. The hostess kneeling next to his table kept filling his glass. He likes women and women like him and he wasn't really surprised to find a slip of paper with her name and phone number in his pocket the following morning. He called her, she came to his hotel and: 'We became friends.' This was said without innuendo. The impression is that whatever else happened or did not happen they really did become friends. On the way to the next concert in Tokyo, he and Budd Johnson and George Duvivier had a long conversation about the meaning of life. Joe found a book on Buddhism in his hotel room. He opened it at random and found a passage that was a more lucid version of their conversation, about how life is governed by the forces of the universe. He put it out of his mind. Coincidence. A few days later, seeing him off at the airport, his hostess friend gave him a present of the same book. Odd. He had not discussed it with her. Fine, he thought, something to read on the plane. His New York lady met him on the other end and said that their friend Cynthia had decided to turn Buddhist. Cynthia, who had been in rather bad shape before he had left, was all smile and rosy cheeks when he saw her again. She looked different somehow, there seemed to be a light shining behind her eyes.

A year later I saw Joe in the Patio Bar of the Meridian Hotel in Paris, where he was starring with a local rhythm section. Less than local. Sweating, he wailed more than said: 'These guys are unbelievable. It's killing my chops, I have to press to pull them along. They're uptight, I don't know why. All I want them to do is swing. Simple, man, swing; that's my style. They get so nervous playing with a so-called "star" they can't play at all. I get nervous too; all the time. My hands sweat and my mouth gets dry. But if you want to be in the bigtime you have to learn control. You can't act little-time and expect to be in the bigtime.'

During the next set Joe got into such a loud argument even the people at rear tables could hear him call the drummer a 'fucking asshole'.

Chant, Joe; pray.

Sonny Stitt followed us on one Nice bandstand. Though you always knew what to expect from Sonny, the expected involved such a high degree of personal elegance and musical purity that his tumbling eighth notes became something like a folk form, with that same sort of timelessness you find in the blues. Coming up in the shadow of Charlie Parker, he was called 'Little Bird' and 'New Bird' but: 'I would have played the way I play anyway. I first met Bird in forty-three in Kansas City. I was playing lead alto with Tiny Bradshaw's band. I was only eighteen and two of the guys had promised my mother to look out for me. When I started to go out of the hotel, one of them asked me: "Where you going, kid?" I said: "I'm going to find Charlie Parker." I'd heard two records he made with Jay McShann. I'd always heard cats talk about 18th and Vine so I went and stood on that corner until all of a sudden I saw this guy come out of a drugstore wearing dark glasses and a blue overcoat with white buttons on it carrying an alto and I asked him: "You Charlie Parker?" He grinned, showed that old gold tooth and said: "Yeah. Who are you?" I said I was Sonny Stitt and I played with Tiny Bradshaw and he said: "I heard about you, kid." We went to this place called the Gypsy Tea Room, took out our horns and started to play some blues, just the two of us. He said: "Man, you sound like me." I said: "You sound like *me*." You know, something a dumb kid would say. We had a lot of adventures together, some good some bad.'

Stitt had long alcoholic bouts, and though he was on the waggon for three years, you could sense a certain fatigue, wariness, the withholding of excess: 'I found out you can have just as much fun and play better abstaining. Anyway I got no choice. You want to die? Drink.'

He drained a quart of Evian water while we talked, but it was too late. He died a year later.

Stitt replaced John Coltrane with Miles Davis in the sixties: 'People have Miles mixed up, saying he's a devil. Actually, he's a sweetheart. I don't care what people say about the man, I love Miles Davis. They put him down, saying he's playing rock. He's just playing what he wants to play. Rock comes and goes but jazz is always there. Jazz is easily listened to by the average human being who likes to groove. There are a lot of fine players in the world, people with good minds. It's a sensible sort of music. You got to swing, tell a story, make sense and take some chances. You can run but you can't hide.'

Like Zoot Sims and Joe Newman, Stitt preferred a succession of local rhythm sections to bandleader responsibilities: 'I'm a single, a loner. I like it. I'm a gypsy. My family understands me. I've been married twenty-two years and I send my kids to private schools. Public school's no good any more. Got a daughter ready to start college, have to pay for all that. I watch a lot of TV and play solitaire; they got some fascinating solitaire games. When I'm home and my kids are in school I hang out with my dogs. I have a standard poodle and a toy poodle. The little black one is called Jazz. You can put him in your pocket.'

At forty-one, our youngest member, Arnie Lawrence was not pleased to hit Munich for Wein's festival there. (At fifty, I was second youngest.) Arnie's eyes reflect the *Talmud*. Taken together with his bushy, untrimmed beard, you can be sure the family name was not always Lawrence. His daughter was studying to be a Rabbi. Arnie played with Blood, Sweat and Tears, Chico Hamilton and, for five years, with Doc Severinson's 'Tonight Show' band. His own group, Treasure Island, played a highly personal, emotional form consisting of collective freedom that passed through what he called 'a succession of doors'. His alto saxophone went from Johnny Hodges to Ornette Coleman adjusting to fit the specific 'door' in question; the other musicians passed through in their own good time and space. One of the doors is called 'Prayer' and its Semitic air led one musician to describe it as 'Jewzz'. He had been in Munich one year earlier with Liza Minnelli's orchestra. Before the concert, Liza asked a German attendant for a fruit juice. The attendant poked his head into the musicians' dressing-room, where the shower fixtures were making Arnie think about Auschwitz, and asked: 'Iz der any jooz left in here?'

Arnie, who has a strong Jewish family attachment, had just broken up with his wife. He stared into space, and when I showed him a photograph of Odile and Marcel, then five, he broke into tears. We were on an airplane, the tears were streaming down his cheeks. The stewardess asked if there was something she could do. The music we were playing, or not playing, had something to do with it. Treasure Island was not getting much work, and working with Liza Minnelli or reading old Duke Ellington classics note-for-note are not healing forces. Arnie and I are more or less in the same musical boat; bebop matured us and we both now live with free and fusion jazz. We see no reason to make a stylistic choice, we want music to reflect our *entire* life. Dick Hyman sprung 'Go up and play whatever you like' on us one night. Total freedom is a terrible responsibility and an irresistible challenge at the same time, and though we both knew out-front it was bound to be a lost effort we could not resist trying. Except for bassist George Duvivier, who could not play an insensitive note no matter how hard he tried, the rhythm section did its best to make freedom a laughing matter. Drummer Bobby Rosengarden banged and clashed and Hyman buried us under an eighty-eight-key earth-quake. To them, freedom means noise, they cannot conceive of peaceful abstraction, or chose not to. Arnie looked like he was about to cry again.

The incident set off a continuing discussion – I hesitate to use the word 'argument' but it is not totally inappropriate. The place: the Munich Jazz Festival. The time: the present. The subject: the past. The protagonist: Bob Wilber.

Wearing a white linen suit cut right out of *The Benny Goodman Story*, Wilber was featured with the NYJRC playing 'Sing Sing Sing' on his licorice stick. Rosengarden's tom-toms sounded just like Gene Krupa and Wilber, presto, became the King of Swing in person. He played 'Black and Tan Fantasy' exactly like Barney Bigard, and he could turn into a Sidney Bechet clone rendering 'Petit Fleur' on soprano sax. When he was a young man hanging around 52nd Street, Wilber was sort of adopted by Bechet and ended up moving into his house. He gets work from the growing 'Jazz Society' circle in America. These are professors, officials, businessmen and suburban nostalgics who gather in motel conference rooms Saturday night. He is also big on the jazz party circuit. Millionaires who in olden days would have commissioned portraits of themselves invite twenty-odd musicians and perhaps 200 of their closest friends for a weekend bash. These people are not thrilled by the search for new traditions.

Tradition is the operative word. Wilber's definition is based on the interpretation: 'The sort of swing on which jazz is based is uniquely American.' Which eliminates a lot of Brazilians, Common Marketeers and Orientals: 'I think it's very difficult for anyone who doesn't know American culture to capture the feeling of swing.' Wilber was raised in New York's Grammercy Park, then in Scarsdale. Now he lives in Massachusetts and likes to spend as much time as possible on Cape Cod; there is in fact a good deal of New England gentility about him. He's clean, you could take him anywhere. He knows how to speak to the press, if sometimes pushing too hard. Whitney Balliett described him in the *New Yorker*: 'Wilber has wavy reddish-blond hair and a small pointed face, and wears glasses, and from the tenth row of Carnegie Hall he looks about seventeen or eighteen. Up close, though, his face reveals miniature signs of wear and his hair is misted with grey . . . He is a small man but he stands with his legs planted wide apart when he plays . . . His manner gives pause to frivolity.'

Many of the adolescents who played jazz in the thirties and forties were frivolous iconoclasts from white middle-class families. Jazz was one way to escape the bourgeois values of their parents. They worked their way through good schools in 'traditional' bands, then became lawyers or brokers. Some went 'wrong', like Roswell Rudd, choosing a messier creative road. We are talking about the white bourgeoisie of course, and when I suggested that perhaps the sort of swing on which jazz is based is uniquely *Afro*-American, Wilber exclaimed: 'That's crazy!'

We were waiting backstage in Munich to follow the trombonist Albert Mangelsdorff. Actually, 'trombonist' is an insufficient adjective to describe him. The trombone never sounded like that before and it will never be the same again. He reinvented the instrument through extensive use of multiphonics, playing one note while singing another. If both notes are in tune, if the sound system is good enough, the acoustics right, if God be willing, a third note is produced through sympathetic vibrations. When this happens Mangelsdorff can play all three parts of Duke Ellington's 'Mood Indigo' by himself.

'It's not jazz. It doesn't swing,' Wilber complained. 'I don't hear the blues in there anywhere.'

'Are you kidding? I hear the blues in every note,' I said.

Wilber was in the process of sorting out some parts at the time, while discussing filing systems with cornettist Dick Sudhalter, who was also the band's librarian (and is jazz critic for the *New York Post*). I must have been furious: 'It might help you to hear if you stopped talking.' I told Wilber then and though he denied it I still think he was really pissed off about a *German* having the nerve to consider himself a jazz musician. Many young trombonists now include multiphonics in their repertoire. Wilber called it a 'gimmick'.

Later I told that to Mangelsdorff and he smiled: 'A gimmick is supposed to be something made easy. This is much too hard to do to be a gimmick. Multiphonics has attracted attention, I suppose, but sometimes it seems like I only really got into music seriously after I began to work with it.' 'Euro-Jazz' is a pejorative term for many American musicians who consider Europeans too intellectual, too conservatory-trained, not funky enough. Mangelsdorff is often the negative example cited. He finds this odd because: 'Whatever I do I want to swing. Swing is a specifically distinct rhythmic intensity. I grew up with bebop and I listen to Sonny Rollins (he records with Elvin Jones) and I believe you have to deal with swing and the blues if you want to remain a jazz musician.'

A definition quite close to Wilber's, but Wilber could not figure out how someone like myself, apparently normal in other respects, could consider Mangelsdorff's 'noises' music. When the houselights came up for the intermission and the sound system carried 'Every Tub' by Count Basie, Wilber sighed: 'A sound for sore ears.'

Nice, Ravenna, San Remo, Milan, Munich, London, The Hague . . . it was like one of those old-time Hollywood movies with calendar pages flying into the past over a montage of buses, planes, nervous impresarios and applauding audiences. Cut to the lobby of the Bel Air Hotel in The Hague; Northsea jazz festival weekend. Besides an

183

unmatched concentration of over 600 musicians performing in three days, what sets the Northsea apart from other festivals is that all of them stay in the same hotel, next door to the convention centre where they perform. It's like a convention itself, with musicians milling and backslapping with ear-splitting smiles. Overheard in the Bel Air lobby: 'This guy gives a strong sleeping-pill to a friend who has insomnia. The next morning he asks how it worked. The friend says he decided not to take it after all. The guy says: "A wilful waste comes to a woeful want. Think of all the sleepy children in India." '

Although drugs no longer play a major role in the world of jazz, drug humour does. Also overheard in the Bel Air: 'This cat has a headache and he's sitting in a restaurant with five codeine pills on the table, trying to get the waiter's attention; he complains: "If I don't have a glass of water soon, my headache will go away." '

Another eavesdrop: 'There's a guy who has a rare disease that can only be cured by eating human brains. His doctor sends him to a special butcher. The man is a bit shy about it but the butcher says not to be and takes him into a back room and points to a tray: "These are lawyers' brains, they cost $30 a pound. Over here we have doctors' brains, $50 a pound." The patient says: "That's pretty expensive. What about those over there?" "I'm afraid those are even more expensive," the butcher replies. "$200 a pound. They're jazz musicians' brains." The patient looks confused: "Why are they so expensive?" The butcher explains: "You know how many jazz musicians it takes to make a pound of brains?" '

Paul Acket, who produces the Northsea festival, said that if he ever retires from his official responsibilities he'd like to spend the weekend just sitting in the Bel Air lobby. In the meantime, he had hands full co-ordinating all those musicians with over 30,000 listeners in three days. There was a choice of ten events for ten hours a day, plus video jazz, jazz films, and stands selling jazz books, records, t-shirts and a variety of consumables. This festival has been criticized by some spoilsports (not me, I love it) as a 'supermarket'. Acket, a soft-spoken grey-haired gentleman, responded: 'Nobody forces you to go to all the concerts. You can take your pick. But I always say that with the Northsea festival you either love it or you hate it. There's no middle way.' It is subsidized by the city of The Hague and the Dutch government. The Dutch

Tourist Office calls it one of their top three draws of the year. 'It's a social happening,' said Acket, 'an evening out. I'm sure that a lot of people who come don't even own jazz records. They come for the party. But then I wouldn't be surprised if they buy a couple afterwards.'

It would probably take less space to list who wasn't playing all these festivals than who was. Europe was swarming with jazzmen from June till August. You could hardly pass through a railroad station or an airport without stumbling over some improviser and his case. Why is that man smiling?

Re-reading the negativity that began this chapter, I was appalled. Do I really feel that negative? Probably not. I considered rewriting it but then decided, let it be. The exploration of emotion in public is a jazz musician's business. So if I wind up more positive than I began, pretend I ended this blues on a high note.

Olé!

20
The Expatriate March

It must have been preordained: an Afro-American named James Reese Europe would bring jazz to Europe.

Before the First World War, Europe ran a booking agency in New York that provided an assortment of black orchestras which could play cakewalks, work songs, comedy numbers, foxtrots, marches and excerpts from the classics. Drafted into the New York Black regiment, he was ordered by the colonel to: 'form the best damned brass band in the US army'.

Europe hired the famous tap dancer Bill Bojangles Robinson as drum-major and sent scouts as far as Puerto Rico to find the right clarinet-player. The band was called the Hellfighters, actually more of a marching than jazz band, when they played in France, old peasant women broke into dances that resembled Walkin' the Dog. Dignified French officers found their toes tapping. German prisoners of war smiled as though they were free.

Lieutenant Tim Brymn's 350th Artillery Corps Band, the 'Seventy Black Devils', created a sensation playing for President Wilson at the peace conference. Lieutenant Will Vodery's band was described by one listener as 'the jazziest, craziest, best-tooting outfit in France'.

Jazz emerged out of the ruins of war; fresh, contemporary, cocky, iconoclastic. The Establishment hated it. The world had barely escaped Establishment-induced Armageddon. Jazz symbolized the general feeling that from now on everything was going to be different.

When the first black musicians toured Europe in the post-war years, it was like the wild west to them. Unexplored territory, romantic, an adventure, a new frontier. They were evangelists, pioneers, and the natives were friendly. Their music, condescended to in the States, was accepted as an art-form and their colour was an advantage rather than a handicap. In his book *Jazz away from Home*, Chris Goddard tells of a black pianist named Elliot Carpenter who, when approached to form a band for a new Paris nightclub in 1920, was sceptical about the enthusiastic stories he'd heard. Opal Cooper and Sammy Richardson had been to Paris, he asked them if they wanted to go back. 'My God, yes!' Cooper said. They told him about the beautiful city and the respect their music received there, and about all the beautiful women who adored jazz musicians: 'Yeah, man, let's go back.' Carpenter reminded them that they had not discussed money yet. Richardson shrugged: 'The hell with that. Let's just get back to Paris.'

Settlers arrived in the twenties. Arthur Briggs and Bill Coleman integrated themselves into French society. Coleman Hawkins became a continental star, Sidney Bechet a French hero. They all returned to the States when the Second World War began (except Briggs, who was interned but survived). The migration, multiracial this time, resumed when it was over.

Guitarist Jimmy Gourley left Chicago, where he had been lost in the crowd, came to Paris in the early fifties and found himself in demand all of a sudden. Adequate European rhythm sections were still rare. He couldn't believe 'all the heavy cats I was playing with all of a sudden'.

One heavy cat, pianist Bud Powell, who was down and out in Paris, eventually came under the wing of Francis Paudras, the kind of dedicated jazz fan only France can produce. There were those who called Paudras a 'super groupie', or accused him of riding on the back of jazz to make a name. Photographer, publisher, amateur pianist in the Bill Evans vein, Paudras says: 'In a sense I was Bud's lover. He came to France because he thought he might be treated like a human being here. As a child his parents told him to play piano and not worry about other things. Then everyone told him he was irresponsible. Oscar Goodstein, who ran Birdland, hired a woman called Buttercup as his guardian. She collected Bud's money and gave him a sort of allowance. He needed her permission to come and visit me. I used to see him on Boulevard St Germain begging like a bum for money to buy a drink. This was one of the musical geniuses of the twentieth century, but he was treated like a crazy man, a freak. Buttercup called me for help once after Bud had passed out drunk and been taken by the police to a hospital. I invited him to live with my wife and I. He said: "You'll have to ask Buttercup." She said OK as long as she went on collecting the money. For about seven months he hardly spoke to us except to ask for the butter or something. A psychiatrist friend of mine said Bud was a classic example of schizophrenia. We would eat in complete silence, other times he'd stay in his room. Then one day I exploded: "Bud, you've got to understand we love you, but we can't help you because you won't say anything. You have to try and communicate." I must have moved him because he took my hand and he looked at my wife and me and said: "Do you love me, really?" We said: "Of course we do." He stopped drinking for six months after that. One night we went to hear Ray Charles. Backstage Bud said to him: "Hey, Ray, it's Bud Powell." They shook hands. Then Bud said: "Ray, you're blind." He went right to the heart of the matter, just like a child. Ray didn't know how to handle it. He mumbled: "Nah nah." Right away Bud's face changed: "Well you look blind." Bud was house pianist at the Blue Note, with Jimmy Gourley, Kenny Clarke and (bassist) Pierre Michelot. The club had been more or less created for Bud. One day I told the owner, Ben Benjamin, to pay Bud directly. I was trying to rebuild a man, trying to make him take his life into his own hands. Everybody found it normal that Buttercup took his money. So they paid him directly for the first time and called a taxi to take him home. They had always paid the driver before leaving, now Bud would have to pay himself. The club called to tell me he had left. I waited, very nervous, until I heard the taxi pull up in front of my house. He was so happy to have his own money. He went out and bought us steak and then kept asking if it was good, as if he was the host. We didn't have very much money then and it was unusual for us to eat steak. Bud said: "You think I'm stupid? You think I can't see you need money?" Then he started to cry. Everybody in the house started to cry. One night our psychiatrist friend who had called Bud schizophrenic came to dinner with her husband and daughter. Her daughter was studying piano. She didn't want to play but Bud convinced her. He told her everybody is afraid, he encouraged her and they played four hands together. Before my psychiatrist friend left, she said to me: "I don't like thinking I could have been so wrong, but I've never seen anybody less crazy than Bud Powell." Bud had tuberculosis and he was in a hospital for a year. He had no insurance. I paid the bills, $50 a day. It took me three years to pay it off. By that time Bud had gone back to the States and died, of malnutrition. I had problems with my in-laws because a black man was living in my house. It was scandalous. Bud Powell was a distinguished person. I consider his music on the same level as Ravel.'

Although an extreme example, this sort of context attracted black musicians to Europe. Kenny Clarke, the father of bebop drumming, first came over with the Edgar Hayes Blue Rhythm Band in 1937, before bebop was born. They played Brussels and then Klook, as he is known: 'just came down to see what Paris was like. I liked it right away. Hell, I even liked Brussels.'

Klook, who was born in 1914, has been living in France so long he can laugh about liking Brussels. The French tell Belgian jokes, which are like Polish jokes. He settled here in the fifties because he wanted a certain quality of life. It was not a matter of money. On the contrary, he had been busy in New York and was running away from the high psychic price money extracts. Klook realized something was seriously wrong when he found himself hiding from Miles Davis, who was offering him work: 'Miles knocked twice on my door so I told the little girl I was with to tell him I was out. He just kept knocking: "Klook Klook, I know you're in there." I just didn't feel like going on that gig. I'd been recording for Savoy Records every day. I was just tired, man, tired. I met Michel Legrand, who was touring with Maurice Chevalier, and I told him how tired I was of New York. He said he could get me on his uncle Jacques Helian's band, "a real jazz band" he called it. I was ready. The following September Helian sent me a first-class ticket on the *Liberté* and I sailed with everything I owned.'

Before leaving, he had recorded with the Modern Jazz Quartet on their first album. The MJQ turned out to be extremely successful, but Klook never regretted leaving that gold mine just before it panned out: 'Never, not for a minute. Well I've thought about that; people say, "Klook, you should have stayed there and made all that money." But money's only good when you need it.'

He has nothing against money. Known to be a hard negotiator, Klook has done well enough in Europe, but he is someone who follows his own inclinations, who wants to take music and life on his own terms. In the late thirties he got tired of playing like Jo Jones – boom boom boom boom on the bass drum. He took the main beat away from the foot and put it up on the ride cymbal. The beat became lighter. The bass drum merely served to kick accents, 'dropping bombs' it was called. In 1940 Teddy Hill fired Klook for dropping bombs with his big band. But one year later, Hill asked him to organize a band for Minton's, a club he was managing on 118th Street in Harlem. Klook hired the eccentric and then unknown pianist Thelonious Monk, and so bebop was born.

Following your own inclinations can be unpopular. This was not a terribly popular thing for a black man to say in 1972, when Klook told fellow drummer Arthur Taylor (for his book *Notes and Tones*): 'To organize you must be organized within yourself first. Because otherwise it turns out like the trade unions, in other words gangsterism. The Black Panthers, for example, that's all gangsterism.' And, commenting on the Afro hair-do craze: 'I think it's a whole lot of needless work. The time it takes to keep their hair in an Afro could be better spent reading.'

In the early seventies, when big bands were about as dead as they would ever be, Klook co-led, with Belgian pianist/arranger Francy Boland, an all-star American and European aggregation that created some of the fattest, most creative big-band music ever. But more important than music, Europe provided Klook with essential perspective: 'If music can help me along the road, so much the better. There's a difference in the mentality here, the social mentality for one thing. People are not afraid to walk in their neighbourhood, to become friends; socially you feel adjusted. I've been lucky. I found a little house in Montreuil (a Paris suburb) about four years after I got here. Things were going good so I just bought it. And when I bought the house, I said to myself: "Well here I am. This is home." '

Steve Lacy, who has been called 'Off-season Charlie', says: 'I don't like to be in a crowd. There are too many cats in New York.' He left New York in the late sixties, starved in Rome, was stranded in Buenos Aires and apartment-sat in Paris (Victor's place). Lacy is an illustration of the fact that following your own discriminations can pay off, even though paying off in the back-alley world of jazz means what normal people take for granted, making a living. He stuck to his own vision through thick and thin, mostly thin, playing the soprano saxophone while it was so out of favour; when there was not even a category for it in the *Down Beat* magazine poll.

During the fifties, Sidney Bechet faded into obscurity, along with dixieland, and only minor figures continued to play old material on the instrument. Lacy recorded with the early formations of Cecil Taylor and Gil Evans and formed a quartet with Roswell Rudd that played Thelonious Monk (who was himself 'off-season' at the time) tunes exclusively. John Coltrane came to hear them at the Five Spot on the Bowery. It is generally acknowledged that Lacy influenced Trane to pick up the soprano and bring the instrument into the vogue it now enjoys. A key to Lacy's personality is that he give the impression of continuing to play soprano *despite* its popularity. It is notoriously difficult to play, with a freak set of overtones and treacherous spots all over the horn. Lacy describes it as being like 'a hysterical woman. You can't control it. You try and calm it down and make it do what you want it to do, but it wants to do something else. It tends to go its own way if you're not careful.'

He has arrived at a personal style that is at once rooted in the past and points to the future. The following definition defines the breadth of his conception: 'A jazz musician is a combination orator, singer, dancer, diplomat, poet, dialectician, mathematician, athlete, entertainer, educator, student, comedian, artist, seducer and general all-around good fellow.'

The breadth involves a desire for greater knowledge of the world. Americans are provincial, though ironically American jazz musicians tend to consider Europe the provinces. Despite the fact that he now wins the *Down Beat* critics' poll, you sometimes hear New Yorkers ask: 'Whatever happened to Steve Lacy?'

Barre Phillips saw no contradiction between being an avant-garde bassist and living in the ruins of an eleventh-century village north of Toulon with neither electricity nor telephone. 'It's that old California feeling,' he smiled, pointing down the hill, 'that old road was built by the Romans. It's mind-blowing to think how many years those stones have been walked on. You wonder about all those people – serfs, crusaders, kings, troubadors. Last week Charlie Mariano walked down there playing his saxophone.'

The late Mezz Mezzrow liked Paris because: 'You can live your own life the way you wish and nobody bothers you.'

A French woman, Dutch plates on the car, a Danish record company, a Swiss agent and plenty of gigs in Germany; it's tailor-made. Tamed as they may seem these days, teaching in universities and concertizing in major halls, jazz musicians retain their outlaw side and Europe still appeals to it. You can duck here, the computer and the tax-collector have trouble tracking you down. It has become something of a tradition, something somehow necessary at some point in a career. The Art Ensemble of Chicago, Ben Webster, Don Byas, Anthony Braxton, Dexter Gordon, Johnny Griffin and Arthur Taylor all spent many years living in Europe. They have in common a tendency to be more open to non-musical experience, to be more interested and interesting than average. But a commitment to Europe is sort of like moving to Las Vegas. There are flickers of doubt – am I only here because I'm not good enough for New York?

New York is the jazz capital of the world – the big time, the trends are still made there and most best players live there. When you leave, those who remain say you weren't tough enough to cut New York. You are considered second-rate. A deserter. They do not wish you well. If you succeed elsewhere, then they are forced to question the wisdom of remaining there. They have a stake in your failure. If you should be forced to come back one day, unless you are a star like Dexter Gordon, you will not be greeted with open arms. You will be made to pay heavier dues than usual to atone for having jumped the sinking ship. And now, dear reader, this story becomes, if not tragic, something of a downer.

The golden age of expatriatism is over. American jazz musicians are no longer automatically welcomed by Europeans. We are considered carpetbaggers rather than evangelists. Inflation has crippled our lifestyle and the competition has become both tougher and less friendly. The level of musicianship has improved to the point where many Europeans are now world-class. They resent the heavy flow of one-way traffic from America. Few French musicians are hired by major French festivals for example, and they almost never tour the States. Yet we exiles are in exactly the same position, we too are taken for granted in France and unknown in the States. A worse position. We have nobody but ourselves to complain to and are not eligible for what meagre subsidies the French government disburses for jazz. We have no lobby; who cares about a few lost jazz musicians? It's worse yet for white expatriates.

The French basically do not believe white people (except French white people) can play jazz. I once overheard two Frenchmen discuss a concert one of them had attended. 'Who was on piano?' '*Sais pas. Un blanc.*' The name doesn't matter, the colour was wrong. Case dismissed.

Sugar Blue arrived in Paris in the late seventies and busked in the metro until Mick Jagger hired him to play harp on the Stones album *Some Girls*. Sugar made his first album as a leader in France. Though happy about the respect the French accord the blues, he is not unaware of social context: 'It's easy for the French to like the blues. They don't have to deal with the reality of twenty million American blacks. Here they have Arabs, and they treat the Arabs and their music just like Americans treat blacks and the blues. Neither the French nor the Americans want to know about their racial minorities' culture on a down-home level.'

The first night of my first visit to Paris in 1958, I checked into the Crystal Hotel and before even unpacking went out with my horn to the caves. I thought about Sartre, Boris Vian, Django Reinhardt, Jean Cocteau. The jazz caves of Paris have a certain romantic image back home, an image that becomes clouded once you spend some time in their pissy, alcoholic, unventilated air. But the image was untinged that first night when I passed a sign in the window of Le Chameleon announcing: 'Allen Eager'. I walked down into that damp cellar with goose bumps and a fluttering heart, walking into history. I asked Allen if I could sit in, he said sure and three hours after arriving in Paris I was already playing jazz. I fell in love with Paris that night, the old Hemingway cliché, walked all over the place for hours, wrote letters in cafés. It did not bother me when I asked for a mineral water in embryonic French and the waiter answered by telling me the time. I knew he had *chosen* not to understand me, speaking French with an accent is considered a laughing matter rather than a good try. I also knew, though, that this city was for me. I loved the grey winters, the illogical tangle of streets, buying cheese in a cheese store and meat from a butcher rather than supermarkets. I made up my mind to come back one day to live. I have now lived in France for thirteen years. The expatriate life agrees with me. Amsterdam and Zurich are an hour's flight away, no comparison to Cleveland and Baltimore. One hour away there's another language, another currency, different food, a new mentality to learn to cope with. Keeps you on your toes. There's a comforting unreality about living in a country that is not your own. You can at least pretend to be less alienated living in the midst of somebody else's alienation.

We Americans here share our alienated alienation, and it brings us together regardless of race, creed or colour. Not that we constitute a close-knit community, we are not in fact very communal. But we are exposed, raw, vulnerable – let's be blunt, lonely over here and we share the European exile experience with those with similar stances. It controls our lives more than where you were born or your colour. Over here we are, ironically, all of a sudden very American; it stands out, we cannot escape it, we re-examine it, and if we finally choose to reject America for a decade or two perhaps that is because we love it too much to cope with its decline. It is becoming more and more difficult to tell La Defense near Paris apart from, say, Dallas. There are no illusions, we have not left America as much as helped bring it to Europe. We may even be cultural imperialists. There is, however, still an inch of difference between value-systems on the two continents. You can be considered a success in Paris without being rich if you have a happy family or do interesting work. It's the inch I live in.

But after a while you begin to wonder if your alienation is perhaps doubled rather than eliminated; you are alien in two places. The French do not enjoy the reputation of being friendly. They are not known for saying 'Have a nice day' to foreigners. A foreigner is anyone who speaks French with an accent, or God forbid, does not speak it at all. (On the other hand resentment of Americans who live here ten years and speak barely enough French to order a meal, not unusual, is understandable.) I speak sloppy, accented but fluent French, I have a French wife, my seven-year-old son corrects my French, I pay French taxes and my teeth have been ruined by French dentists but a foreigner I remain. I will always remain a foreigner.

I formed a drumless trio called 'Not Much Noise' with a texture modelled after the fifties trio of Jim Hall, Jimmy Giuffre and Bob Brookmeyer. Christian Escoudé, guitar, and bassist Alby Cullaz soon formed a chique. A two-man clique in a trio means trouble. We played a festival in Ivrea, Italy. I discovered a year later that the two of them had made a duo record there. The trio broke up shortly thereafter. How could they have done that without me knowing, and worse, why? I assumed it was because I was American, not in their clique, a foreigner. Then I began to suspect a more disconcerting reason; they did not like my playing. I have recorded with Eric Dolphy, John Lewis, Jimmy Garrison, Archie Shepp and Thad Jones, to name a few. How could I be good enough for them in New York and not good enough for Escoudé and Cullaz? Maybe I'd lost it. Maybe the unfriendly atmosphere contributed to my losing it. Obviously there was something other than music involved. Ever since then I've hired Americans whenever possible. I had a quartet with four nice young Frenchmen (the young are not yet bitter) for a while. Producing a concert series for the American Center, a cultural foundation, I avoid hiring the French. My trade with them is monumentally out of balance in their favour. I have become a protectionist. Buy American is my motto, 'fucking Frog' my refrain. It's not my fault, it's survival. The French consider me a complainer.

A few years ago a Parisian club offered a programme called 'Forty French musicians in fifty-five days'. The club generally booked touring Americans and the idea was to give local musicians a chance. Admirable. The problem was the definition of local – anybody with a French name. I was appalled by such blatant discrimination. Why not also divide people by race or sex? It's the same thought-process. Being an American in Paris, I was excluded from the club's normal policy as well as its exception. It seems I was excluded everywhere from everything. I grew morose during the fifty-five days of French jazz. I thought . . . Hey, what about me? I live here too. I like to play too. We're *neighbours*.

The French and American jazz communities in Paris are anything but neighbourly. They rarely play together or even attend each other's concerts. Language plays a part in that. Americans have trouble learning French. It took me five years to stop saying '*Je suis fini*' (meaning 'I'm all washed up' or 'I'm dead' rather than the intended 'I've finished', '*j'ai fini*') after washing the dishes. On the other hand French musicians are reluctant to use their English for patriotic and cultural reasons. You might call it a communications breakdown.

The Dutch have a system that provides subsidies to jazz musicians who are 'Dutch citizens or residents'. 'Resident' is defined as someone who has settled in Holland more or less indefinitely. It is not a question of papers or official sanction. If you have rented an apartment and are living with a Dutch woman you obviously intend to stay a while. This is jazz not banking, after all. We all live outside the law, even if only in our head, to some degree or other, or should if we're serious about playing this music. Burton Greene, Wilbur Little and Irv Rochlin benefit from Dutch subsidies as much as Hans Dulfer and Martin van Duynhoven. Rochlin tells the story of how he was playing with a Dutch band one night and the leader made an announcement to the effect that they were now going to prove that the Dutch could play jazz as well as Americans. The band broke up laughing looking at Rochlin, who was flattered: 'I'd been living here fifteen years. This guy obviously considered me Dutch. They make you feel wanted here.'

Many American expatriates prefer Holland, Germany or Scandinavia, where the weather may be lousy but they feel welcome. English is widely spoken and everything works in those places. In France there's always some sort of social disorder. The French have a secret love affair with disorder; they call it a '*bordel*'. '*Quel bordel!*' Odile exclaimed joyfully when leftist students jumped on-stage to disrupt a concert protesting what they considered outrageous ticket-prices. This instinctive anarchist streak is one of their more endearing traits – one reason, now that I think of it, why the French make good jazz musicians, and why I continue to live among them.

21
The Long-Distance Jump

I've started this chapter several times but it got either too maudlin or intellectual, I could not stand reading let alone writing it so I'm trying to bang it out fast like a letter to be rid of the willies once and for all. Shook by the willies, reduced to a blithering lump by the willies. The Willies, capitalized.

The Willies arrived in force after adventure-induced destability. Destabilization is perhaps a small enough price to pay for adventure (it is basic to adventure, after all), but it wasn't my adventure. At least at first. First there was the shock of recognition. I had been so smugly mature, strong, under control, feeling more complete with advancing age – cool, cooler, coolest – until the bridge lowered, the boom. Boom! Dumped on.

Enjoying an absolutely astonishing late-thirties blossom – yoga-hardened curves, misty mobile eyes, a smooth funky lope, God knows where she found it – friendly-thighed Odile made up her mind (once made up it stays made) to find a lover. '*Ça swing pas assez ici,*' she said, fair warning unheeded. How could I know that her swing was about to toss all my fine-feathered 'jealousy is negative energy, everybody should be free to do what they like with their own body' talk through my fine-feathered panic-bar. Blind panic, white fear. 'Mike, I found a lover,' she whispered. In bed. Words spoken with hushed reverence. This was obviously no one-night stand but a real occasion. She had to tell me, she could not lie to me. It was also an unconscious brag, she had the offensive. *Voilà!* I was a victim. I'd rather she had lied, said she needed extensive dental work. Same thing anyway, one drilling or another.

Adventure was not unlike me, a journalist; played piano yet. He had an important editing job on a big daily paper, financial security, and I knew how my hairy freelancing unsecured Odile. Actually it was going well, my phone was ringing, but Adventure was French, another point for him. And he was new. 'Please don't leave me,' I pleaded, a classic case of self-created disaster. Verbalize something and it immediately becomes an objective fact, something to deal with. Expressing the possibility only served to reduce my odds. The thought had never occurred to her, it was an adventure. I tried fixing the odds by a stab at liberation: 'Is he on top or the bottom?' What she said then was not as funny as it may read now: 'I hope you're happy, I couldn't come.' Yes I was happy, but if I really love her why? Ought her frustration to please me? I should wish her to come every time so long as I remain number one comer, as it were. It was no joke, believe me, I had trouble following her advice: 'Try to keep your sense of humour.'

Marcel was ready to study piano. It so happened 'A' knew a teacher. I went to see him. 'So you're a friend of "A"'s,' he said pleasantly.

'Actually, he's a friend of my wife.' I civilized my face. The teacher seemed just fine and we set a date for the first lesson. He would come to our apartment. Late that night, very late, the gremlins spoke to me and in the morning I told her: 'I don't want "A"'s teacher. I don't want "A" in my house. He's already in my wife.'

She groaned: 'You certainly are making life complicated.'

'You told me to keep my sense of humour. I thought that was a pretty funny line there.' Then the indecency of it struck me: '*I'm* making life complicated?!'

She suggested I go out and find 'a nice girl, but not too nice'. I was writing this book, articles, playing music; I had neither energy nor need for another woman (though I did find a nice brief affair). Odile and I began making love more often, and better. Passion bequeaths passion. After eleven years, our passion was apparently still renewable. The, excuse the expression, hot breath of competition may have had something to do with it. We talked about all this and drew closer. For our own reasons – me to win her back, her to reassure me – we worked harder at the relationship. But while we had both taken occasional lovers before, it was never while in the same city. I was popping Valium like bon-bons. Even stuck in the victim role, I knew deep-down that the only way to come out of this situation alive was to let adventure run its course. There was no choice anyway, she was hell-bent on it. The only possibility of permanent damage came from my jealous and useless nagging. I suppose all nagging is useless by definition, but I double-nagged. I sighed, panted, cringed, wrung my hands. One defeat promises others. With defeat in the air, I wrote an article that was far from the style of the expensive house written for. I wrote it anyway. My style is better than your style. Being stuck in a dull house-style is your problem not mine so fuck you. You can imagine just who got fucked.

Defeat was more than in the air. It was all over my face. Even Count Basie noticed it: 'You seem to be expecting bad things to happen,' he told me.

Born in Red Bank, New Jersey, in 1904 Bill Basie replaced Fats Waller with 'Liza and her Shuffling Sextet', toured Oklahoma with Gonzelle White on the Keith circuit, and took over Walter Page's Blue Devils in Kansas City. Jazz thrived under Boss Pendergast's political machine in the wide-open after-hours Kansas City of the thirties. I asked Basie to talk about it.

'I'd like to but I can't,' he said; 'You see I'm writing a book about my life and there are a lot of things I won't be able to tell you. We'll have to do a lot of curving.'

'What's it like leading a big band for over fifty years?'

'What do you mean what's it like?'

'Do you still enjoy it?'

'Of course. If I didn't have a band I'd be washing dishes. What else is there to do?'

I was beginning to feel pushed: 'Other people form combos or move to Vegas. There are alternatives.'

'Maybe for some people. Not for me.'

(Could she be doing *that* with *him*; *now*?) I tried the best I could: 'What was Lester Young like when he joined your band?'

'The same as always. Lester never changed.' Flat statement. Period. Silence.

Silence is Basie's medium. He says 'One more time' in a voice that sounds like a brass section in bucket mutes and his roaring pneumatic machine breaks into the coda of 'April in Paris' again, but the part we remember is the space between the notes.

He looks like his sound – somehow fat and lean, clean and funky, black and grey, quiet and loud, serious and funny at the same time. Once I might have added 'slow and fast', but he's definitely slow now. Seventy-eight, he walks with a cane. He undergoes therapy for arthritis in his Bahamas home. Arthritis is a serious ailment for a bandleader who wants to keep moving, worse for a piano-player.

Fortunately Basie has never moved his fingers very much. Space has always been his main material. With Miles and Monk, he is a master of minimalist jazz. Sitting at the keyboard in front of his powerhouse, dropping the essential plink here and perfectly placed plunk there, he seems to be doing nothing and yet it becomes everything. The music implodes around him like the eye of a hurricane.

There was a storm brewing. I was already pushed to the limit. It was getting too heavy, or rather too light. I said: 'You know you shouldn't be afraid to tell me things that will be in your book because . . .'

'I'm not afraid to tell you, I'm just not going to tell you.'

My face got red.

'Now don't go getting red in the face.'

I got up to leave: 'Let's just forget it.'

He looked at me and hung his mouth open: 'Well you must be kidding. You're the first journalist that ever acted that way with me.'

'I'm not like other journalists.'

'You're wrong,' he said. 'Come on, sit down. I just said that I can't tell you and you took offence.'

'That's right, I took offence.' I sat down.

'That's where you were wrong. You should have asked me another question and come back to it. I would have answered you. First of all, you must always be looking for something like that to happen. If that's your attitude, any little thing is likely to get to you. Just be happy all the time. Don't look for reasons to be unhappy. I don't – ever. That's the reason all down through my life, no matter what went wrong, I always felt all right. That way nobody nowhere on earth can ever offend you. Because I try to get along with everybody and everything.'

'OK. What was Kansas City like in the thirties?'

He laughed: 'I can see that you're going to fool around and try and trick me into telling you anyway. I can see that.'

It was time to disappear for a while. Even through the willies I could see I was losing touch with reality. The willies were about ending up old, cold and alone on a park bench. The willies, plural. One little willie had none.

Not run away. Never leave your territory undefended, unless of course you have another territory to fall back on. Crass, perhaps, but practical advice. Don't surrender under fire. Retreat to gather strength, orchestrate a manoeuvre. Someone in San Francisco had proposed a possible screenplay but I was told the possibility no longer existed. A country house had been offered for the purpose of writing this book, but willies multiply alone in the country.

Then my lucky star appeared. We all have lucky stars, the problem is recognizing and following it quickly enough. Lucky stars are to be pounced on. This time my star did not even wear a disguise. It was a star – Jean-Louis Aubert, lead singer and song-writer with the number one French rock group Telephone. I interviewed him, we chatted. I said I played trombone. Just-like-that, as if every rock band is in dire need of one, he said: 'We're looking for a trombone-player. How would you like to visit France with a rock band?'

Just-like-that, I heard myself answer: 'Sure. I need a change of air.'

How did he know I wasn't some *schmuck* who played dixieland Saturday nights with ad-agency stompers? How did I know he wasn't one more spaced-out rocker? He has a strong, intelligent face and sparkling eyes. He saw me, I saw him. Had I questioned it, said I'd think about it and call him tomorrow, the star would have vanished. In the five seconds it took me to answer, my muse had been beeping . . . chapter chapter chapter.

Presto! I was no longer a victim. *I* was the one with the adventure. You may not have heard of them, but Telephone sell 400,000 copies of their albums, big for a small country; they are superstars in this country, recognized everywhere. Odile knew that 'A' would never leave his dependable job for this sort of juvenile lark. There was respect on her face, when, less than a week later, she watched our big bus with 'STARCRUISER' painted on it pull out of the Porte de Champerret.

I watched her drive off in the opposite direction, sure she was on the way to a tryst (note the relationship between 'tryst', assignation of love, and '*triste*', sad), knowing she had lost the initiative, whether she knew it or not. Big bucks, name in the papers: '*Un Jazzman Chez les Rockers*', the best hotels, autographs, champagne. My musical career had been stalled, not a gig in sight, not a scribble on the calendar, and then suddenly there I was in front of 11,000 people (Lyon), half of them holding lit lighters high above their heads in tribute. Have you ever performed for 11,000 people? You feel their energy flow over you, it is physical not mere atmosphere. Sock it to me. So what if she's doing *that* with *him*. Playing at night supported writing this during the day. It was like a subsidy. Riding 'STARCRUISER' out of Rennes, Jean-Louis closed the Henry Miller book he was reading and said with a degree of pride only a French rock star could have about it: 'We must be the only rock band in the world with a resident writer.'

Right Disappearance strews wreckage. Jazz musicians said, 'I see you crossed over.' They were serious, I had committed a crime against Right Music. 'It's just something to do,' I told them. 'It's fun.' A man I freelanced for screamed at me, fired me even though I owed him no money or work. He was stuck behind his desk while I went out playing with rock stars. 'You have no sense of responsibility,' he shouted. I shouted back: 'I'm a freelancer. I'm fucking free!'

Daily two-way love letters: 'You are my sunshine, and I suppose my rain too . . . Please don't be too unhappy and jealous, I'll always be here, you know that . . . You smile when you come. Other women grimace, groan, shout, cry. You smile. Do you smile like that with him? . . . I feel great love coming from you. You are a handsome man, you have a wonderful smile, you are a great fuck . . . Every time I throw on my Odile switch the "A" switch goes on with it. There's got to be a way to wire those two switches on separate currents. I would like to kiss your switch, bitch, or do you need an electrician? . . . Hi kid, be happy but not too happy . . .'

Meanwhile, Jean-Louis Aubert took a flying leap out into the cheering sea, started way back by the drum-kit and jumped full-tilt like it was a watery sea. 'Jeezus!' I asked him. 'Do you do that often?' He smiled enigmatically: 'From time to time.' People who perform for 11,000 people are different from people like you and me. It's easy to get hooked on the sound of 22,000 hands clapping. I've played often for hundreds, but it's not the same thing; a difference in kind rather than quantity. You begin to suspect the whole world loves you. My articles in the *Herald Tribune* may be read by, say, 100,000 people, but I don't see them. I'm not sure they are applauding. One wonderful thing about both writing words and playing music for a living is the balance between lonely work communicating one-on-one over great distances and collective energy immediately fed back. Yin and yang. This was yang plus. Cheap energy in a zappy package. Warning: jazz snob at work. Before the Beatles I automatically associated pop music with massive bad taste; pink Cadillacs, trailer-parks, permed hair, shallow minds and Bel Aire. At best it was still disposable, lightweight – pop was a murder mystery, jazz Hemingway. *Sergeant Pepper* changed all that for a while, and though I have come a long way back to my original distaste for pop music (the music's fault not mine), when Jean-Louis picked up his guitar one rainy morning on 'STARCRUISER' near Toulouse and started to strum 'I Am the Walrus', I sang along with everybody: 'Choking smokers don't you know the joker laughs at you-ou-ou-ou? . . . hahahahah.'

Impossible. It was never supposed to happen. No rock group had ever come close to surviving singing in French. Yet Telephone was drawing like Bruce Springsteen, mobs of bright kids, kids next door with eager faces who had stood for hours waiting for the doors to open and pushed to get down front, overjoyed finally to have role models who speak their own language. In the past French has been too proud to accept the servile role rock often demands of language. The Rolling Stones swing first, sing second. What Jagger sings is often less important than how he swings singing it. Jimi Hendrix liked to sing verbal licks, word riffs. When the Beatles sang, 'She Came in through the Bathroom Window', texture and time were more important than meaning. Rock appeals to the body first, the head second. The French *chanson* appeals to the head first, often only the head. The strength of the *chanson* is language – words are the painting, music the canvas. But Marcel Proust called language 'a sealed fortress' and language sealed French off from Western pop culture until Telephone figured out how to do without long-distance calls.

Before performing for still one more joy-stricken, sold-out house, Corine Marienneau, who plays the bass guitar, said: 'It's getting too easy. We could just go out and stand there and they'd cheer.' She was having a hard time coping with 'STARCRUISER', being protected by a security corps, and the sense of isolation that seems to be the inevitable price of fame. She was having a particularly hard time coping with the groupies (apparently normal men twisted their faces into lecherous smiles asking me: 'Is it really true about groupies?') who pop up painted after each show. Presto. Here are four not-bad-at-all young things just dying to suck your cock. Not mine. One nice thing about passing fifty is you don't need it that much any more. An evening of wasted conversation in return for half an hour of possible physical bliss no longer seems a good deal. I had an eye on Corine for a while but only her shell was visible. To call her absent would be to imply more presence than she had. Looking into her eyes was like staring into space. I told her about Odile's adventure, hoping to make her see me, but her walls were too high, her locks too sturdy. 'What's happening to us?' she asked more than once, trying to analyse the evils of stardom. They had once lived a communal existence in the same apartment, they were an extended family with multi-levelled relationships and fame was putting a great deal of stress on it. She played the roles of sister, mother (she was the oldest, thirty) and mistress. She hated groupies. How could her family couple with groupie after groupie like animals? She felt sullied somehow. A journalist asked her: 'Isn't it hard being a woman on the road with a rock band?' She looked hard and answered: 'Yes, it's hard.' One night we all came back to the hotel at two, starving. The bar was open but not the kitchen. The barman said there were makings in there and be my guest. Corine immediately left to make sandwiches and a salad and brought it all out to the bar. Not one of the men budged to help her. Still trying to reach her then, I asked how she felt about all of a sudden assuming woman's traditional servile role: 'The rest of the time you're all buddies, but when it comes to the kitchen you're automatically the cook.' You could see the family close ranks as she said softly: 'I don't really mind. They'd never do it, and I was hungry. Besides, they're really only children.'

They are four children in the process of buying the candy store. Inordinate success had come only a year earlier. They were just beginning to deal with the size of it, and with accumulation of great sums of money. Headlines (on page one, not the inside entertainment page) screamed: 'Telephone: a triumph more than a success'. Drummer Richard Kolinka is most childlike of all, and that's a compliment. There's a certain innocence about him, a child's ability to focus total attention in one direction. He knew he wanted to be a drummer the moment he found out he had the same birthday as Ringo Starr. He always smiles playing the drums, even without an audience, and when not playing he's smiling banging and tapping on something.

After bowling over 8,000 people at the Porte de Pantin circus tent in Paris, Louis Bertignac beat Yannick Noah, number one French tennis pro and now French Open champion, at ping pong backstage. There must have been some mistake at the hospital; Louis should have been born American. He absolutely *has* to win. He is over-motivated, desperate to win. He stood about a metre back from the table and slammed that little white ball unmercifully at poor Noah, who was trying to be a good sport about it. Louis would probably agree with Richard Nixon, who has said: 'Show me a good loser and I'll show you a *loser*.' He was not hesitant about using stardom's perks; people were always carrying and going to fetch something for Louis. Tour manager David Wernham dubbed him 'King Louis'. Louis called David 'Roastbeef'. This French group touring France had an English agent, two English buses and drivers, English light and sound men working English equipment hauled in English lorries driven by English drivers, and English stage and tour managers. ('English road crews work twice as hard as the French and cost half as much,' Wernham explained.) King Louis and Roastbeef got along quite well after a while. Louis hugged him and said: 'I want you to take care of the rest of my life.' A tough gig, Louis takes life seriously. He is highly-strung and brittle and I wasn't all that surprised when he fell off the stage in Montpelier and broke his collar bone in two places and the second half of the tour had to be postponed three weeks as a result.

I arrived in Paris very early Sunday morning after three weeks out. Odile and 'A' had begun to take their evenings together for granted. Not a day too soon. Louis's collar bone may have saved my marriage. A Saturday-night date had been hastily cancelled. 'A' did not like returning to number-two man. He complained. By the time I left again the adventure was going out of Odile's adventure.

My big Telephone number was a tune called 'Le Chat', about a cat who leaves home and comes back again. I played the cat, dressed in black. First I room with a guy who smells like catfood, then I *am* a cat. I'm allergic to cats. Life is comprised of such unexplainable connections. You figure it out. I made bluesy cat music with my plunger mute. One night I could feel it click hard, the band moved up a notch behind me and we all found the same slot. This is an improviser's dream, to pick up your rhythm section single-handedly, a feeling of great power. Calling these four French rockers 'my rhythm section' does not exactly describe our relationship with much accuracy, a fact brought home to me the following day on 'STARCRUISER' when I said to Jean-Louis: ' "The Cat" went really well last night.' He looked surprised: 'Did it? I couldn't hear you, my monitor wasn't working.'

Anything that does not come through electric wiring isn't worth mentioning. The gulf between us yawned. I learned the limits of our relationship. Listening together to the Rolling Stones track 'Neighbours', on which Sonny Rollins has a solo, I was the only one still listening when it arrived. Sonny Rollins was like a commercial to Telephone, time to talk. The hole in their Swiss cheese was my Swiss cheese. 'Hey, that's Sonny Rollins!' Nothing. One day I arranged with the bus-driver to put on my cassette of Willie Nelson singing 'On the Road Again' just as we pulled away from the hotel. They had told me they did not know Nelson's work, and I thought his happy song about the same experience we were all living so intensely would give them a kick, but Louis took it off without a word in favour of their heroes the Police.

Everything in the same three or four keys with spin-offs of the same three- or four-chord progressions. It astounded me that the audience was not bored by them, to say nothing of the band. Every song performed they had already recorded, and they were performed in the same order every night. Like working in a bank. Telephone made me aware of one major difference between rock and jazz – rock musicians would rather play a mediocre concert for 10,000 people than a great one for 100, jazz musicians basically play for each other.

I carried my baggage through the door like a dusty cowboy at the end of a gruelling but profitable 2,000-mile cattle drive. 'Boy!' Odile hugged me. 'You sure do know how to disappear.'

22

A Big-Buck Cakewalk

Music is not work. You do not 'work' music, you 'play' music. It's a game, some people are embarrassed getting paid money for having so much fun.

Jimi Hendrix could not believe how much money he was making just to play music. Offered $50,000 for a concert in Cleveland, he spent days trying to figure out why they were willing to pay him so much. Music came first for Hendrix, before women and drugs, though he did love them all. But he slept with his guitar and would rather jam than anything. He never related to business; the fact that the $50,000 concert might involve direct and indirect costs of $60,000 did not occur to him.

When I was eighteen I played on a cruise boat from New York to Buenos Aires and back for $65 a week plus room and board, good money at the time. I would have done it just for room and board. The passengers were paying to take the same trip, and they didn't even get to play music. This sort of value-system has led me to leave a lot of money on the table over the years.

I try to discipline myself to ask for what I consider a high figure, but this is usually considered low by the person asked. You can tell by the way they answer. Mention a price and if they snap back an 'OK' right away, you know you're low again. But even if I'd always managed to get top dollar, it would not have amounted to much. Jazz musicians are paid in inverse proportion to the enjoyment of their work, which, as we now know, isn't really work at all.

Alexis Korner hired me to play for his fiftieth birthday party, a media event in the garden pavilion of the Pinewood film studios near London. That this homage was organized, paid for and filmed by West German TV rather than the BBC is revealing of

Alexis, an obscure legend of mixed ancestry. 'The father of the English blues' was sired in France by a Greek-Turkish mother and an Austrian cavalry-officer father. He went to school in Switzerland, became more popular in France and Germany than on his own island, and speaks fluent French and German. He was having trouble translating the song-title 'Honky Tonk Woman' into either language. He looked at the journalist who had asked him to do it with a sort of desperation, finding the precise meaning seemed important to him, until he finally shrugged coming up with: 'A honky tonk woman is open, she drinks, she smokes, she stays up all night and God bless them all.'

He threw me a sneaky smile. We are about the same age. I refer myself to his fine mental and physical shape when down about being past fifty. He agrees that insecurity is a fountain of youth: 'Too easy is boring. You've got to keep stretching it. I don't like music where there are no mistakes. How can rock bands play the same music night after night? It would drive me absolutely bonkers.'

Ironic, because playing the blues for three days almost drove me bonkers. A blues band basically plays the same tune all the time. (Alexis says it is such a rich and varied 'tune' that to view it as the 'same tune' totally misses the point.) But after two days rehearsing riffs on top of that tonic-sub-dominant-tonic-dominant-tonic twelve-bar sequence, riffs grew hard to come by. John Surman, who played baritone sax with us, thought of a solution: 'Let's call rent-a-riff.'

The blues as a money-making industry can be traced back to Alexis. He does not much approve of what happened, he hates guitar heroes and in general feels personal responsibility for having fathered a lot of shitty music. In 1960 he formed Blues Incorporated, probably the first white electric blues band. This credit might appear to have too many qualifications to be meaningful, but it in turn fathered the Rolling Stones, Cream, John Mayall and the rest. At the time, English popular music was dominated by 'Trad' (traditional dixieland) jazz. Electrifying the blues was greeted with cries of 'sell-out', similar to those Muddy Waters received some years earlier in Chicago for doing the same thing. But 'Trad' had become fixed, boring, predictable. Youth was ready for something new. Ginger Baker replaced Charlie

Watts on drums with Blues Incorporated, Jack Bruce played bass, singers included Mick Jagger, Eric Burdon and Paul Jones. Keith Richard, Eric Clapton and Brian Jones were all Korner sidemen at one time or another: 'Everything was so free and open at the beginning. Anyone who said they could play the blues was allowed a go. One go. We could tell fast enough if they were telling the truth. It was such a beautiful give and take. The only difference between the audience and the players was that the players got paid ten shillings a night.' (You can't beat fun.)

After the rehearsals and the party-concert on the third day, German TV continued to shoot while some stars who once played with Alexis started to jam. Eric Clapton unpacked his guitar. Surman and I were standing at the foot of the bandstand stairs, smoking. He turned surly saying: 'Certainly we're not expected to *jam* too. I mean, enough's enough. The gig's over, right?'

I scowled: 'The motherfuckers always expect you to play for free. Three days of the bloody blues are enough.'

Then the two of us looked at each other, wondering how we had allowed ourselves to be trapped in that stupid loveless professional musician number. 'You know,' Surman said, 'I wouldn't mind playing with Eric Clapton.'

'Neither would I.' And we played again.

Cut to the Sologne, rolling farm country south of Orleans.

As opposed to fashion
The passion of blood brothers
Imbues this effort with controlled contrast,
A movement next to no movement,
Fireworks but don't look for them.
'Think of your ears as eyes' (Gertrude Stein).
A terrific whale imitation
Touches you where you've never been touched
Since Buddy Bolden went mad
Or I'm more off-base than an AWOL GI. A seagull cry,
The sound of a heavy lorry revving up on a narrow street.
Go along get lost,
But don't stop there.

Those lines were cut-up out of what has been written about and by ECM Records over the years in publications, releases and catalogues. Scraps of paper cluttered my floor. Cutting up words is one way to use your ears like eyes. Now hear this. The music sounds like it comes from a snowy tropical plain where new dreams mix with old over solitude cocktails, where science-fiction is neither scientific nor made-up, where Brazilians play Norwegian folk songs with Americans and John Coltrane stars with Edward Munch in a film by Eric Rohmer. Is that obscure?

Go on get lost.

Friends of my in-laws had loaned us their small, turreted château, Venay, for two weeks. We watered the flowers and tried not to stain the antiques. Surrounded by gold-leafed leather-bound volumes and period prints hanging on fluffy wallpaper in the library, I was writing about ECM's president Manfred Eicher, who created the 'ECM Sound', described above.

As opposed to fashion.

Eicher issued a two-record album of Keith Jarrett's solo acoustic piano in 1975. *Köln Concert* has by now sold almost a million copies, unheard-of for a solo acoustic double jazz album. Jarrett said: 'That was a far-out risk. Everybody said Manfred was crazy to do it. But that is one of his rare qualities. He isn't afraid to take risks when he believes in something.'

A movement next to no movement.

Outside the window behind my typewriter, Marcel flew by on his bicycle, followed by Nicholas brandishing a Zorro sword on another bike, followed in turn by a black and white puppy and cute little Thomas on his tricycle. Figure out what real life has to do with a comic strip.

Fireworks but don't look for them.

In the distance, fat brown cows grazed in the mist by a thick green forest. Listening to Egberto Gismonti, admiring the poetry of that name, I turned up the volume and worried about how it has come to pass that at the age of fifty-two the only luxury that ever enters my life is borrowed.

But don't stop there.

An aperitif named 'Swing' came on the market during the German occupation of France, not such a swinging time. 'Êtes-Vous Swing?' and 'Mon Heure de Swing' were hit songs. The sartorial fad modelled after Cab Calloway's zoot suits was called 'Swing', and the youngsters who wore them (hippies of their day) were known as *Les Petits Swings*.

Since the time of slavery in the United States, swing has been a metaphor or that disorderly, robust state called 'freedom'. At no time was it more symbolic than under the Occupation.

The Nazis banned jazz after America entered the war. Charles Delaunay, and his Hot Club de France, began to emphasize that jazz was now an international phenomenon, a mixture of French, African, Spanish and Anglo-Saxon influences. Hot Club concerts were billed as 'Jazz Français'. The Germans wanted French collaboration and they leaned over backwards to respect French culture. Delaunay pointed out in articles and interviews that jazz had French roots in the form of traditional New Orleans airs, and that 'Tiger Rag' was based on the nineteenth-century French quadrille 'Praline'.

French jazz musicians went right on playing their old repertoire, only changing the names. 'St Louis Blues' became 'La Tristesse de St Louis', 'Honeysuckle Rose' 'La Rose de Chevrefeuille', 'Sweet Sue' 'Ma Chère Susanne'. The Germans may have suspected what was going on, but they had more pressing problems.

Gypsy guitarist Django Reinhardt, a relatively obscure cult hero before the war, became a superstar overnight. His song 'Nuages' (Clouds) was whistled on the street. He was as well-known as Maurice Chevalier. His picture covered many Parisian walls. When he arrived in a town to play, it was like the liberation; people knew something happy was going to happen for a change. His concerts were always packed. Django lived in sumptuous apartments, gambled heavily in posh casinos, ate well in expensive restaurants. His fame protected him while other gypsies were being shipped to camps with the Jews. More and more pressure was exerted on him to tour Germany, something he desperately wanted to avoid. When it seemed inevitable, he tried to cross into Switzerland but was caught. The German officer began his interrogation: '*Mon vieux Reinhardt, que fais-tu?*' A jazz fan, he freed Django with a warning.

His inaccessibility made Django a sort of legend in America, where the press had reported several rumours of his death. Soon after the liberation, a group of American officers invited him to play for a party. He had heard Charlie Parker records that were smuggled in from Sweden during the war, he knew being cut off from the mainstream was hurting him artistically. He had played with people like Duke Ellington and Rex Stewart when they toured Europe, but had never visited the home of the music he played so well. He tried hard to impress the Americans at the party. However he was cool answering an officer who asked how much he'd want to tour the States. Django had learned something about the value of swing: 'How much does Gary Cooper make? I want the same thing.'

'Ah, Music! What a beautiful art! But what a wretched profession!' Georges Bizet.

'Romanticism and sorrow and greed – they can all be put into music. I can definitely recognize greed. I know when a man is playing for money.' Coleman Hawkins.

'What you said hurt me very much. I cried all the way to the bank.' Liberace.

'I have learned from experience that it is easier to make a businessman out of a musician than a musician out of a businessman.' Goddard Lieberson.

'I want to tell the mothers and fathers of our great country never to permit their children to become professional musicians, because if they do, they are going into a starvation business.' James C. Petrillo (former president of the American Federation of Musicians).

'Plenty corrupts the melody that made you famous once, when young.' Alfred, Lord Tennyson.

'A musical profit can put you way ahead of a financial loss.' Edward Kennedy 'Duke' Ellington.

I read in this week's *Time* magazine that Philip K. Hwang, forty-six, chairman of TeleVideo Systems Inc. has decided to go public. Hwang fled North Korea to the south during the Korean war and served in the South Korean army. Fifteen years ago he was sweeping floors in a Lake Tahoe casino working his way through engineering school. He started TeleVideo in his northern California garage. His investment bankers believe that when TeleVideo goes public the 700,000 shares Hwang plans to sell will bring him $12.5 million cash, and his remaining 28.2 million shares will be worth $507.8 million.

There's a man who knows how to appear.

Talking money with the manager of Telephone before the tour, I asked for a figure higher than I had ever earned since leaving Dome Steel. This time I would not leave anything on the table. When he balked, I had an answer ready: 'You can probably find some kid to go out for less, but I have experience and a name. Besides, if I don't make good money with a hot rock band I'll never make good money.' We laughed and shook hands. I was proud of myself until I ran into a picker from Austin, Texas, who said he was sick and tired of being exploited by country music stars who make $30,000 a night and 'only' pay him just about exactly the figure I was making with Telephone.

Right Disappearance has no price.

Marcel came out with us for a couple of days. Kids are good luck on the road and the members of Telephone, kids themselves, carried him on their shoulders, played ping pong with him, rolled around the dressing-room floor together. During concerts he sat right on stage, behind an amp, next to Richard's drums. Richard likes to dress and paint his face like a pirate, performing. He painted Marcel's face like his own. Marcel found a bandanna exactly like Richard's to put around his head. Watching Richard toss and twirl his sticks and have such outrageous fun playing drums, Marcel pointed to his own head and twisted his index finger the way the French do when they use a pejorative to express respect: 'He's really nuts, that guy.'

He watched the video on 'STARCRUISER', played the band's Atari games with them. His mouth hung open watching them give interviews and sign autographs, which they do more out of pleasure than duty. Wherever Richard went, Marcel was two steps behind. 'My shadow', Richard called him.

Ever since, Marcel has been banging and tapping on everything in sight. He plays Telephone records one after the other. I was appalled hearing myself ordering him as my father once ordered me with another kind of music: 'Turn that down!'

'I don't like jazz,' he said to me. 'Rock swings more, don't you think?'

What did you want me to tell him? Read Hugues Panassie? We found a clean young classical pianist from Tennessee, a Baptist, to teach Marcel. One reason we chose him was because an American is less likely to kill a youngster's love of music by laying too many rules on him at the beginning. We seemed to agree that motivation was the only essential to start with, he should learn to speak the language before learning its rules. But the teacher began to spend most of the lesson on scales and fingering and I soon had to nag Marcel to the keyboard. He likes to play standing up. The teacher said: 'Now Marcel, sit down. You can't stand up and play piano, like – what's his name? – Jerry Lee Lewis.' Stern stuff, the Baptist in him, he made his disapproval clear. I got in the habit of repeating: 'Sit down, Marcel.' And: 'Third finger, not fourth.' More stern stuff. Then I remembered how Monk's fingers flew finding their own logic, how he sometimes stood up to play when the spirit moved him, and how Keith Jarrett raises himself off the bench with improvisational intensity. Marcel is little, it may be easier for him to play standing up, more like a game; probably can't get a good view of the keyboard sitting down. He'll sit down when it's easier to sit down. Now there's alienation for you. You assume mainstream values unconsciously, repeat what you hear all around you. Everybody wants to drag you into the hole that they're in. I kicked myself. What are you trying to do, asshole? Take the game out of his game? Make play work?

I leafed through the Real Book, an encyclopaedia of jazz standards, looking for easy tunes. I found 'Blue Monk'. Should have thought of that earlier. My friend saxophonist Jean Cohen and I play it in our duo. I fooled around with it on the piano.

'I know that,' Marcel said, running in and forgetting all about the cartoon he'd been watching on TV. 'You play that with Jean.' The next day Marcel know 'Blue Monk' by heart. Then I found Mingus's 'Nostalgia in Times Square'. He memorized that just as fast. He played it over and over again until I was beginning to get good and tired of 'Nostalgia in Times Square'.

'I thought you didn't like jazz,' I said.

'Oh is that jazz? How can you tell the difference between jazz and rock?'

A tough question. 'Well,' I began, 'jazz is better music. I only play rock for the money.'

'What?!' His little face lit up. 'You mean you get *paid* to play music?!'

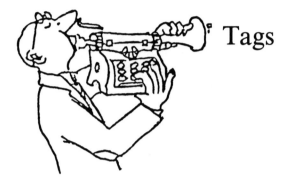

Tags

Tag One: Chet Baker

You do not generally feel like jumping up and shouting 'Yeah!' after a Chet Baker trumpet solo. All that tenderness, turmoil and pain has driven you too far inside. He reaches that same part of us as a late Beethoven string quartet, a spiritual hole where music becomes religion.

Though small by industry standards, Baker's audience is select and passionate. 'Chet cares for each note and makes it sing,' said Manfred Eicher, head of ECM records (for whom Baker does not record). 'He approaches phrasing and harmony in a highly aesthetic fashion. He was one of my most important influences when I first started listening to jazz. And he still is, more than ever.'

Keith Jarrett said: 'Chet's unique combination of sound, form and time is a remarkable unified artistic statement. He is concerned with being himself rather than new or different or avant-garde.'

John Vinocour, Paris correspondent for the *New York Times*, once called me though we do not know each other. He asked me where Chet Baker lives, does he have an agent and so on. I asked him if he was writing an article on Chet, odd because Vinocour is a political writer. 'No,' he answered, 'but somebody should. I heard him the other night in Bonn and I've rarely been so moved by music.'

Baker looked depressed: 'It's kind of depressing to realize that so much of what I'm trying to do and say is going by completely undetected. It's really very complicated but it looks easy. I'm sure that ninety-five per cent of the audience is unaware that I've said anything unique or that there's more depth to it than there was twenty-five years ago.'

Chesney Baker was born of poor parents in Yale, Oklahoma, in 1929. One of his problems may well be that the world is not, and may never be, ready to accept a redneck jazz musician. But that's not the main problem. He has been his own worst enemy, and drugs were the weapon. When he made his big splash in 1952 in Los Angeles with the revolutionary pianoless Gerry Mulligan Quartet ('One day the piano-player didn't show up for rehearsal and we decided it was better without a piano'), it seemed as if his combination of James Dean's looks and Miles Davis's talent would take him far. He could even sing, and on the basis of his first vocal album *Chet Baker Sings*, tied Nat King Cole for third place in the *Down Beat* magazine poll. By the time he came to Europe in 1959, he was putting most of his assets into his veins. After doing fourteen months for a drug offence in jail in Lucca, Italy, where he learned fluent Italian, he went back to the States in 1964. His teeth were knocked out in 1968 in a San Francisco brawl. On methadone and welfare, he lived with his wife and three children at his mother's house near San Jose, California.

Gradually, painfully, he learned to play again with dentures ('I use a product called "Fast Teeth"; sticky stuff'), and when he started a comeback in 1974, critic John S. Wilson wrote that Baker had acquired 'more range and assertiveness within the wistfully ruminative style with which he has always been associated'.

Although the similarity is only in superficial texture, Baker has been accused of being a Miles Davis rerun. Responding to this, he just smiles at its irrelevance and says: 'I'm a Miles Davis fan.' Some critics accuse the recording industry of having tried to push him as a sort of great white hope. Hopes were dashed by bad habits. Now Baker records with just about anyone who asks him and plays with anyone who happens to be around in any joint that happens to have an opening. They are usually small joints, usually packed. He did six nights in New York's Village Vanguard and a week at Fat Tuesdays (with Ron Carter); both stints sold out. He works whenever he wants to but rarely primo venues. He is hard to reach and does not always return calls.

He likes Europe because, 'People are nicer to each other here. In New York it comes down to half the people pimping off the other half. A lot of people hurting one another.' His limping speech and weak physical state give the impression that there is perhaps not room for much more hurt.

To his fans, Baker becomes the measure by which to judge the honesty-quotient in others. He goes for feeling first, with just as much technique as he needs. Other improvisors try and overwhelm the trumpet; blast it fast, screech down the walls of Jericho. Baker builds new walls. He needs them for protection.

He always plays seated, folded into a question-mark. Between solos, he sits, trumpet resting on his crossed legs, without moving. You almost say to yourself – my God, he's passed away up there. Then, ever so slowly, he raises the instrument to his lips and when those sweetly burned innocent notes bloom again it's a relief, almost as though you've made it through one more winter.

Chet Baker is summertime, but the livin' isn't easy.

Tag Two: John Cage

Trying to write 1,000 words about John Cage reminds me of the old Monty Python routine where a quiz-show contestant is to give a thirty-second résumé of Proust's *Remembrance of Things Past* starting . . . now.

Explorer, adventurer, philosopher, musician, Cage is talking about silence: 'Thoreau and the Indians and I have said all along that the sounds all around us are equivalent to music. In India they say that music is continuous; it only stops when we turn away and stop paying attention. Thoreau said that silence is like a sphere with sound bubbles on its surface. I want to keep from interrupting the silence that is already here.'

He once composed a piano sonata titled 'Four Minutes, Thirty-three Seconds', consisting of four silent movements of different lengths. As the audience began to suspect that the pianist, who was looking at a stopwatch, was not ever going to play 'music', they started to giggle, fidget, nudge each other, cough and blow their noses. These sounds, plus street-sounds from outside, became themselves music. As Pop Art helped people recognize everyday objects as art, Cage revealed music where before there was only noise – or silence.

He studied with twelve-tone composer Arnold Schoenberg and

the Zen philosopher Suzuki. He is a macrobiotic vegetarian and a mycologist: 'a hunter of mushrooms and sounds'.

He arrived early for his first piano lesson in Los Angeles, where he was born. The teacher said he was early and would he please come back on time. Cage walked around the neighbourhood and returned five minutes late. The teacher told him to come back next week, explaining 'the importance of time for somebody involved with the art of music'.

'When I began to study composition,' Cage says, 'there were only two possibilities. Schoenberg and Stravinsky. Now we are lucky – we live in an age where everything is possible. Once we had the Mona Lisa, now we also have the Mona Lisa with a moustache.'

Here we come to the 'prepared piano'. In the early forties, Cage placed nuts and bolts and other objects (now he does it mostly through electronics) in the strings, his way of painting a moustache on the piano. Thus the piano was enlarged to equal a variety of instruments with previously unknown textures that could be altered between movements or compositions. He wrote a composition for twelve radios. On the occasion of his seventieth birthday, 5 September 1982, French Minister of Culture Jack Lang, noted for tirades against American cultural imperialism, presented him with a medal, saying: 'You represent everything that is pure and creative in the United States.'

Cage lives in a loft in the former B. Altman department store on the Avenue of the Americas, which, like all good New Yorkers, he calls by its old name: 'I love living on Sixth Avenue. It has more sound, and totally unpredictable sound, than any place I've ever lived. Some people call it noise, but I've always been interested in noise. It goes on night and day and at first I couldn't sleep through it. Now I enjoy it as much as a concert.'

Somebody once said that all musically talented people have large ears, and Cage's are very large and exquisitely folded. He is calm, yet there is an inner spring that uncoils into the loudest silent laugh you ever did not hear. The face is absolutely exploding, splitting itself with laughter and yet there is only silence. The silent laughter comes frequently and finally breaks into its inherent joyous component: noise. He speaks slowly, with precision and often poetry: 'If you want to be free of that thing that defines the ego, you must leave both the things you like and dislike. If you have learned to flow, the question of likes and dislikes might come up but they won't be important, whereas if it comes up before that, they are extremely important, and they stop the flow.'

For flow he composes with what he calls 'chance elements', and chance is like 'sitting cross-legged. Only instead of going inwards towards the dreams it goes out through the sense of perception and effects the sound of my music. It enlarges the field in which my work operates. If I just used my tastes, my likes and dislikes, my work would get ever more refined and narrow. And, you see, I have what I think is an advantage. I don't hear music in my head. I hear it when it's audible. So I do not hear my music as I write it. When I'm writing, I'm writing; when I'm listening, I'm listening. Which is wonderful because that way I can write something I've never heard before.'

One more noisy silent laugh.

About reaching the age of seventy: 'Obviously I have less time left now, so I should become involved in more things rather than less. I started gardening a few years ago (there are over 200 plants in his loft) and now I make etchings and I've become, they say, interesting.'

He can admit to being considered interesting without giving the impression that he is really interested in being interesting; 'People think that things are not in themselves interesting, that human beings have to do something in order to make them interesting. To force them to be interesting. This isn't true. A speck of dust is interesting.'

He gave up smoking by 'dividing myself. You become two people, one who knows he's stopped and the other who still smokes. The one who knows laughs at the one who doesn't know. Which is how I feel about getting this (French) medal. The one who has done his work accepts the medal, and the one who has not yet finished working must disregard it so he can continue.'

There are those who consider Cage's compositions unlistenable, even a fraud. Yet, regardless of taste, to speak of him as a composer is missing the point. His real strength is the pervasiveness of his influence.

Film music is a good example. When the movies began to talk, music was everywhere. When action flagged, the solution was to tell the composer: 'More fiddles, Max.' Over the last decade or two, the sound of on-screen action has increasingly replaced traditional instrumentation. We hear footsteps, the sea, traffic, office machinery, coffee pouring. Movie music is no longer necessarily 'music', and John Cage is somewhere behind all that.

After Jack Lang presented Cage with his medal, there was a concert of his music. Outside later it was pouring down rain. Instead of complaining about or running from it, one listener turned to his companion and said: 'Listen to the rain. Isn't it beautiful?'

Tag Three: Manfred Eicher

The man who created what has come to be called the 'ECM sound' describes it as: 'The most beautiful sound next to silence', 'a movement next to no movement' and 'controlled contrast'.

The sound is as much due to Manfred Eicher, a thoughtful, thirty-eight-year-old German, as to his eclectic collection of artists. More if you consider that he chose the collection in the first place: the Art Ensemble of Chicago, Pat Metheny, Keith Jarrett, Don Cherry, Charlie Haden, Egberto Gismonti, Jan Garberek, Chick Corea, Gary Burton, Steve Swallow and minimalist composer Steve Reich to cite a few.

Eicher, who produced 245 of ECM's 250-album catalogue, quotes the late pianist Glenn Gould to define the producer's role: 'The work of a great producer should be as distinctive in the sound of a record as are the works of composer and performer. And to a sensitive listener, the producer's work should be aesthetically as significant.'

Even an insensitive listener can recognize the most obvious element of the distinctive ECM sound. We won't use the word echo. Echo implies technical fiddling to juice up music once it has been recorded. Eicher does not like that word. It implies something he disapproves of, placing technology before music. But there is a distinctive personality on all of Eicher's productions, a reverberating brilliance. Although few would argue with the statement that, taste aside, ECM is the most creative jazz label today, some criticize what they call the 'monotony' of this texture.

224

Eicher replies that he is out to capture 'the entire aural panorama, the complete musical picture', and if he utilizes reverb it is first and foremost to be able to 'hear all the details. I want to capture each musician's individual musical personality. We use different microphone placement and pairing for Chick Corea and Jarrett for example. Many jazz recordings sound flat to me, compressed, limited. It's important to get depth and dimension into music. But the music is always first. I've worked closely with the same engineer for fifteen years, we have developed a sensitivity towards the individual sound of each musician, to get closer to their ideas. I would never throw out what we agree is a great take for technical reasons. We'll find a way to make it technically acceptable if the music is superb. There were technical problems with the tape of Jarrett's *Köln Concert* but we knew there was a story there that we would never get again and this was much more important than any technical consideration. I am fascinated with musical detail, I want to hear the overtones and contours of the instruments and the individual touch of each musician. This comes from my experience with classical music.'

Eicher began to study violin at the age of six. He switched to contrabass when he was sixteen and spent one year with the Berlin Philharmonic. In his teens he began to listen to the cool jazz of people like Gil Evans and Lee Konitz. In the early sixties, the pianist Bill Evans became 'one of the strongest influences on my musical thinking. When I first heard his records, something important happened to me.'

He began to understand the unique dimension of jazz reading Bill Evans's liner notes for the Miles Davis album *Kind of Blue*: 'There is a Japanese visual art in which the artist is forced to be spontaneous. He must paint on a thin stretched parchment with a special brush and black water paint in such a way that an unnatural or interrupted stroke will destroy the line or break through the parchment. Erasures or changes are impossible.'

As he listened to jazz with increasing respect, Eicher began to notice that classical music was recorded with more stringent technical standards. During the pressing process, for example, quality on classical records was controlled about twice as frequently as with jazz. In 1969 a record-store owner named Karl Egger invested 16,000 marks to help Eicher launch a company that would try to 'treat jazz as classical music'.

The first ECM (Editions of Contemporary Music) release was Mal Waldron's *Free at Last*. Eicher has produced about twenty albums a year since them. The undisputed locomotive of the catalogue is *Köln Concert*, which hooked a lot of classical music fans who yearned for simpler, more constant times.

Jarrett's 'contract' consists of a handshake – not unusual at ECM.

Gary Burton once spoke of Eicher: 'That I would become good friends with my record-company president and/or producer is something I would never have expected to be possible. They've always been people of a completely different breed; I would no more expect to become friends with my booking agent or a concert promoter... I mean, it's a different type of personality, a different approach that they have to music. But Manfred was a musician first; he operates from a love for the music.'

The business end does not really interest Eicher, who, when asked, is hard-pressed to come up with sales figures. He discusses business with reluctance. He made world-wide distribution deals and the business now more or less takes care of itself. Business is good. He says 1982 was a better year than '81, rare in today's depressed industry; 'Our catalogue offers music which is not based on time-cycles. We do not record disposable music. I'm not working for big hits. Sure, Pat Metheny sells very well but, remember, we developed him over a period of seven or eight years.'

Another secret is a small-is-beautiful business philosophy. The modest ECM office in an anonymous modern building over-looking an *autobahn* and a car park in a Munich suburb is staffed by four executives and two secretaries: 'That's as big as I want to get. We'll stay like that. Everything gets done, but with more intensity than in a big company, where work often gets delegated to people who may not always be in tune with company policy.'

Eicher finds himself listening to classical music again now, he reads more now – playwrights Botho Strauss and Peter Handke for example. He has begun recording classical music; Steve Reich's 'Music for Eighteen Musicians' and 'Tehellim', and is planning to record violinist Gidon Kramer playing pieces by the

Lithuanian composer Arvo Pärt.

'Jarrett recently performed Bartok's Second Piano Concerto, as well as works by Colin McPhee and Lou Harrison, and he will do a Samuel Barber work in Stuttgart soon. You can hear the influence of this music in his recent solo improvisation recordings. It really bothers me when people say Keith always sounds the same. Each concert is different from another and he's always searching for new elements. We just recorded Jarrett playing standards like "All the Things You Are" with Gary Peacock and Jack DeJohnette. The standards are just vehicles, they go in and out of strict form, but you can always feel respect for the source.'

Studio ambience, which includes motivating the musicians, is one of a producer's principal responsibilities. The choice of the studio itself is important. Eicher prefers a studio in Oslo because: 'Environment stimulates improvised music. The isolation you find in Oslo is very intense. Egberto Gismonti was totally disoriented when he arrived in Oslo directly from Brazil. I don't think he'd ever seen snow before. I'm sure that had something to do with the music. The Edward Munch museum is very close to the studio; looking at Munch paintings can change a musician's head. I love cold grey places, I'm fascinated by the endless light or endless darkness of northern Europe.'

Recording 'Two Folk Songs', side one of Pat Metheny's *80/81*, Mike Brecker was not even aware he was recording. He thought it was a rehearsal. But part of the producer's job is to know when to run the tape, it's as basic as that. 'Two Folk Songs' were not intended to run together, they were planned as two separate tracks, but when Brecker finished, Eicher motioned for the musicians to continue, Metheny played and then Charlie Haden soloed. The entire double album was done in two days of studio time.

'Recording is a very intimate situation that should remain intimate. It's so delicate, there are a lot of stories I would never repeat outside the studio. The role of the producer is to hear the connections musicians cannot possibly hear listening to themselves over earphones. To make a good record is a collective experience, and I think the producer also has the right to find his own language.'

Tag Four: Jimmy Gibson

When Jimmy Gibson was five he popped up from behind the piano finger-pointed and thumb cocked for his big line: 'Stick 'em up.'

Jimmy's father, a sub-underground fifties hero known as Harry the Hipster, turned around at the keyboard and asked: 'Stick what up?'

'I don't know, this is my first gig,' little Jimmy said. The audience roared.

Harry the Hipster is perhaps best remembered for his hit 'Who Put the Benzedrine in Mrs Murphy's Ovaltine?' He was a singer, jazz pianist, accompanist (for Mae West) and monologuist (Jimmy calls his father's routine 'Harry's rollin' up and benny act') who, though never breaking out of the saloon circuit, managed to keep working with his 'Rock, Boogie, Bluesjammers' in joints like the Melody Room, the Happy Hour, the Four Deuces and the Jumpin' Pizzeria.

'We never had a home,' Jimmy said, 'I was always in a hotel or backstage. I used to sleep under pianos.'

There would be four months in Las Vegas, a winter in Miami, a few weeks on Sunset Strip, a term in school here and there. Jimmy Gibson's been on the road since he was five: 'I learned right away that I was different from other kids. I had to make friends quickly and get something together because I wasn't going to be around that particular place too much longer. I learned how to make the best of the present, and to leave possessions.'

As with Lord Buckley and Lenny Bruce, Harry's fans were strippers, musicians, bartenders, car-park jocks and night people. Someone once said of Buckley, hero to beatniks and pre-freak freaks: 'Before Mort Sahl, before Lenny Bruce, Richard Buckley was lord of the hepcats.' He had a famous monologue about 'the Naz', a hip version of the Trinity, and 'the Hip Gan', about Gandhi. He influenced the humour of the sixties as Muddy Waters influenced the music of the sixties. Buckley was Jimmy Gibson's godfather.

Jimmy's only friends his own age were Buckley's kids, Laurie and Richie: 'Richie would be reciting Shakespeare or something and Laurie and I would be playing knights of the round table. I'd be Prince James. Growing up for me was like a long party. Buckley and Harry would be rapping and making up stories and they'd send us to bed but, you know, we'd be up all day and night sometimes.'

Harry the Hipster displayed a giant horse hypodermic needle on the piano; in those days it could still be considered a humorous prop. Drugs were not an epidemic then. There was a sort of innocence about it all – drugs were more a symbol of underground outlook than an escape-route. In any case little of it seems to have rubbed off on Jimmy, who may be a bit footloose but is ebullient, fresh-faced, well-fed, alert – certainly no layabout. From his energy and values you'd never guess that he grew up under a piano with a horse hypodermic on it.

He plays bass (electric and acoustic), guitar, saxophone, flute and piano. When somebody asks if he knows 'Indiana', he just starts playing the song. He's always heard it, known it, there was no need to learn it. He learned music as a language, he has always been around music and there were always instruments available. He can play rock, jazz, the blues, pop or boogie – he doesn't care which as long as he can have them all at one time or another.

But music is also more than music to him. These are instruments of freedom and adventure, the means to 'try and open every door in the world. My environment is where my next gig is. I want to see everything. I'd like to spread myself thin.'

Don't look for Jimmy Gibson's name on a marquee. Lack of itinerary is the only itinerary, he'll go wherever his axes take him. He's been riding his instruments to Greece, Holland, France, West Germany and Switzerland since he came to Europe seven years ago (he's thirty-four now). One band follows another and sometimes he's a one-man band.

The current vehicle is the Jukes, four young Americans who play the blues and 'just get into a town, go to a club and say "Hey, we're a band and we're here to play. You want us to set up?" It's wide-open territory out there. There's a whole bunch of clubs just empty. They don't want you to send them cassettes and they won't answer letters. But all you got to do is to be there and you start making some change. It's like a travelling salesman, you got to get your foot in the door.'

When Jimmy was ten: 'Harry left me with friends on a ranch

near Vegas. I chopped wood and rode desert ponies. I hung out with aunt Sally Rand – you know, the stripper, she was like family in Vegas – and Harry would send people like (alto-player) Eddie Shu to make sure I was all right.'

Jimmy picked up a guitar, put a band together, and 'played my way off that ranch. I always manage to play my way out of any situation.'

Driving cross-country, Harry would say: 'Hey, Jimmy, light me a cigarette.' Jimmy, who was maybe eight, lit it up and passed it. This is obviously terribly bad for a kid. Jimmy doesn't smoke. You figure it out.

He's also up to his chops in the work-ethic. The thing he wants to avoid more than anything else is what Thelonious Monk called 'dead time', the time between sets: 'I hate dead time. Dead time is when you're not playing music.'

He has an obvious attachment to his father, who is seventy-one and semi-retired in St Petersburg, Florida: 'Whenever Harry gives me the call, I go see him. Every so often he sends a message, "You'd better come over and hang out for a while." I always say OK.

'Me and Harry ran away from Chris, Mama, one time in Miami. Harry was on a health-kick. He didn't have any gigs on so we went out to Matheson Hammock, in the mangroves there. We waded out it must have been miles and built a little tree house and ate peanut butter and jelly for four days. There was a kind of whirlpool nearby and one day Harry threw me in it. He stood there watching while I swam out. Then he told me: "See, that's the experience you need to survive. When your old man throws you in the current, you got to learn to swim out." '

Tag Five: Elvin Jones

Elvin Jones was sitting at the bar of the Five Spot Café on the Bowery, looking at his watch. The Pepper Adams/Donald Byrd Quintet which he was working with had a deal. Anyone who showed up late bought the others a drink. Elvin sometimes stood two rounds a night. This night, however, he was still alone when the minute-hand hit ten. 'Bartender!' he called out, 'a quadruple

Old Bushmills on the rocks.'

That was the old Elvin Jones, a super wildman who could seemingly go on forever absorbing chemicals and still keep smiling time with one of the strongest heartbeats known to jazz. For years now he has been clean, positive, reliable, no longer a threat to himself or others. The heartbeat could get out of hand. The new Jones was due partly to his petite Japanese wife Keiko, also his manager, who travelled with his 'Jazz Machine' ten months a year on the road. She explained simply: 'I'm afraid of that man when he drinks.'

Elvin was one of the principal bridges between the worlds of art, theatre and jazz when they mingled during a creative spurt in New York in the late fifties and early sixties. Larry Rivers painted his portrait. He jammed with Larry in loft sessions, played a gunfighter in the underground film *Zachariah*, had a role in Jay and Fran Landesman's off-Broadway musical *The Nervous Set*, mixed easily at parties with playwright Jack Gelber (*The Connection*) and painter Willem de Kooning.

His albums sell in the upper five figures, his quartet is offered more work than it can handle, he has met with the Japanese Minister of Culture to discuss 'the upgrading of jazz in general'. Yet last month this superstar toured Germany and Switzerland with the George Gruntz Concert Jazz Band as a sideman.

Before playing the Atlantic Club in Basel, I asked him why he had agreed to do it: 'I like George's music,' he answered, musician rather than star. 'I like playing with big bands. It's good discipline, gives me a chance to brush up on my reading (he's self-taught). This is the first big band I've played with since Duke Ellington.'

That was in 1966, when he'd left John Coltrane after six historic years. Ellington had, for reasons unclear to Jones, hired a second drummer. There was always heavy political manouevring on that band: 'It's not one of my more pleasant experiences. It was only two weeks, and I didn't get a real chance to play. Although Duke has always been the person I've most admired since the beginning of my musical life . . .'

He trailed off in melancholy recollection. You sense tremendous vulnerability in the man, despite a rather fierce exterior, and his empathy, expressed in frequent shouted laughter and rib-crushing bear-hugs, impresses everyone who knows him. But there remains something fundamentally untamable about Elvin, something it must require great discipline to control. You can hear it when he plays; perhaps no other drummer combines so much force with so much nuance. His elastic, breathing time is immediately recognizable; it has influenced modern jazz drumming as much as Trane influenced modern tenor saxophone-playing. You can also sense his sensitivity towards others; he always listens to fellow musicians, adjusting to and inspiring them. He calls it 'putting it in the right place. Drumming is complementary. It isn't supposed to be dominating. It should embellish.'

One morning Alan Skidmore, a British saxophonist also with Gruntz, walked into the breakfast-room of our hotel where we were eating before an early departure. Everybody was half asleep, staring into space or coughing. Without breaking stride, he put his face up close to Jones (Skidmore wears glasses with thick lenses) and announced; 'Elvin, it sure is good to wake up in the morning and see *you*.'

Jones had conducted four drum-clinics recently in Japan: 'Attendance was 930 a day. We had to use a concert hall. One of the questions I'm always asked at clinics is what it's really like to be a professional musician. All those kids know is their fantasies. I think this is one of the responsibilities in being a professional, to prepare the younger generation by passing on some of our knowledge and experience.'

'But there's no bloody work!' I said. 'Where are all those 930 drummers going to play?'

Elvin's laughter roared: 'You don't have to enter the *Tour de France* to enjoy riding a bicycle.'

Tag Six: Jaco Pastorius

Jaco Pastorius is called the Jimi Hendrix of the bass guitar, even its Paganini. Critic Joachim Berendt thinks he is 'the most important jazz discovery in recent years'. He says of himself: 'Nobody can do what I'm doing on the bass guitar. I have no competition.'

He decided to play the instrument because it was easy. He accompanied the Temptations, Della Reese, Lou Rawls, the Supremes. David Bowie told him he was doing something fresh and exciting. He worked around Miami with the celebrated, 'undiscovered' at the time, trumpeter and reedman Ira Sullivan. Pastorius calls him 'one of the greatest musicians on the planet'. He had offers from some big people along the way, but 'I decided I wasn't ready yet. If the roots of a tree aren't deep enough, the first wind will blow it over.'

By 1976, ready, he joined the hot, high-priced fusion group Weather Report. Then he was a relatively obscure sideman, now his instrument will never be the same.

In the early days, tubas played the bass-line. As jazz matured they were replaced by more flexible plucked bass violins. A purely foundational function was expanded by such soloists as Jimmy Blanton and Oscar Pettiford. Slam Stewart introduced bowing and the role expanded further. Young bassists like Scotty LaFaro and Gary Peacock began to play speed, diversity and range the instrument had not been thought capable of.

There was one problem. Except for recording sessions where balance could be adjusted, the bass, the foundation, the hardest working member of the group, often remained inaudible. Then the Fender Corporation invented the (electric) bass guitar. Traditional bass violin-players considered it too easy, a machine rather than a musical instrument. They doubled on it only when it brought them work, with condescension. When electric pop music began to get fancy in the sixties with people like Hendrix and the Beatles, bass-lines grew more melodic and elaborate. Paul McCartney, a pioneer on bass guitar, chose notes more carefully, integrated them into the melodies themselves.

At the same time 'soul music' record labels like Stax/Volt in Memphis and Motown in Detroit began to mix the bass at a higher level. It was an exciting, physical sound, conducive to dancing, and other producers picked up on it. Spurred on by the exposure, bass guitarists expanded their technique.

Jack Bruce of Cream played jazz on it. Woody Herman's band switched to bass guitar. Steve Swallow played bass guitar with Gary Burton. The bass guitar learned how to 'walk'. Stanley Clarke found new harmonic possibilities by using his thumb. Some players had the frets removed, which made the instrument much harder to play in tune but true vibrato and glissando became possible.

Pastorius took the implications of all this one step further: 'I had to invent my own fingerings. There was no place I could go and learn how to play a Bach Chromatic Fantasy of Charlie Parker's "Donna Lee". I figured it out myself. The overtone series on the instrument was totally unexplored. It can sound like a guitar, an electric plane, an entire choir by using half and quarter strings.'

He is an overwhelmingly confident young man who explains his sudden popularity like this: 'I'm the first cat that can really play the instrument. It's as simple as that.'

A well-known jazz musician, asked what he thought of Weather Report, replied; 'Cloudy'. Like the group itself, Pastorius is often considered too flashy, slick, cocky, conveniently commercial: 'I think it scares people to hear something so different all of a sudden. Weather Report is really contemporary, and we reach a lot of people. I think some guys are just jealous. Anyway, I don't use technique for itself. I use it to make sounds that have never been heard before.'

Bass violinists like Ron Carter and Aladar Pege can play at least as wide a variety of sound. With improved pick-up mikes and amplification techniques, they also can produce enough volume for large halls. And it is doubtful whether production-line metal can ever equal the rich vibrations of aged wood.

However Pastorius has made the bass guitar respectable, and he is hot: 'A year ago I'd never even made a record, now everybody's talking about me. When we played in Yugoslavia, I was treated like a king. Sometimes I can hardly believe it's happening. And it's funny. I started to play bass guitar because it was an easy instrument. Then I went and made it hard for myself.'

Tag Seven: Adolphe Sax

After the Belgian inventor Adolphe Sax patented the saxophone in 1846, Hector Berlioz wrote: 'Its principal merit is the beautiful variety of its accent; deep and calm, passionate, dreamy, melancholic, like an echo of an echo . . . To my knowledge no existing musical instrument possesses that curious sonority perched on the limit of silence.'

In his autobiography *Father of the Blues*, W.C. Handy – who claimed to have been the first to use a saxophone in an American orchestra, in 1909 – describes the instrument as 'moaning like a sinner on revival day'. For Arnold Bennett, the saxophone was the 'embodiment of the spirit of beer'.

It combines the speed of woodwinds with the carrying-power of brass and at the beginning Sax intended the seven instruments in his new family for marching bands, replacing clarinets, oboes and bassoons. It was an easy instrument to learn; each village could now have its own band. You can produce a tone in an hour, learn a simple tune in a day. Faced with embouchure problems, brass-players may take weeks to reach the same point; violinists even longer. Fingering is much less delicate than on older reed instruments. For the first time one wind-instrument-player could play from the top to the bottom of the piano keyboard.

Sax also invented families of brass instruments called saxhorns, saxtrombas and saxtubas; an enormous organ powered and pushed by a steam locomotive for public events; a design for an egg-shaped concert hall, an air-purifier for sufferers of respiratory diseases . . . forty-six patents in all. But he is principally remembered for the saxophone family, which in range, homogeneity, speed and subtlety, became the wind equivalent of the violin family, and the sound of the twentieth century.

Adolphe Sax was born in Dinant, Belgium, on 6 November 1814, the son of Charles-Joseph Sax, whose factory employing 200 workers was the largest wind-instrument producer in Europe. At the age of twelve, Adolphe was an apprentice there. He studied flute at the Brussels Royal Conservatory of Music and won a prize playing the revolutionary fingering system devised by Theobald Boehm. His first patent was for a redesigned bass clarinet, giving it more flexibility and power. He demonstrated his first saxophone in 1840, behind a curtain because it was not yet patented. It caught the attention of the government of King Louis Philippe of France, which ordered its military officials to equip their bands with Sax's new instruments. There were newspaper articles pro and con, his competitors used their influence and filed law-suits against him. A battle of the bands – one conducted by Sax, the other using traditional instruments – on the Champ de Mars in Paris resulted in a jury prize for Sax. The press was almost unanimously favourable. He won large contracts.

Sax moved to Paris. The revolution of 1848 installed a republic and ended the monarchy, including its support of Sax, who filed for bankruptcy in 1852. But the Second Empire followed shortly and in 1854 Napoleon III granted Sax a subsidy. As political fortunes changed, he went bankrupt again, continuing his manufacturing business on a smaller scale. He was in reduced circumstances when he died in 1894, and few would have been willing to bet on the future of the saxophone.

The saxophone was never seriously integrated into classical music, aside from isolated works by Berlioz, Stravinsky, Milhaud and a few others. Then came jazz. At the beginning, the dominant instruments were trumpets and cornets; Buddy Bolden, King Oliver, Freddy Keppard, Louis Armstrong. Slowly the saxophone began to take over. In 1918 a clarinet-player named Sidney Bechet was seduced by a soprano saxophone in a London shop window. In his autobiography *Treat It Gentle*, Bechet writes: 'This was a piece of good luck for me because it wasn't long after this before people started saying they didn't want clarinets in their bands no more.'

The saxophone was described as 'throbbing' or 'wailing' as soloists like Bechet, Adrian Rollini (bass saxophone) and Johnny Hodges discovered it in the twenties. Its melodic capabilities were developed by Coleman Hawkins, Ben Webster and Lester Young in the thirties. Saxophone sections were the real stars of dance bands. Charlie Parker played it harder and faster in the forties. Lee Konitz and Paul Desmond cooled it out in the fifties. Serge Challoff, Gerry Mulligan and Pepper Adams picked up from Ellingtonian Harry Carney and explored the under-exposed baritone sax. Steve Lacy rediscovered the soprano, which had been neglected after Bechet.

Louis Jordan, King Curtis and Junior Walker introduced the saxophone to rhythm and blues. John Coltrane and Eric Dolphy stretched the physical and emotional range of the saxophone in the sixties, while Archie Shepp, Pharoah Sanders and Albert Ayler coaxed it to play sounds never before heard.

With rock, the instrument went into eclipse like jazz itself. The electric guitar took over. But to approach the subtlety and variety of saxophones, guitarists had to employ auxiliary equipment such as wah-wah peddles, phasers and flangers. The synthesizer, the first major new instrument invented since the saxophone, served technopop well, but people need warm streams of air too and the saxophone combines human breath with the speed of a guitar or keyboard. In the mid-seventies. Andy McKay with Roxy Music and David Payne with Ian Drury introduced the saxophone to rock. Saxophones soon became integral parts of such hot young groups as Dexy's Midnight Runners and Q-Tips. Clarence Clemmons's tenor is essential to the power of Bruce Springsteen's rock. Phil Woods's alto has been prominently featured on Billy Joel hits.

So those who never knew it left will be pleased to learn that the saxophone has come back. Its continuing contemporary appeal can be illustrated by a sixteen-year-old music student named Charles who recently switched from guitar to tenor sax, giving as his reason: 'I want to play an instrument I can kiss.'

Tag Eight: Sun Ra

The twenty-five piece Solar Space Intergalactic Myth-Science Arkestra has shrunk to a baker's dozen. Where are all the dancers and singers, the gold lamé shirts, the burnooses, turbans, Robin Hood caps and Ra's Egyptian helmet? Have they shrunk too? Will there still be a fire-eater? What about the tinkles, flutter-tongues and sweet melodies fit for a wedding on Venus? Can only thirteen people re-create the sound of an inter-planetary war? Has Sun Ra returned to his previous incarnation, Sonny Blount?

In answer to these questions, Sun Ra smiled enigmatically: 'I've been promoted. I'm dealing with the omniverse now.'

Ra was sitting in an earthbound hotel near the Place de la Republique, in a tacky room with sickening wallpaper. The ghosts of lonely sailors haunt this room, and Ra had not quite succeeded in exorcizing them by hanging blue cloth with bright yellow and red swatches everywhere. Somewhat optimistically, he said: 'Bright colours give off good energy.'

For the past twenty-seven years Sun Ra has mixed his UFO brand of free jazz with communal living, mythology, heiroglyphics, astronomy, theatricality, the Bible, ontology and Fletcher Henderson. There is nobody quite like him; certainly nobody who

237

speaks quite like him and he speaks so well it would be best to let him speak for himself.

As always when Ra speaks he is surrounded by disciple musicians. Some, like Marshall Allen and John Gilmore, have been around him since 1955. They shared a house on New York's lower east side, then moved with him to Philadelphia. They listen attentively as Ra speaks, smiling often, gasping with a shock of recognition. Ra reclined on his bed, called for grape juice, which looked suspiciously like *vin rouge*, and spoke: 'People call music the universal language, but I'm saying it's the language of the universe. I have to eliminate a lot of musicians out of the scheme of things because playing universal music they have not become universal beings. My music has not done them any good. So they can't possibly do anybody else any good. They are earth-minded.

'The omniverse consists of all the universes together, including the black holes. Music of the omniverse tries to get people to rise above human beings to be omnibeings. We sing a song that says: "First stop Mars". Then there's "Take a trip to Jupiter". "Why just go to the moon? Stop off at Pluto, too." And "Have you heard the latest news from Neptune?"

'The Iranian government said that music was impure and they banned it. Well they were not entirely wrong, but why not just put out some music that's pure? The people who play pure music tend to stay out of the way, they don't want to get hurt by people's crude remarks. There's a lot of pure music hidden away, but I'm the only one brash enough to jump out and face the world.

'Black people haven't really latched on to what I'm talking about. They're talking about freedom, I'm dealing with discipline. We're on opposite poles. Freedom sounds like a nice word, but it kills people. Peace is another word like that. A gun is also a piece.

'People think they are going to be saved by God. God is love, they say. Which limits God, you know. I'm giving God a chance to be more than love. The only way we know there is a God is from all the bad things happening to people. What really happened in the Garden of Eden? We haven't heard God's side of the story. Maybe Eve did not eat the apple at all, maybe she just told Adam she did so he'd eat it and she could see what would happen to him first. Then Adam told God she ate it too to protect himself. And he punished them for lying.

238

'Sure there's a spiritual revival in America. But they've got it all wrong. If they were really spiritual, they'd shut down every church in the country one Sunday and have a real Sabbath. Don't pray, don't sing, don't say anything to God. God might speak down from heaven and say "Thank you".

'People always come up to me and talk. One day in Harlem a teenager on the street said: "Hi Sun Ra, I'm God."

'I said: "Hi God. It's nice of you to visit me."

' "That's why I like you, Sun Ra," he said, "because if I had told anybody else I was God they would have denied me. You never deny me. That's why I will always come to you."

'He started to walk away. I said: "Bye God."

'He said: "Bye Sun Ra." '

Index

242